Shelley's style

Engraved by W. Sharp.

Dum brevis efse laboro, obscurus fio.

Published Jan. 1. 1798. by John Horne Tooke, Wimbledon, Surry.

Shelley's Style

WILLIAM KEACH

Methuen
New York and London

First published in 1984 by
Methuen, Inc.
733 Third Avenue, New York NY 10017

Published in Great Britain by
Methuen & Co. Ltd
11 New Fetter Lane, London EC4P 4EE
733 Third Avenue, New York, NY 10017

Printed in the USA

Library of Congress Cataloging in Publication Data
Keach, William, 1942–
    Shelley's style.

    Includes bibliographical references and index.
    1. Shelley, Percy Bysshe, 1792–1822—Style.
I. Title.
PR5444.K4   1984   821'.7   84–1151
ISBN 0–416–30320–X

British Library Cataloguing in Publication Data
Keach, William
    Shelley's style
    1. Shelley, Percy Bysshe—Criticism and interpretation
    I. Title
821'.7   PR5438

    ISBN 0–416–30320–X

To Sheila Emerson

CONTENTS

ACKNOWLEDGEMENTS

I want first to thank Sheila Emerson for her strong, animating sense of what this book could be, and for her deeply imaginative and generous work in making it what it is. She reads Shelley like she reads Ruskin, and so much else – with breath-taking intelligence and wit. Her help meant, and means, the most to me.

It is a great pleasure to thank Christopher Ricks for his initial responsiveness, his discerning comments on the manuscript, and his abiding encouragement. Stuart Curran's early and continuing interest in the project mattered importantly. Donald Reiman gave me the benefit of his remarkable knowledge of Shelley and Shelley's text as well as access to the resources of the Carl H. Pforzheimer Library, New York. To him, and to the staff of the Pforzheimer Library, I am very grateful. Susan Wolfson read a draft of the book with keen critical sympathy and was in every way a tirelessly supportive colleague. Among many others who contributed information, ideas and encouragement, I should especially like to thank Barry Qualls, Richard Poirier, Hans Aarsleff, Derek Attridge, Timothy Burnett, Maurice Charney, James Guetti, Daniel Harris, George Levine, Laurence Lockridge, Peter Manning, Stuart Peterfreund, Arden Reed, John Richetti, Samuel Schulman, Thomas Van Laan, William Walling and Andrew Welsh. At every stage and for every aspect of this study, the writing and teaching of William K. Wimsatt provided a source of inspiration and a standard of judgement.

For two invaluable and timely leaves, thanks are due to the Rutgers University Faculty Academic Study Program.

Parts of Chapter III appeared in an earlier form in the *Keats–Shelley Journal*, 24, 1975, 49–69; most of Chapter VI first appeared in *Romanticism Past and Present*, 6, 1982, 23–42. I am grateful to the editors for permission to reprint.

The frontispiece to John Horne Tooke's *ΕΠΕΑ ΠΤΕΡΟΕΝΤΑ, or, The Diversions of Purley* is from a copy in the Pforzheimer Library.

NOTE ON ABBREVIATIONS AND TEXTS

Standard works referred to parenthetically in the text have been abbreviated as follows:

PP: *Shelley's Poetry and Prose*, ed. Donald H. Reiman and Sharon B. Powers, New York, Norton, 1977.

PW: *Shelley: Poetical Works*, ed. Thomas Hutchinson, corrected by G.M. Matthews, Oxford, Oxford University Press, 1970.

CW: *The Complete Works of Percy Bysshe Shelley*, ed. Roger Ingpen and Walter E. Peck, London, Ernest Benn; New York, Charles Scribner, 1926–30.

Letters: *The Letters of Percy Bysshe Shelley*, ed. Frederick L. Jones, Oxford, Clarendon Press, 1964.

Mary Shelley's Journal: *Mary Shelley's Journal*, ed. Frederick L. Jones, Norman, University of Oklahoma Press, 1947.

Wherever possible, quotations of Shelley's poetry and prose are taken from *PP*. All other quotations of Shelley's poetry, except where specifically indicated in the notes, are from *PW*. Other quotations of Shelley's prose are from *CW* unless otherwise indicated in the notes. Titles of journals in the notes are abbreviated according to the Master List of Periodicals given in the *MLA International Bibliography*.

INTRODUCTION

What exactly did Wordsworth mean when he called Shelley 'one of the best artists of us all: I mean in workmanship of style'?[1] Commentators, literary historians and anthologists often cite Wordsworth's judgement as if its meaning were apparent, yet for many readers it is neither apparent nor central to their sense of why Shelley's poetry matters. There have been some finely detailed readings of individual poems, and a few useful studies of particular stylistic features. But the larger question of Shelley's 'workmanship of style' has for the most part been either set aside as an old and no longer very interesting debate initiated by Eliot and Leavis and prosecuted by the New Critics, or absorbed into kinds of reading for which the terms 'artist', 'workmanship' and even 'style' itself have become quaint mystifications that prevent our accepting the indeterminate play of all writing, including – or especially – Shelley's. This study grew out of a conviction that the old debate about Shelley's characteristic ways of using language needs to be revived and kept alive. It argues that while he recognizes in his own terms the problems inherent in the relation of words to thoughts and things, his writing is shaped by his working as an artist against, as well as in knowing submission to, what he calls 'the limitedness of the poetical faculty itself' (PP, 504).

Shelley's poetry does present special stylistic difficulties – even his most loyal admirers have had to acknowledge that. Consider this passage from Frederick Pottle's classic advocacy in 'The case of Shelley':

> He employs pronounced, intoxicating, hypnotic rhythms that seem to be trying to sweep the reader into hasty emotional commitments. He seldom uses a firmly held, developed image, but pours out a flood of images which one must grasp

momentarily in one aspect and then release. He is fond of figures within figures. He imposes his will on the object of experience: he does not explore 'reality', he flies away from it. He seldom takes a gross, palpable, near-at-hand object from the world of ordinary perception and holds it for contemplation: his gaze goes up to the sky, he starts with objects that are just on the verge of becoming invisible or inaudible or intangible and he strains away even from these.[2]

It is easy to see from this partial and by no means self-validating inventory – Pottle concedes too much too quickly – why Shelley's writing has attracted the interest of theoretically minded post-structuralist critics (all the essays in *Deconstruction and Criticism*, not only those of Paul de Man, Jacques Derrida and J. Hillis Miller, were originally to have focused on Shelley).[3] But while traditional Shelleyans have often granted that his style must seem problematic to modern readers and have then directed our attention towards other aspects of his poetry, post-structuralist Shelleyans – stimulating as much of their work is – have been too little concerned with distinguishing the elusive activity peculiar to Shelley's writing from the problematic condition of language generally. That certain verbal difficulties, idiosyncracies and extravagances may be intrinsic to the 'workmanship of style' that Wordsworth admired is a possibility yet to be thoroughly explored.

A stanza from *The Witch of Atlas* will help exemplify the critical situation I have just described. Shelley concludes his account of the 'magic treasures' stored in the Witch's cave with these lines:

And wondrous works of substances unknown,
    To which the enchantment of her father's power
Had changed those ragged blocks of savage stone,
    Were heaped in the recesses of her bower;
Carved lamps and chalices and phials which shone
    In their own golden beams – each like a flower
Out of whose depth a fire fly shakes his light
Under a cypress in the starless night.

(201–8)

In *The Quest for Permanence*, David Perkins cites lines 205–6 as an instance of Shelley's 'frequent resort to an imagery lacking in individuation', of 'his incredibly high-handed use of metaphor':

For it sometimes seems in Shelley's poetry that virtually anything can be compared to anything else. . . . If one brings a visual imagination to bear, such metaphors become far-fetched not to say grotesque, and the fact that Shelley used them suggests that there was little awareness of the identity of the things compared.[4]

But what seems 'high-handed' and lacking in awareness to Perkins, with his expectations of referential specificity and cogency in figurative language, becomes an occasion for exuberant celebration in Jerrold Hogle's provocative Derridean essay, 'Metaphor and metamorphosis in Shelley's "The Witch of Atlas" ':

> Whether it emphasizes the metaphoricity of personal thinking or the metamorphosis of figural orders across recorded time, the cave of the Witch's birth and education is a collective unconscious of ciphers on ciphers without beginning or end, all of them 'wondrous works of substances unknown' (l. 201) building up the treasury of desire. Metaphor commands the Human Repository far more than any single figure or consciousness . . .[5]

Both these divergent responses raise important questions about Shelley's style. But neither of them conveys much detailed concern with the writing in this stanza. Perkins does not pause to explain why he thinks it 'incredibly high-handed', even 'grotesque', to compare lamps and chalices to flowers, or to substantiate his assumption that a 'high-handed' or 'far-fetched' use of metaphor necessarily implies an absence of attentive discrimination. Hogle, for his part, does not show how the beginningless and endless play of figures he finds in this stanza differs from such activity elsewhere in the poem, or in other Shelley poems, or even in poetry generally. One problem with believing that *The Witch of Atlas* 'is "about" (in the process of) the sheer release of further transfigurations from the potentials of existing metaphors'[6] is that the writing may come to seem sheer when it is dense or resistant. Such a belief may encourage us – as it sometimes encourages Hogle – to look through or past, not at or into, the particular configurations of language in a given passage.

While the objects 'of substances unknown' in the Witch's cave are ontologically indeterminate, as 'wondrous works' they have an author in the Witch's father, Apollo, whose double figurative identity as sun and as artist is suggested in the lines near the beginning that tell how the Witch was conceived:

Her mother was one of the Atlantides –
   The all-beholding Sun had ne'er beholden
In his wide voyage o'er continents and seas
   So fair a creature, as she lay enfolden
In the warm shadow of her loveliness . . .
   He kissed her with his beams, and made all golden
The chamber of grey rock in which she lay –

                                    (57–63)

Conception, natural and imaginative, is imaged here as the filling of an enclosed space – a womb, a cave – with light, and the figurative pattern is recapitulated in the later stanza: the sun-god has stored his daughter's cave, once her mother's before she 'dissolved away' (64), with replicas of her own begetting. The characteristic reflexive image of the Witch's mother lying 'enfolden / In the warm shadow of her loveliness' when she and the cave were 'made all golden' by the sun's light is precisely traced and transmuted in the later image of vessels that 'shone / In their own golden beams'. These vessels, like the cave and like the new-born Witch herself – 'A lovely lady garmented in light / From her own beauty' (81–2) – derive their mysterious power of self-illumination from Apollo's enchanting power. Shelley gives this sequence of metaphorical transformations a fictional and figurative origin that is important to the poem's playful allegorical exploration of artistic generation and process. Beings and objects are made to shine in the light of their own beauty by virtue of Apollo's creative (pro-creative) desire and power. One might question the stability of the sun-god's own mythical identity and emphasize the capricious erotic impulse that marks his initial appearance in the poem, but such considerations do not contradict the status Shelley gives him as originating figure.

The 'wondrous works' in the Witch's cave – the 'carved lamps and chalices and phials' – are like each other in being vessels, and each, Shelley goes on to say, is 'like a flower'. 'High-handed' or 'far-fetched'? Think of such familiar flower names as 'buttercup' and 'wine-cup'. Shelley is reversing Shakespeare's metaphor of 'chaliced flowers' from a familiar song in *Cymbeline* ('Hark, hark, the lark', ii.iii.20ff). He would have been reminded by Erasmus Darwin's *The Botanic Garden* that the outer whorl of sepals enclosing a flower is called the *calyx*, a word commonly though mistakenly derived (in Johnson's *Dictionary*, for instance) from Latin *calix*, 'cup', the etymological source of 'chalice'.[7]

Elsewhere in Shelley's poetry flowers are figured as dew-filled cups –
and as lamp-like sources of light:

> And the wand-like lily, which lifted up,
> As a Maenad, its moonlight-coloured cup
> Till the fiery star, which is its eye,
> Gazed through clear dew on the tender sky.
>
> (*The Sensitive Plant*, 'Part First', 33–6)

Shelley's figurative transformation of the vessels into flowers is
prefigured in Apollo's transformation of 'those ragged blocks of savage
stone' into 'wondrous works', as if the poem's mythological fiction and
its ongoing verbal activity were reciprocally confirming. Rhetorically,
however, the transformation in lines 205–8 is not metaphorical, as both
Perkins and Hogle assert. The simile here ('each like a flower'), as so
often in Shelley's writing, makes explicit a difference and separation
between the main terms of the figure. In this sense Shelley preserves,
rather than collapses, the distinct identity of the 'things' (I would prefer
to say 'thoughts') compared; the poet's power to produce flowers is
both like and unlike the power of the sun-god he imagines. This
acknowledgement of difference has to do, I think, with the subsequent
direction of Shelley's multiply coherent simile. In the last two lines of
the stanza, earlier references to Apollo's transforming sunlight give way
to a nocturnal scene that is at once lyrical and incipiently funereal
('under a cypress in the starless night'). Shelley's flowers do not, as it
turns out, shine 'In their own golden beams' like the
vessels which they otherwise resemble. They shine with the borrowed,
intermittent light of a fire fly, whose appearance here deep within the
flower simile recalls a kindred creature in Shelley's introductory stanzas
'To Mary (On Her Objecting to the Following Poem, Upon the Score
of Its Containing No Human Interest)':

> What hand would crush the silken-winged fly,
>   The youngest of inconstant April's minions,
> Because it cannot climb the purest sky
>   Where the swan sings, amid the sun's dominions?
> Not thine. Thou knowest tis its doom to die . . . .
>
> (9–13)

In a way that seems to me richly illustrative of Shelley's 'workmanship
of style', the flower simile extends the 'wondrous works' of an idealized
creative power with inventive precision, while at the same time

acknowledging an incomplete, imperfect relationship to such a power. The writing does not sacrifice an awareness of individual identity on behalf of an 'earnest pursuit of Intellectual Beauty' or 'the One'.[8] Nor, for all its playfulness, does it blithely and indiscriminately indulge in an 'utter submission to metaphor-making'.[9] It unfolds with an audacious, opportunistic purposiveness – notice the pointed rhyming – that is self-delighting but not self-satisfied.

A premise of this book is that the difficulties and extravagances of Shelley's style reflect a divided, often agitated understanding of language. I want to investigate that understanding and the stylistic features most directly related to it in terms derived, as far as possible, from Shelley's own writing and reading. He sometimes writes about language in ways that seem to anticipate ideas familiar in modern linguistic and critical theory. But what he says about language, including some of those remarks that may sound strikingly advanced, is rooted, at times precariously or wilfully, in the poetry and philosophy he read and reread: in Plato and Dante, in Bacon and Locke (yes, Locke), in Wordsworth himself. About language as about almost everything else, Shelley could write with visionary optimism. In Act IV of *Prometheus Unbound*, the Earth proclaims that 'Language is a perpetual Orphic song, / Which rules with Daedal harmony a throng / Of thoughts and forms, which else senseless and shapeless were' (415–17). Important though this is as an expression of Shelley's linguistic ideal, it is not, I believe, indicative of his prevailing attitude or of his poetic practice. Shelley's style is not the product of an imagination for which language was 'a perpetual Orphic song'. Rather, it is the work of an artist whose sense of the unique and unrealized potential in language was held in unstable suspension with his sense of its resistances and limitations. All the chapters that follow are designed to show how the antithetical impulses in Shelley's disposition towards language pressure and energize each other.

There are a number of styles within Shelley's 'Style', and many different kinds of questions could be asked about each of them. I have tried to be alert to the particular stylistic aims and conventions that distinguish intimate lyric from formal ode, or metaphysical dramatic allegory from mythological verse fable, while at the same time locating characteristics of Shelley's writing common to his performances in different genres. I have not tried to address all aspects of Shelley's styles, but have instead concentrated on those that seem to me to show most fully his distinctive sense of the verbal medium, and that in some instances have been either neglected or taken for granted. After the first chapter, which is devoted to Shelley's writing about language in *A Defence of Poetry* and elsewhere, the book moves mainly from questions of imagery and figuration to questions of syntax and versification. The final chapter departs from the scope and approach of the previous five by looking at a closely related group of poems from the end of Shelley's career, and by adjusting a deliberately selective focus on style to take fuller account of biographical and historical complications.

The emphasis of this book is openly, but I believe not narrowly or exclusively, formalist. Criticism of Shelley's poetry may be said to have gone beyond formalism without ever having been there – without ever having given the formal features of his writing adequate attention. The speculative subtlety of some of Shelley's own critical remarks about form works against one's being naive or complacent about what it means to define such features and to bring them into the foreground of interpretation. My purpose is not to slight the important mythopoeic, philosophical, political and biographical commentary which has predominated in Shelley studies over the past twenty-five or thirty years, but to argue that much remains to be done to show how the forces and values revealed through that commentary get articulated in his language.

I THE MIRROR AND THE VEIL: LANGUAGE IN SHELLEY'S *DEFENCE*

Studies of Shelley's poetics have paid too little attention to what he says about language.[1] Even studies focused on his exalted notion of metaphor have been more concerned, in ways Shelley himself might well have approved of, with acts of mental apprehension and relation than with acts of articulation. The reasons for this are clear enough: Shelley never wrote as extensively about the language of poetry as Wordsworth did in his prefaces, or as Coleridge did in the *Biographia Literaria*. The initial and ultimately the dominant impulse in *A Defence of Poetry* is to consider poetry in its most unlimited 'general sense' (*PP*, 480); even when he narrows the perspective to 'poetry in a more restricted sense' (*PP*, 483), Shelley devotes just six paragraphs to the question of the verbal medium before moving on to a broader historical and conceptual plane. But despite – and also because of – Shelley's tellingly brief and apparently tangential treatment of language in the *Defence*, his way of writing about it there and elsewhere in his prose and verse asks for more detailed scrutiny than accounts of his poetics have given us.

Shelley clearly cared about both the idea and the fact of language. In 1812 he cared enough about recent developments in the study of language to order editions of the three most important English theorists and philologists of his day: Lord Monboddo, Horne Tooke and Sir William Jones (*Letters*, I, 344–5). What Shelley later says about language indicates a characteristically free and eclectic familiarity with these and other linguists, ancient and modern. And then Shelley was himself a gifted linguist in that other, more primary sense of the term: he was, as Timothy Webb's study has shown,[2] perhaps the most versatile and ambitious translator among all the Romantic writers. That someone so consistently involved in translation could speak of 'the vanity of translation' (*PP*, 484) in the *Defence* is itself indicative of an attitude towards language that needs to be investigated.

The *Defence* is Shelley's most important and familiar piece of critical prose, and its treatment of language, although in some respects sketchy and underdeveloped, provides the best vantage point we have for looking at what he says elsewhere and for assessing his general attitude. My argument develops from the conviction that Shelley's attitude towards language is deeply divided, and that this division is rooted in the fundamental relationship between words and the thoughts they signify. On the one hand, Shelley argues in the *Defence* that language is entirely a product of mind and is therefore more fully and precisely expressive of thought than any other medium. On the other hand, he implies in certain passages of the *Defence* and says explicitly elsewhere that words, once they are spoken or written, separate themselves from the mind that produced them and are therefore inherently imperfect signs of thoughts. This basic division in Shelley's attitude is crossed and complicated by a recognition, encouraged by many eighteenth- and nineteenth-century writers on language, that the relation of thought and language is in fact reciprocal and circular – that if language is the product of thought, thought is also the product of language. Shelley's sense of this latter circumstance, of what is now commonly referred to as the constitutive function of language, is intimately linked to his shifting attitude towards the verbal medium of poetry. For while it leads him to imagine in *Prometheus Unbound* that Prometheus 'gave man speech, and speech created thought, / Which is the measure of the Universe' (II.iv.72–3), it also leads him to acknowledge in the *Defence* that language inevitably tends to harden into a system in which verbal signs limit thought to a sphere of established, habitual, 'dead' relations, a tendency which it is the poet's work to counter.[3]

For Shelley a poet is necessarily involved, as Richard Cronin has recently said, in a linguistic 'predicament', in an inevitable 'struggle against' an artistic medium whose unique and inherent expressive virtues he must also realize.[4] In its argument and in its imagery, *A Defence of Poetry* may be read as both a determined defence against and a disguised revelation of Shelley's version of this linguistic predicament. With respect to its account of language as the medium of poetry, the *Defence* is at once bravely confident and radically unstable: some of its soaring celebrations of the poetic imagination turn upon daring, even desperate, transvaluations of a linguistic skepticism which is all the more revealing for its latency. What Shelley says about language is sometimes genuinely contradictory and obscure. We need to be able to recognize this without closing ourselves to the possibility that some forms of contradiction and even obscurity may be necessary to the reflections of a volatile verbal sensibility. Although he read widely in the philosophy of language, in the *Defence* he writes not primarily as a linguistic philosopher but as a poet, whose convictions about language fluctuate as his polemic moves between the extravagance of the ideal and the frustrations of the actual. In following these fluctuations we need to avoid what Shelley calls the 'vulgar error' of distinguishing 'between poets and prose writers' (*PP*, 484) and read the prose of the *Defence* as the 'vitally metaphorical' (*PP*, 482) poetry that it is – as writing which generates its meanings through a fusion of argumentative and lyrical rhetoric, extended figuration, syntactic and even phonetic patterning. In the discussion that follows I want to approach Shelley's critical essay as an unfinished poem in prose, organized in three main movements.

I

Despite its rhapsodic enthusiasm and frequently digressive manner, the *Defence* has a clear argumentative superstructure.[5] Shelley begins the first movement synoptically by distinguishing 'two classes of mental action, which are called reason and imagination', and by considering poetry 'in a general sense' as simply ' "the expression of the Imagination" ' (*PP*, 480). With the fifth paragraph he narrows the argument to consider 'poetry in a more restricted sense' (*PP*, 483), which 'expresses those arrangements of language, and especially metrical language', created by the imagination. Poetry in this 'more restricted sense' remains his primary concern in the long historically organized second movement of the *Defence* announced in the transitional eleventh paragraph: 'Having determined what is poetry, and who are poets, let us proceed to estimate its effects upon society' (*PP*, 486). But Shelley's interest in the verbal medium itself is only sporadically explicit in this section. When it emerges, as in the paragraphs on Dante that culminate Shelley's historical survey, it does so in ways which suggest why language has not been kept in the foreground of the argument. This averted relation to language also characterizes the third movement of the *Defence*, where Shelley leaves what he calls 'a critical history of Poetry and its influence on society' to take up Peacock's charge that poetry is delightful but not useful (*PP*, 500), and extends through the three-paragraph coda. These later sections contain passages of an intriguing indirect relevance to the early discussion of language – intriguing partly, as we shall see, because of the ways in which they put into question and signal an underlying precariousness in Shelley's opening linguistic confidence.

In the first four paragraphs of the *Defence*, this confidence depends mainly on Shelley's determination not to restrict poetry to that mode of imaginative expression whose medium is language. Much of what he says in these opening paragraphs does have an important anticipatory bearing upon the discussion of language that follows. By claiming in the second paragraph that 'poetry is connate with the origin of man' (*PP*, 480), for instance, Shelley aligns himself with the 'primitivist' strain in eighteenth-century accounts of the origin of language – with Thomas Blackwell and William Louth, and with Rousseau and Herder.[6] But the image of the 'Aeolian Lyre' which intervenes between this claim and Shelley's invocation of those favorite eighteenth-century models of linguistic origin – the 'child at play' and the 'savage' (*PP*, 480–1) – suggests that his initial emphasis will fall not on the medium of primitive poetic expression, but on that fusion of mimetic and expressive 'mental action' which runs throughout the essay. Shelley imagines a mode of expression for both child and savage which circumvents the distinction between the linguistic and the pre-linguistic: between 'voice and motions' in the child; between 'language and gesture, together with plastic or pictorial imitation', in the savage. The questions which necessarily arise, say, for Condillac or Monboddo in attending to the differences between arbitrary linguistic signs and natural pre-linguistic signs, and to their probable interrelation in the development of language, are here put in abeyance. This is true even when Shelley moves on in this paragraph to consider 'Man in society' as he comes to respond retrospectively and self-referentially to his own previous expressive representations: 'language, gesture, and the imitative arts, become at once the representation and the medium, the pencil and the picture, the chisel and the statue, the chord and the harmony' (*PP*, 481). Shelley distinguishes 'medium' from 'representation' only to say that in the simultaneous development of human culture and poetic expression they are in fact the same. And while he finds specific images to evoke this double existence of the expressive mode in painting, sculpture and music, he is notably unspecific about it in poetry whose medium is language.

Shelley takes an important step towards addressing the verbal medium near the end of the second paragraph when he observes, as if it followed logically from his Rousseauean remarks about the 'social sympathies', that 'men, even in the infancy of society, observe a certain order in their words and actions, distinct from that of the objects and impressions represented by them, all expression being subject to the laws of that from which it proceeds' (*PP*, 481). The recognition that all expressive media have their own intrinsic formal, non-representational 'order' distinct from, although not independent of, mimetic and expressive representation, is extended in the next paragraph:

> although all men observe a similar, they observe not the same order, in the motion of the dance, in the melody of the song, in the combinations of language, in the series of their imitations of natural objects. For there is a certain order or rhythm belonging to each of these classes of mimetic representation, from which the hearer and the spectator receive an intenser and purer pleasure than from any other.
>
> (*PP*, 481)

Shelley's later remarks about rhythm, meter, versification and even 'the vanity of translation' are contained here in embryo. But while Shelley emphasizes the idea of the formal distinctiveness of each kind of art, he has as yet said nothing specific about what that distinctiveness consists in. It is worth noticing, therefore, that this attention to the non-representational formal 'order' peculiar to each medium allows Shelley to grant the various media a kind of parity which he will later revise when he comes to compare them more specifically with respect to their expressive, representational resources. One may also notice just a shadow of doubt in Shelley's celebrating the formal 'order' distinctive to each medium. The clause 'all expression being subject to the laws of that from which it proceeds' may embrace, as John E. Jordan says, the Coleridgean ideal of 'organic unity and inward determination',[7] but the phrase 'subject to' also hints at an inevitable limitation on expression which will haunt later passages of the *Defence*.

Shelley's definition of a poet 'in the most universal sense of the word' turns upon his conviction that each expressive medium has its own peculiar formal 'order or rhythm' capable of yielding a unique kind of pleasure, in its own way supreme. 'Every man in the infancy of art', he says, 'observes an order which *approximates* more or less closely to that from which this highest delight results' (*PP*, 481; my emphasis). In poets the same capacity 'is very great', even 'exists in excess', and yet is still a 'faculty of approximation to the beautiful' (*PP*, 482). As Shelley goes on to imagine the relation of primitive poet to society through this shared 'faculty of approximation', his emphasis shifts back again from the strictly formal to the representational aspect of poetic expression, and – for the first time in the *Defence* – from a general consideration of the question of artistic medium to the resources peculiar to the linguistic medium. Poets 'in the most universal sense' suddenly become poets whose medium is language:

> Their language is vitally metaphorical; that is, it marks the before unapprehended relations of things, and perpetuates their appre-hension, until the words which represent them, become through time signs for portions or classes of thoughts instead of pictures of integral thoughts; and then if no new poets should arise to create afresh the associations which have been thus disorganized, language will be dead to all the nobler purposes of human inter-course. These similitudes or relations are finely said by Lord Bacon to be 'the same footsteps of nature impressed upon the various subjects of the world' – and he considers the faculty which perceives them as the storehouse of axioms common to all knowledge. In the infancy of society every author is necessarily a poet, because language itself is poetry.
>
> (*PP*, 482)

This is a remarkable passage. But to see what is genuinely distinctive in it requires some sense of historical context. The idea that poetic language was in the beginning 'vitally metaphorical' is hardly new; throughout the eighteenth century one can find conjectural accounts of linguistic origins which assert that all language was originally metaphorical. The view figures so prominently in Thomas Blackwell's *An Enquiry Into the Life and Writings of Homer* (1735) that some linguistic historians have insisted, contrary to all evidence, that Blackwell must have read Vico:[8] 'it is plain that any Language, formed as above described, must be full of Metaphor; and that Metaphor of the boldest, daring, and most natural kind.'[9] Characteristic later extensions of this view may be found in Rousseau's *Essay on the Origin of Languages* ('As man's first motives for speaking were of the passions, his first expressions were tropes')[10] and in Hugh Blair's popular *Lectures on Rhetoric and Belles Lettres* ('the early language of men being entirely made up of words descriptive of sensible objects, it became, of necessity, extremely metaphorical').[11] Among Shelley's contemporaries it is Wordsworth who makes the most of this particular aspect of primitivist theory, and Shelley's movement from language which is 'vitally metaphorical' to language which is 'dead' may well have been inspired by the Appendix to the 1802 Preface:

> The earliest poets of all nations generally wrote from passion excited by real events; they wrote naturally, and as men: feeling powerfully as they did, their language was daring, and figurative. In succeeding times, Poets, and men ambitious of the fame of Poets, perceiving the influence of such language, and desirous of producing the same effect without being animated by the same passion, set themselves to a mechanical adoption of those figures of speech, and . . . frequently applied them to feelings and ideas with which they had no natural connections whatsoever.[12]

What distinguishes Shelley from Wordsworth (and also from Blackwell and Rousseau) is the cognitive emphasis in his account of metaphor, the intense specificity with which he imagines the decline from an original metaphorical vitality, and the implication that the process he describes applies to language as a whole, or at least to all written language ('In the infancy of society every author is necessarily a poet, because language itself is poetry'). To catch the full force of Shelley's thinking on all three of these points, we need to look closely at his own metaphorical writing in this passage.

The language of poets is 'vitally metaphorical', Shelley says, when 'it marks the before unapprehended relations of things'. As John Wright argues in *Shelley's Myth of Metaphor*, Shelley here attributes a rudimentary organizing and constitutive power to metaphor. Metaphor appears to be a way of thinking, not merely a vehicle for expressing or articulating thoughts. 'The most important and novel element', Wright says, 'came from his insight into the nature of metaphor and its role in the formation of experience. . . . metaphor is a vital form of language only to the extent that it is first a specific form of relational apprehension. . . . metaphor is essentially an integral thought made by the mind.'[13] Wright's sense that metaphor is for Shelley a category of thought as well as of language is true to Shelley's own language at the beginning of the passage. 'Vitally metaphorical' language '*marks* the before unapprehended relations of things' (my emphasis) in the double sense of both *noticing* such relations and of *designating* these relations by marks or signs. But as Shelley's passage continues, the second of these senses becomes momentarily dominant, and the enthusiasm with which the sentence begins gives way to an account of what Wright aptly calls 'semantic entropy' ('the principle that the elements of cognitive and emotive organization tend through time . . . toward disorganization of the relationships once unified or integrally apprehended').[14] What Wright does not sufficiently emphasize, however – and this seems to me true as well of Jerrold Hogle in his important recent essay, 'Shelley's poetics: the power as metaphor' – is that for Shelley this tendency is inherent in the historical condition of language. To perpetuate his apprehension of before unapprehended relations, the poet must 'mark' or 'represent' them with words which inevitably become 'signs for portions or classes of thought instead of pictures of integral thoughts'. The process Shelley speaks of is not to be written off simply as linguistic corruption or decadence. Language as we know it and as we use it every day – even as poets know it and use it – depends upon the evolution of vital metaphors into signs. But for Shelley this tendency of language leads to deadness, and 'through time' it increasingly becomes the poet's task not just to 'mark' new relations of things, but to revitalize old markings, 'to create afresh the associations which have been . . . disorganized' in the course of linguistic evolution.

Shelley's remarks on metaphor come prematurely in the *Defence*, in that he has not yet restricted his attention to poetry whose medium is verbal. It would therefore be misleading to see this passage as Shelley's definitive comment on metaphorical language. But there is a significant anticipatory shift in what Shelley says here, from an enthusiastic confidence that depends upon thinking of metaphor as an originating 'form of relational apprehension' (Wright) or as a 'picture [ ] of integral thoughts' (Shelley), to an anxiety that arises as soon as his attention turns to the actual circumstances of human language and to the fact that 'pictures of integral thoughts' depend for their initial intelligibility on being represented in words, in pre-established verbal signs. The shift is from an ideal perspective in which linguistic categories are essentially mental (Wright's title, *Shelley's Myth of Metaphor*, is indicative of his own mentalistic emphasis), to a perspective which acknowledges the necessarily external, temporal and systematic dimension of language. Both perspectives, we may notice, assume a constitutive function of language. But whereas in the first case vital metaphor constitutes thought ('marks . . . before unapprehended relations') in a positive creative act, in the second case dead metaphor constitutes thought negatively by tending to determine and confine it within an established frame of reference. At this point in the *Defence* the shift in perspectives and the ambivalence it indicates may be felt as only an undertow running beneath the ongoing rush of Shelley's exuberant purpose. 'Their language is vitally metaphorical' dominates the key sentence grammatically and rhetorically to such a degree that the anxious complexity of what follows is subsumed within its authority.

Shelley's appropriation of Bacon in this passage on metaphor involves a similar deflection of latent linguistic skepticism. Along with Plato and Dante, Bacon is one of the heroes of the *Defence*; this is his first explicit appearance, and it is worth considering in some detail. In thinking of metaphor as a mode of knowing, not just of saying, Shelley looks back past Vico and quotes from Book III, Chapter 1 of the *De Augmentis Scientiarum*, where Bacon does indeed speak of certain 'similitudes' as relational precepts common to different branches of knowledge and thus characteristic of that 'one universal science' or '*Sapience*' he is attempting to define: 'These similitudes or relations are finely said by Lord Bacon to be "the same footsteps of nature impressed upon the various subjects of the world"[15] – and he considers the faculty which perceives them as the storehouse of axioms common to all knowledge.' Bacon's own cunning metaphor of 'footsteps', with its attendant imagery of impressing and imprinting, appears later in the *De Augmentis*, in a context which places Shelley's quoting him as a celebrator of 'vitally metaphorical' language in an uncertain light. In Book VI Bacon describes the 'philosophical' study of grammar as man's attempt to overcome the 'second curse of the confusion of tongues'.[16] While he asserts that such grammar may inquire into 'the analogy between words and things, or reason', for 'Certainly words are the footsteps of reason' ('Vestigia certe rationis verba sunt'), his entire argument grows out of a recognition that words are only faint and deceptive 'footsteps' ('traces', as Shelley will come to say in the *Defence*):

But the Idols of the Market-place are most troublesome; which have crept into the understanding through the tacit agreement of men concerning the imposition of words and names. Now words are generally framed and applied according to the conception of the vulgar, and draw lines of separation according to such differences as the vulgar can follow: and where a more acute intellect or a more diligent observation tries to introduce a better distinction, words rebel. And that which is the remedy for this evil (namely definitions) is in most cases unable to cure it, for definitions themselves consist of words, and words beget words. And although we think we govern our words . . . the juggleries and charms of words disturb the judgment, and (after the manner of the Tartar bowmen) shoot back at the understanding from which they proceeded.[17]

In the parallel section of *The Advancement of Learning*, Bacon goes on to confess 'that it is not possible to divorce ourselves from these fallacies and false appearances, because they are inseparable from our nature and condition of life'. This skeptical strain in Bacon's attitude towards language is obviously contrary to Shelley's main rhetorical purpose in the sentence from the *Defence*. But Shelley often echoes Bacon's mistrust of words elsewhere in his writing, and even in this paragraph his notion of what happens when vital metaphors or 'similitudes' become signs betrays an affinity with Bacon's characteristic mistrustfulness. Shelley's Englished quotation from Book III of the *De Augmentis* stands unstably against the pressure of the larger Baconian context it evokes.

The way in which Shelley raises fundamental questions about language only to dissolve them within his larger emphasis on 'mental action' continues to characterize the end of this third and all of the fourth paragraph of the *Defence*. 'To be a poet', he claims, 'is to apprehend the true and the beautiful, in a word the good which exists in the relation, subsisting, first between existence and perception, and secondly between perception and expression' (*PP*, 482). The very distinction Shelley makes here implies that the issues of verbal articulation are in need of separate consideration from those of mental apprehension. But he quickly resurrects a primitivist perspective which collapses that distinction: 'Every original language near to its source is in itself the chaos of a cyclic poem: the copiousness of lexicography and the distinctions of grammar are the works of a later age, and are merely the catalogue and the form of the creations of Poetry.' To see lexicography and grammar as 'merely the catalogue and the form of the creations of Poetry' is to subordinate the second of Shelley's relations ('perception and expression') ruthlessly to the first ('existence and perception'). He may be thinking here of the view, familiar in eighteenth-century language theory, that languages developed their syntactic and grammatical complexity at the expense of original utterances which were powerfully condensed and concrete. Diderot imagined language as evolving from a 'natural order', in which single utterances conveyed the complex simultaneity of thought, towards an 'order of institution', in which the complex simultaneity of thought is 'decomposed' into elaborate sequences of signs;[18] Adam Smith argued that entire 'events' or 'matters of fact' expressed in primitive languages by single verb-like utterances were subsequently 'artificially split' and 'expressed by a sort of grammatical circumlocution' requiring sequences of nouns, verbs and objects.[19] Shelley wants to keep poetic 'perception' (the common term in his two relations) or conception in the foreground, and for him, as for Diderot and Smith, imagining the primitive condition of language provides a fiction in which 'perception and expression' are naturally and spontaneously unified.

The radical philosophical principle underlying Shelley's thinking at this point in the *Defence* had been made explicit in the essay 'On Life', where Shelley asserted that from the perspective of the 'intellectual philosophy' advanced most clearly and vigorously in Sir William Drummond's *Academical Questions*, linguistic structures necessarily falsify the true unity of all mental experience, of the mind with its objects:

> Nothing exists but as it is perceived. The difference is merely nominal between those two classes of thought which are vulgarly distinguished by the names of ideas and of external objects. Pursuing the same thread of reasoning, the existence of distinct individual minds similar to that which is employed in now questioning its own nature, is likewise found to be a delusion. The words, *I, you, they*, are not signs of any actual difference subsisting between the assemblage of thoughts thus indicated, but are merely marks employed to denote the different modifications of the one mind. . . . The words *I*, and *you* and *they* are grammatical devices invented simply for arrangement.
>
> (*PP*, 477–8)

Shelley is conscious of the contradiction involved in trying to use language to reveal delusions inherent in language: he goes on to acknowledge that 'It is difficult to find terms adequately to express so subtle a conception as that to which the intellectual philosophy has conducted us. We are on that verge where words abandon us' (*PP*, 478). But Shelley was capable at times of not worrying about being abandoned by words. He returns to the dizzying conceptions of 'On Life' in the fourth paragraph of the *Defence*, as he drops the primitivist fiction but continues to depreciate the structural particularities of poetic language:

> A Poet participates in the eternal, the infinite, and the one; as far as relates to his conceptions, time and place and number are not. The grammatical forms which express the moods of time, and the difference of persons and the distinctions of place are convertible with respect to the highest poetry without injuring it as poetry.
>
> (PP, 483)

The clause that needs emphasizing here is 'as far as relates to his conceptions'. Just how far this is, is the question which Shelley has so far been reluctant to bring into sharp focus. His doing so in the paragraphs that follow will mean, among other things, that his confidence in the convertibility of the 'grammatical forms' in 'the choruses of Aeschylus, and the book of Job, and Dante's Paradise' (*PP*, 483) will give way to his sense of 'the vanity of translation', an idea which insists both on the arbitrariness and imperfection of language and on its irreducible importance.

II

Shelley finally commits himself in the fifth paragraph of the *Defence* to a direct consideration of language as the medium of poetry by adopting a familiar eighteenth-century procedure, the formal comparison of the different arts:

> Language, colour, form, and religious and civil habits of action are all the instruments and materials of poetry; they may be called poetry by that figure of speech which considers the effect as synonime of the cause. But poetry in a more restricted sense expresses those arrangements of language, and especially metrical language, which are created by that imperial faculty, whose throne is curtained within the invisible nature of man. And this springs from the nature itself of language, which is a more direct representation of the actions and passions of our internal being, and is susceptible of more various and delicate combinations, than colour, form, or motion, and is more plastic and obedient to the

controul of that faculty of which it is the creation. For language is arbitrarily produced by the Imagination and has relation to thoughts alone; but all other materials, instruments and conditions of art, have relations among each other, which limit and interpose between conception and expression. The former is as a mirror which reflects, the latter as a cloud which enfeebles, the light of which both are mediums of communication. Hence the fame of sculptors, painters and musicians, although the intrinsic powers of the great masters of these arts, may yield in no degree to that of those who have employed language as the hieroglyphic of their thoughts, has never equalled that of poets in the restricted sense of the term.

(*PP*, 483)

What is so striking about Shelley's comparative argument is not that he claims the superiority of poetry, but that he does so on the basis of unique resources in language. From the more broadly generalizing perspective of the beginning of the *Defence*, Shelley was able to say that 'there is a certain order or rhythm belonging to each of these classes of mimetic representation, from which the hearer and the spectator receive an intenser and purer pleasure than from any other' (*PP*, 481). But from the comparative and expressive perspectives dominant in this paragraph, the verbal medium of poetry is seen to be capable of producing the most intense and the purest imaginative pleasure of all.

Shelley is drawing on a long tradition of defining the special powers of poetry in comparison to the other arts. Addison initiated one aspect of that tradition in *Spectator* 416 when he argued that words have a greater power than sight itself to arouse certain Secondary Pleasures of the Imagination, because through verbal description of an object or scene 'the Poet gives us as free a View of it as he pleases, and discovers to us several Parts, that either we did not attend to, or that lay out of our Sight when we first beheld it.'[20] Among later theorists who took off from Addison's argument, the most important and influential was Burke; he claimed a unique evocative power for poetic language not because of its descriptive freedom, but because of its peculiar affective potency:

But as to words; they seem to me to affect us in a manner very different from that in which we are affected by natural objects, or by painting or architecture. . . . Such words are in reality but mere

sounds; but they are sounds, which being used on particular
occasions, wherein we receive some good, or suffer some evil . . .
and being applied in such a variety of cases that we know readily
by habit to what things they belong, they produce in the mind,
whenever they are afterwards mentioned, effects similar to those
of their occasions. . . . the sound without any annexed notion
continues to operate as before.[21]

Burke's locating the distinctive power of language in the capacity of
words to function as 'mere sounds' and to evoke an emotion by
association or habit 'without any annexed notion' is the opposite of
Shelley's sense that language is unique because it represents 'the actions
and passions of our internal being' and 'has relation to thoughts alone'.
A view closer to Shelley's was put forward by the linguist James Harris
in the second of his *Three Treatises* (1765), 'A Discourse Concerning
Music, Painting, and Poetry':

> *Poetry*, having the *Ear* also for its *Organ*, as far as *Words* are
> considered to be no more than *mere Sounds*, we can go no farther in
> Imitating, than may be performed by *Sound* and *Motion*. But then,
> as *these its Sounds stand by Compact for the various Ideas, with which the
> mind is fraught*, it is enabled by this means to imitate, *as far as
> Language can express*; and that 'tis evident will, in a manner, include
> all things.
>
> (ch. 1)

> POETIC IMITATION includes every thing in it, which is
> performed either by *Picture-Imitation* or *Musical*; for its Materials
> are *Words*, and *Words are Symbols by Compact of all Ideas*.[22]
>
> (ch. 3)

Harris's celebration of the verbal medium, like Shelley's, depends upon
thinking of words as signs for thoughts or ideas, and while he begins
with a strong mimetic emphasis, he goes on to elaborate his argument
from an expressive angle as well:

> Not only therefore is *Language* an adequate *Medium of Imitation*,
> but in *Sentiments* it is the only *Medium*; and in *Manners* and *Passions*
> there is no other, which can exhibit them to us after that clear,
> precise, and definite Way.[23]
>
> (ch. 5)

One can see in passages like these why Kathleen Coburn cites Harris as a possible source for Coleridge's remarks on language in the lecture notes which have come to be titled *On Poesy or Art*:

> Poetry likewise is purely *human* – all its materials are *from* the mind, and all the products are *for* the mind. . . . In this way Poetry is the ~~Perp~~ Preparation for Art: inasmuch as it avails itself of the forms of Nature to recall, to express, and to modify the thoughts and feelings of the mind – still however thro' the medium of *articulate speech*, which is so peculiarly human that in all languages it is the ordinary ~~distinction~~ phrase by which Man and Nature are contra-distinguished.[24]

Coleridge dated these lecture notes 10 March 1818, the day before Shelley and Mary left England for the Continent, so it is highly unlikely that he was a direct influence on the passage in the *Defence*. What Coleridge and Shelley unmistakably share, however, is the conviction that the verbal medium is uniquely '*from* the mind' and '*for* the mind'.

As Shelley narrows his focus to consider 'the nature itself of language', he expounds his sense of the relation of mind and language with considerable exactness. He begins by saying that language 'is a more direct representation of the actions and passions of our internal being' than other artistic media, and thus more subtly responsive to the mind's expressive activity. This clearly implies that the mind's thought and feelings exist prior to the words originally created or subsequently employed to articulate them. As a 'representation' of our 'internal being', language presupposes an anterior presence or presentation of mental 'actions and passions'. That language might play some constitutive role in determining what those 'actions and passions' are in the first place is not part of Shelley's thinking here. It is resolutely thought that constitutes or produces language:

> For language is arbitrarily produced by the imagination and has relation to thoughts alone . . .

Shelley is likely to sound surprisingly modern to a reader who believes that the arbitrariness of linguistic signs is an idea discovered by Ferdinand de Saussure and first asserted in the *Cours de linguistique générale*.[25] But in fact it is considered at length in Plato's *Cratylus* and had become axiomatic in most serious linguistic theory since Locke's *Essay Concerning Human Understanding*.[26] Despite his decidedly un-Lockian emphasis on imagination, the main principles underlying Shelley's conception of language could have been derived from Book III of Locke's *Essay*: first, that words are created by the mind as the signs not of things but of thoughts ('*Words, in their primary or immediate Signification, stand for nothing but the* Ideas *in the mind of him that uses them,* how imperfectly soever, or carelessly those *Ideas* are collected from the Things, which they are supposed to represent', III.ii.2); secondly, that the relation between words and the thoughts they signify is not natural but arbitrary ('*Words* . . . came to be made use of by Men, as *the Signs of* their *Ideas*; not by any natural connexion, that there is between particular articulate Sounds and certain *Ideas*, for then there would be but one Language amongst all Men; but by a voluntary Imposition, whereby such a Word is made arbitrarily the Mark of such an *Idea*', III.ii.1).[27] Shelley had none of the antipathy to Locke assumed to be characteristic of Romantic writers, and it is quite possible that Book III of Locke's *Essay* had an immediate influence on the language of the *Defence*.[28] That he read Locke enthusiastically and quoted him approvingly during and just after his time at Oxford is not surprising.[29] More significant is the fact that he kept reading Locke throughout his life. In September 1815 he wrote to his bookseller: 'I have the 2nd volume of the 21st Edition of Locke's Essay on the Human Understanding. I should be obliged if you could procure me the 1st vol. which is deficient' (*Letters*, I, 431).[30] Mary Shelley's *Journal* shows that Shelley read Locke regularly from November 1816 to January 1817, and that he returned to him again in March 1820, less than a year before he began the *Defence* (*Mary Shelley's Journal*, 68–74, 131).

Shelley's basing his celebration of the verbal medium of poetry partly upon the arbitrariness of linguistic signs is striking, and in several respects risky. Wordsworth repeatedly associates the arbitrariness of language with its corruption, as in the Preface of 1800 ('arbitrary and capricious habits of expression'),[31] and with its inherent limitations, as in the Essay Supplementary to the Preface of 1815 ('language; a thing subject to endless fluctuations and arbitrary associations').[32] Coleridge accepts the principle that words are arbitrarily related to the thoughts they signify, but he chafes against it on behalf of an organically conceived ideal:

> Is thinking *impossible* without arbitrary signs? & how far is the word 'arbitrary' a misnomer? Are not words &c parts & germinations of the Plant?[33]

Coleridge's sense that there may be something arbitrary about the term 'arbitrary' is shrewd and points to one source of potential uncertainty in Shelley's assertion. Locke uses 'arbitrarily' to mean 'by a voluntary imposition', and this seems to be Shelley's main sense of it too: language is created by a voluntary act of mind. But this use of the word in the eighteenth century is confined to linguistic theory. Johnson's *Dictionary* gives the two more familiar senses: '1. Despotick; absolute; bound by no law; following the will without restraint . . . 2. Depending on no rule; capricious.'[34] Shelley incorporates and transforms the first of these senses when he refers to the imagination as 'that imperial faculty'. But the possibility that the arbitrariness of language can be imperious and despotic lurks within the terms of Shelley's celebration; it is certainly something one is made to feel by Shelley's customary way of using the word 'arbitrary' and its variants, even within the *Defence* itself:

> Let us for a moment stoop to the arbitration of popular breath . . .[35]
>
> (*PP*, 506)

That 'arbitrarily produced' might come to mean 'capriciously produced' is an idea which also shadows Shelley's language here. It was implied in his previous depreciation of 'the copiousness of lexicography and the distinctions of grammar' as being 'merely the catalogue and the form of poetry', and therefore 'convertible with respect to the highest poetry'. It emerges explicitly elsewhere, as we shall see, when he thinks about a poet's having to work with words which have already been 'arbitrarily produced'.

Shelley might have been guided towards his positive appropriation of Locke's idea of arbitrary signs by Monboddo's incisive discussion of what he calls 'this so curious subject' in Part II, Book I, Chapter 16 of *The Origin and Progress of Language*. Monboddo immediately refers his reader to the most important consideration of the question in classical antiquity, Plato's *Cratylus*, a text which Shelley himself almost certainly knew.[36] 'It is . . . from Plato only,' Monboddo says, 'that I have got any light upon this subject.'[37] Yet he goes on to insist that 'notwithstanding this inspiration, the dialogue concludes sceptically as to the question in dispute betwixt the parties.'[38] After showing how Socrates exposes the untenable exaggerations of both Hermogenes (names are arbitrary) and Cratylus (names are natural), Monboddo bases his own position on an interesting distinction between the arbitrariness of 'original words' and the rule-governed 'art' required for the subsequent refinements and complexities of language as we know it. He implicitly suggests a basis for Shelley's positive ideal of linguistic arbitrariness when he recalls that 'Socrates proceeds upon the supposition, that those lawgivers in language, as he calls them, were philosophers of the sect of Heraclitus, who maintained that everything was in constant flux and motion.'[39] It is certainly consistent with Shelley's idea of poets as 'unacknowledged legislators' to think of words as originally produced by the imagination of *arbiters*, 'lawgivers' of language.

But what about poets who inherit a language produced by previous arbiters, a language inevitably fraught, as Shelley has reminded us in the passage on metaphor, with the despotic, capricious arbitrariness of dead metaphor? The ways in which the dark possibilities of the arbitrary cloud Shelley's brilliant celebration of it are confirmed when we look at the images he uses in comparing the relation between 'conception and expression' as it is affected by language on the one hand, and by 'all other materials, instruments, and conditions of art' on the other: 'The former is as a mirror which reflects, the latter as a cloud which enfeebles, the light of which both are mediums of communication.' The mirror is one of Shelley's favorite figures for the mind itself; that it here becomes a figure for the capacity of language to reflect the mind dramatizes Shelley's emphasis on the special connection of words and thoughts.[40] But to say that language is 'as a mirror which reflects' without saying anything about the adequacy of that reflection is sufficient only in a passage which compares mirrors to clouds. The ambiguity of the mirror image is made apparent by Shelley himself four paragraphs later:

> The story of particular facts is as a mirror which obscures and distorts that which should be beautiful: Poetry is a mirror which makes beautiful that which is distorted.
>
> (*PP*, 485)

The movement from the simile of a distorting mirror to the metaphor of an idealizing one is revealing, since in the earlier passage language is '*as* a mirror' (my emphasis), and since neither a distorting nor an idealizing mirror exactly reflects the light it receives. While in comparison to other media language may be an idealizing mirror, in relation to thought or conception itself it may necessarily be as obscuring as the cloud to which it is here contrasted – or as the veil or vestment which replace the mirror as Shelley's favored metaphors for words later in the *Defence*. Language is created in the first place, Shelley has told us, by 'that imperial faculty, whose throne is *curtained* within the invisible nature of man' (my emphasis).

Shelley brings his comparative celebration of the verbal medium to a close with yet another image which reveals some latent uncertainty in the basic terms of his argument. Poets 'in the restricted sense of the term' employ 'language as the hieroglyphic of their thoughts'. One can see immediately that 'language as . . . hieroglyphic' suits Shelley's rhetorical purpose very well. In the present context it reconciles the comparative antithesis of the verbal medium and other artistic media. In the larger perspective of the entire essay it looks back to and bridges the gap between live metaphors as 'pictures of integral thoughts' and dead metaphors as 'signs for portions or classes of thoughts'. The image also looks forward: to the inseparable fusion of verbal form and signification which makes translation vain (here again Diderot provides an interesting precedent, with his claim that lines of poetry 'are not merely a chain of vigorous words which express the thought both forcibly and nobly, but a series of hieroglyphs, one after another, which picture the thought to us visibly'),[41] and to Shelley's concluding ideal of poets as 'the hierophants of an unapprehended inspiration'. Yet despite its complex rhetorical function, the notion of language-as-hieroglyph confuses the distinction between the natural forms and materials of the other arts and the arbitrary signs of language so central to this paragraph. Even if Shelley had read William Warburton's seminal account in *The Divine Legation of Moses* (1737–8) of how the originally natural signs of Egyptian hieroglyphs came to be used as arbitrary signs,[42] the fact remains that the forms of hieroglyphic symbols are residually natural and are not 'arbitrarily produced by the imagination' with 'relation to thoughts alone'. Shelley wants to celebrate the radical distinctiveness of language as a completely human and mental creation. But he also wants to give language a pictorial immediacy and unity, and this urges him in the direction of natural and material forms. A writer entirely secure with the arbitrariness of words would have no need to blur an argument based upon it by having recourse to the notion of words as hieroglyphs.

With the sixth paragraph of the *Defence* Shelley narrows his focus still further 'to determine the distinction between measured and unmeasured language; for the popular division into prose and verse is inadmissible' (*PP*, 484). He has already laid the grounds for his argument in the second and third paragraphs with his claim that 'men, even in the infancy of society, observe a certain order in their words and actions, distinct from that of the objects and the impressions represented by them.' In poetry, this 'certain order' is now said to take the form of

> a certain uniform and harmonious recurrence of sound, without
> which it were not poetry, and which is scarcely less indispensable
> to the communication of its influence, than the words themselves,
> without reference to that peculiar order. Hence the vanity of
> translation; it were as wise to cast a violet into a crucible that you
> might discover the formal principle of its colour and odour, as
> seek to transfuse from one language into another the creation of a
> poet. The plant must spring again from its seed, or it will bear no
> flower – and this is the burthen of the curse of Babel.
>
> (*PP*, 484)

Shelley's metaphor of the violet stands in striking contrast to what he
has just said about 'the nature itself of language': the connection of
articulate sounds to the thoughts they signify may be fundamentally
arbitrary, but the poet creates what Cythna in *The Revolt of Islam* calls 'a
subtler language within language' (VII.3112) and gives those arbitrary
connections a new integrity which can be expressed only as a natural
organic unity. But while a poet's words may be like violets in this sense,
as entities 'arbitrarily produced by the imagination' they can never fully
be the natural things that violets are. Once again Shelley extols the
resources of language by reminding us of and then transvaluing the
limits of language. His remark about 'the vanity of translation',
although offered in support of the indissoluble fusion of thought and
articulate sound in poetry, recalls Locke's remarks about the limits of all
translation between languages whose signs are the arbitrary creations of
particular cultures and not 'the steady workmanship of nature' (*Essay*
III.v.8).[43] And his reference to 'the burthen of the curse of Babel' recalls
Bacon's words about 'the second curse of the confusion of
tongues'.

Shelley is able to write openly here near the end of the first
movement of the *Defence* about the general limits of language because,
paradoxically, he draws confidence from the particular formal aspect of
language – the 'uniform and harmonious recurrence of sound' – which
is his immediate subject. He is closer to Wordsworth than to Coleridge
in affirming that the 'distinction between poets and prose writers is a
vulgar error', but his reasoning is quite different from both of theirs.
Shelley goes beyond Wordsworth's qualification of meter as the point
of distinction between verse and prose ('nor is this, in truth, a *strict*
antithesis; because lines and passages of metre so naturally occur in

writing prose')[44] by claiming that prose no less than verse may contain the 'measured language' proper to poetry. His examples are Plato, Cicero and Bacon:

> Lord Bacon was a poet. His language has a sweet and majestic rhythm, which satisfies the sense, no less than the almost superhuman wisdom of his philosophy satisfies the intellect; it is a strain which distends, and then bursts the circumference of the hearer's mind, and pours itself forth together with it into the universal element with which it has perpetual sympathy.
>
> (*PP*, 484–5)

The rhythm of Shelley's own sentence, although certainly un-Baconian, illustrates the point that while poetry often does make use of 'metre, or a certain system of traditional forms of harmony of language', it is 'by no means essential that a poet should accommodate his language to this traditional form'. The proper distinction in Shelley's view is between the more systematic and traditional forms of measured language we call meter, and the less systematic and traditional forms of measured language ('rhythm') available to the prose writer.

Shelley sees that there are both special advantages and special obligations in adopting the traditional systems of meter. He is vague here about the advantages: that these are particularly apparent 'in such composition as includes much form and action' leaves open the possibilities both of congruence and of counterpoint between subject and systematic rhythm. Yet the language in the characterization of Bacon's 'sweet and majestic rhythm' about 'a strain which distends, and then bursts the circumference of the hearer's mind' conveys none of Wordsworth's sense of meter as a pattern which checks and tempers 'excitement . . carried beyond its proper bound',[45] nor of Coleridge's notion that meter has its origin in 'the balance in the mind effected by that spontaneous effort which strives to hold in check the workings of passion'.[46] About the special obligations incumbent upon the poet who employs meter Shelley is more precise: 'every great poet must inevitably innovate upon the example of his predecessors in the exact structure of his peculiar versification.' Shelley's interest in formal innovation and experimentation is as strong as that of any Romantic poet. Here we have that interest articulated as a principle.

III

Shelley's attitude towards language as the medium of poetry in the first movement of the *Defence* is ostensibly celebratory and confident. Yet the more specific he becomes in examining its unique resources, the more likely he is to reveal an underlying linguistic skepticism that runs throughout the *Defence* like a counterplot. This skepticism about the adequacy of language to express the conceptions of the poet is no submerged counterplot elsewhere in Shelley's writing – it appears openly, frequently and often with a clear indication of its origins in the philosophical traditions he most admired. The combined influence of Bacon and Locke is evident in a letter to Godwin of 29 July 1812:

> You say that words will neither debauch our understandings, nor distort our moral feelings. . . . But *words* are the very things that so eminently contribute to the growth & establishment of prejudice: the learning of *words* before the mind is capable of attaching correspondent ideas to them, is like possessing machinery with the use of which we are so unacquainted as to be in danger of misusing it. But words are merely signs of ideas, how many evils, & how great spring from the annexing inadequate & improper ideas to words.
>
> (*Letters*, I, 317)

Sometimes in his early prose Shelley is more distinctly Baconian and emphasizes the prevalent confusion of words and things, as in the notes to *Queen Mab* ('By the vulgar mistake of a metaphor for a real thing, of a word for a thing', *PW*, 812); sometimes he echoes Locke's emphasis on the connection of words and ideas:

> Let us analyse the ideas and feelings which constitute the contending beliefs, and watchfully establish a discrimination between words and thoughts.
>
> ('Essay on a Future State', *CW*, VI, 205)

Shelley's philosophical convictions change in the years that follow, but skepticism about language remains conspicuous.

> We do not attend sufficiently to what passes within ourselves. We combine words, combined a thousand times before. In our minds we assume entire opinions; and in the expression of those opinions, entire phrases, when we would philosophise. Our

whole style of expression and sentiment is inflected with the tritest plagiarisms. Our words are dead, our thoughts are cold and borrowed.

> (*Speculations on Metaphysics, CW*, VII, 62)

I have found my language misunderstood like one in a distant and savage land.

> ('On Love', *PP*, 473)

These words are inefficient and metaphorical – Most words so – No help –

> (Shelley's note to 'On Love', *PP*, 474)

How vain it is to think that words can penetrate the mystery of our being.

> ('On Life', *PP*, 475)

[The 'intellectual philosophy'] reduces the mind to that freedom in which it would have acted, but for the misuse of words and signs, the instruments of its own creation.

> ('On Life', *PP*, 477)

Names borrowed from the life; and opinions of Jesus Christ were employed as symbols of domination and imposture. . . . Not his doctrines, for they are too simple and direct to be susceptible of such perversion – but the mere names.

> (*A Philosophical View of Reform, CW*, VII, 5)

The same mistrust of language is recurrent and familiar ('too familiar, no doubt, to some', says one recent critic)[47] in Shelley's poetry, from the *Hymn to Intellectual Beauty*:

> That thou – O awful LOVELINESS,
> Wouldst give whate'er these words cannot express.
>
> (71–2)

to *Epipsychidion*:

> The winged words on which my soul would pierce
> Into the height of love's rare Universe,
> Are chains of lead around its flight of fire. –
>
> (588–90)

In all these instances Shelley locates the inadequacy of language precisely where, in the *Defence*, he sees its unique expressive potential – in its capacity to represent 'the actions and passions of our internal being'.[48]

In the second main movement of the *Defence* Shelley turns from the intrinsic resources of poetry itself 'to estimate its effects upon society', and the verbal medium of poetry, which has finally come to the fore in the last six paragraphs of the first movement, again moves into the background. But precisely because Shelley is no longer immediately concerned with a celebration of language, the uncertainty in his attitude towards it occasionally emerges more openly. There is, for instance, Shelley's conviction that the poets of every era have to contend with the linguistic deceptions characteristic of false religious dogma. He introduces this idea in the first major paragraph of the second movement:

> Every epoch under names more or less specious has deified its peculiar errors. . . . But a Poet considers the vices of his contemporaries as the temporary dress in which his creations must be arrayed, and which cover without concealing the eternal proportions of their beauty. . . . The beauty of the internal nature cannot be so far concealed by its accidental vesture, but that the spirit of its form shall communicate itself to the very disguise, and indicate the shape it hides from the manner in which it is worn.
>
> (*PP*, 486–7)

Shelley returns to this idea in a later paragraph when he takes up the 'poetry in the doctrines of Jesus Christ, and the mythology and institutions of the Celtic conquerors of the Roman empire':

> It is unfortunate for those who cannot distinguish words from thoughts, that many of these anomalies have been incorporated into our popular religion.
>
> (*PP*, 496)

In these two passages, as in the earlier account of metaphor, specious or dead semantic relations have to be exposed – thoughts must be distinguished from words – if the poet is to escape the corrupting power of language. But in the first of the two passages quoted above it is clear that he does not escape completely; his 'creations' are 'arrayed' in and partly hidden by the 'temporary dress', the 'accidental vesture', the 'disguise' of the language he necessarily shares with his society.

The figure of language as the dress, vestment or veil of thought becomes extremely prominent in this second movement of the *Defence*. It stands, as we noted earlier, in apparent antithesis to Shelley's previous figure of language 'as a mirror which reflects' rather than hides 'the light' of imaginative conception. Both figures are antithetical to characteristic Romantic ways of imaging language. The impulse is strong in both Coleridge and Wordsworth to see language as the incarnation of thought, to see words as symbols through which thoughts become present to the senses as things. 'I would endeavour to destroy the old antithesis of *Words* and *Things*,' Coleridge wrote to Godwin in 1800, 'elevating, as it were, words into Things, and living Things too.'[49] For Coleridge a word ideally acquires 'a *feeling of reality* – it heats and burns, makes itself to be felt. If we do not grasp it, it seems to grasp us, as with a hand of flesh and blood, and completely counterfeits an immediate presence.'[50] In Wordsworth this impulse is tempered by a recurrent sense of what in *The Prelude* he calls 'the sad incompetence of human speech', but it is none the less strong.[51] A well-known passage from the third *Essay Upon Epitaphs* explicitly rejects the figure of language as clothing or vestment in favor of language as the embodiment or incarnation of thought:

> Words are too awful an instrument for good and evil to be trifled with: they hold above all other external powers a dominion over thoughts. If words be not (recurring to a metaphor before used) an incarnation of the thought but only a clothing for it, then surely will they prove an ill gift; such a one as those poisoned vestments, read of in the stories of superstitious times, which had power to consume and to alienate from his right mind the victim who put them on.[52]

Wordsworth makes clear the source of the words-as-clothing metaphor he here attacks in a previous passage in the same paragraph, where he contrasts 'the artifices which have overrun our writings in metre since the days of Dryden and Pope' with 'expressions which are not what the garb is to the body but what the body is to the soul'.[53] Wordsworth knows very well that language can function, as it does for Pope in *An Essay on Criticism*, as 'the dress of thought'.[54] But when it does it becomes 'a counter-spirit, unremittingly and noiselessly at work to derange, to subvert, to lay waste, to vitiate, and to dissolve'.[55]

In contrast to Wordsworth and Coleridge, Shelley freely appropriates the idea of language as dress or vestment to express his sense that the poet must inevitably articulate his conceptions in words not entirely of his own making, in words which, though they have 'relation to thoughts alone', can never be those thoughts. He generally avoids speaking of language as the embodiment, incorporation or incarnation of thought. When he does use this figure, as in the Preface to *The Cenci*, it is to idealize the mental power which produces language, rather than language itself:

> In a dramatic composition the imagery and the passion should interpenetrate one another, the former being reserved simply for the full development and illustration of the latter. Imagination is as the immortal God which should assume flesh for the redemption of mortal passion.
>
> *(PP, 241)*

In the one instance where 'incarnation' appears in the *Defence*, there is no direct reference to the verbal medium:

> [Poetry] transmutes all that it touches, and every form moving within the radiance of its presence is changed by wondrous sympathy to an incarnation of the spirit which it breathes.
>
> *(PP, 505)*

Much more frequently and characteristically, Shelley inverts the figure of linguistic incarnation and sees imagination, conception or thought as the naked body clothed or veiled by language.[56] To return to the long paragraph which begins the central movement of the *Defence*:

> Few poets of the highest class have chosen to exhibit the beauty of their conceptions in its naked truth and splendour; and it is doubtful whether the alloy of costume, habit, etc., be not necessary to temper this planetary music for mortal ears.
>
> *(PP, 487)*

What is so deeply characteristic in this sentence is Shelley's way of transmuting the language-as-clothing/veil idea from a figure expressive of his suppressed linguistic skepticism to a figure by which he celebrates the inexpressible 'truth and splendour' of poetic conception in its naked purity. Notice that Shelley is ambiguous as to whether the verbal clothing or veiling of conception is a matter of the poet's choice, or simply a 'necessary', ineluctable condition of even the highest poetry.

Shelley's preference for language-as-vestment (and language-as-mirror) over language-as-incarnation provides yet another indication of his intellectual ties to the eighteenth century. But these recurrent Shelleyan figures carry the associations of other sources as well. The most important for this particular movement of the *Defence* is Dante.[57] In the Advertisement to *Epipsychidion*, written immediately before he drafted the *Defence* in February and March of 1821, Shelley quotes *La Vita Nuova* XXV:

> gran vergogna sarebbe a colui, che rimasse cosa sotto veste de figura, o di colore rettorico: e domandato non sapesse denudare le sue parole da cotal veste, in guisa che avessero verace intendimento.[58]

> [it would be a great shame to him, who should rhyme anything under the vestment of figurative language, or of rhetorical colors: and, being asked, would not know how to denude his words of such a vestment, in such a way as they might have true understanding.]

Figurative and rhetorical language is a garb or vestment ('veste') not only of the poet's thought, but of a clear and direct verbalization of that thought. The poet must be able to strip that vestment away from what are still his words ('denudare le sue parole da cotal veste') and convey his meaning directly.

In the paragraphs which conclude Shelley's historical survey of poetry's 'effects upon society', he adopts the key metaphors from *La Vita Nuova* XXV and applies them to Dante himself. In doing so he radically transforms those metaphors in ways which reveal a recurrently fluctuating attitude towards language. Having praised the lyric poetry of the *Vita Nuova* as 'an inexhaustible fountain of purity of sentiment and language' (*PP*, 497), Shelley goes on to celebrate Dante as 'the second epic poet' (*PP*, 499) after Homer (Milton is his chief rival). Dante's achievement, more conspicuously in Shelley's view than either Homer's or Milton's, was linguistic:

> he created a language in itself music and persuasion out of a chaos of inharmonious barbarisms. . . . His very words are instinct with spirit; each is as a spark, a burning atom of inextinguishable thought; and many yet lie covered in the ashes of their birth, and pregnant with a lightning which has yet found no conductor. All

high poetry is infinite; it is as the first acorn, which contained all oaks potentially. Veil after veil may be undrawn, and the inmost naked beauty of the meaning never exposed.

(*PP*, 499–500)

As with other extended passages from the *Defence* we have looked at, the volatility and agitation of Shelley's thinking about language are revealed most tellingly in the shift and drift of his metaphors. At first Dante's words are not just signs related to his thoughts; they are '*instinct with spirit*'. This idea gets expanded in the imagery and etymological play of the second clause: 'each is as a spark, a burning atom of *inextinguishable* thought' (my emphasis). For a moment Dante's words are seen not just to reflect the light of the imagination, as in Shelley's previous celebration of the verbal medium, but to partake of and burn with that light. Yet as the sentence continues and we move into the third clause, Dante's burning words come to be partly 'covered in the ashes of their birth'. The metaphorical transition recalls the end of *Ode to the West Wind*, where words are 'Ashes' of 'dead thoughts' as well as 'sparks' from 'an unextinguished hearth' (63–7), and it anticipates the account of 'the mind in creation . . . as a fading coal' later in the *Defence*.[59] Here, having acknowledged metaphorically that words may necessarily obscure the imaginative light with which they burn, Shelley sets about transmuting an apparent limitation into a strength. He does this by diverting attention from the actual to the potential: the very fact that the sparks of creative thought with which words are instinct 'lie covered in . . . ashes' gives those sparks a much greater potential, the potential of 'lightning which has yet found no conductor'. The infinite potential meaning of poetry is seen to depend upon the inability of words ever completely to conduct and therefore to discharge the mental energy they signify. So when Shelley goes on to transfigure words-as-ashes into words-as-veil, he does so not to lament the discrepancy between thoughts and words, but to expand his claim that 'All high poetry is infinite.'

In the third main movement of the *Defence*, as Shelley turns to consider more directly Peacock's attack on the 'utility' of poetry, he keeps the question of language even more resolutely in the background. When the question does emerge, Shelley's impulse is still to try to convert his sense of the inadequacy of language into an ideal of inexhaustible poetic meaning, as he had done in the passage on metaphor from the first movement, and in the passage on Dante from the second. The metaphors of ash and fire, veil or vestment and naked body, shadow and reflection continue to provide the vital elements of the transvaluations. But the effort of defending poetry from the limitations of its own medium takes its toll, and in the most famous extended passage of the *Defence*, the process of transvaluation falters.

That paragraph begins with the confident assertion that 'Poetry is indeed something divine' (*PP*, 503). But as Shelley comes to consider the movement from conception to composition, from inspired thought to articulated word, the 'spark' and 'ashes' of the Dante passage fuse into a 'fading coal'. Between conception and composition falls the shadow:

> A man cannot say, 'I will compose poetry.' The greatest poet even cannot say it: for the mind in creation is as a fading coal, which some invisible influence, like an inconstant wind, awakens to transitory brightness: this power arises from within, like the colour of a flower which fades and changes as it is developed, and the conscious portions of our natures are unprophetic either of its approach or its departure. Could this influence be durable in its original purity and force, it is impossible to predict the greatness of the results: but when composition begins, inspiration is already on the decline, and the most glorious poetry that has ever been communicated to the world is probably a feeble shadow of the original conception of the poet.
>
> (*PP*, 503–4)

Shelley's principal focus is on the unpredictability and evanescence of inspired conception 'in its original purity'. But the consciousness of that pure original potential, and the proof of the unpredictability and evanescence which are its hallmarks, come only 'when composition begins', when the poet attempts to give his conception verbal form. The verbal composing of thought thus confirms a process of fading and decline which begins prior to composition. As Shelley goes on to say, the limits of language mark and reveal a more fundamental limitation:

> The toil and the delay recommended by critics can be justly interpreted to mean no more than a careful observation of the inspired moments, and an artificial connexion of the spaces between their suggestions by the intertexture of conventional

expressions; a necessity only imposed by the limitedness of the poetical faculty itself.

The inadequacies of language accentuate but resist being completely transvalued by Shelley's lyrical idealizing of 'the original conception of the Poet'. The 'toil and the delay' of composition are not, finally, aspects of a corrupt fiction which betrays the limitedness of critics. They are 'a necessity' which betrays 'the limitedness of the poetical faculty itself'. The language of poetry succeeds when it articulates by 'careful observation' its own idealized failure. Poetry as it actually exists records the failure of an ideal expressive completeness.[60]

The relation of this entire paragraph to Shelley's definition and celebration of 'the nature itself of language' in the fifth paragraph of the *Defence* can only be described as subversive. Instead of language 'as a mirror which reflects' (in contrast to 'a cloud which enfeebles') the light of imaginative conception, we have language as 'a feeble shadow' of a mind which burns with the 'transitory brightness' of a 'fading coal'.[61] The shift from 'mirror' to 'shadow' – from an object which figuratively intercepts and returns light, to an image produced when light is intercepted and obscured – epitomizes the shift in Shelley's sense of what it means to think of language as a 'representation of the actions and passions of our internal being'. And while in the earlier passage Shelley could confidently see the arbitrariness of words as a product of imagination and as an indication that words have 'relation to thoughts alone', he now relocates that arbitrariness in 'the intertexture of conventional expressions' which serve mainly as the 'artificial connexion of spaces between' moments of inspiration.

At the end of the paragraph Shelley even reverses his previous comparison of language to other artistic media. With the question of medium in the foreground, he had claimed that language is 'a more direct representation of the actions and passions of our internal being, and is susceptible of more various and delicate combinations, than colour, form, or motion, and is more plastic and obedient to the controul of that faculty of which it is the creation'. But with this later emphasis on the 'instinct and intuition of the poetical faculty' in its 'original purity', all media are seen to fall short of, and at best to produce 'a feeble shadow' of, 'the actions and passions of our internal being'. This is a truth, Shelley says, 'more observable in the plastic and pictorial arts' than in verbal poetry.

a great statue or picture grows under the power of the artist as a child in the mother's womb; and the very mind which directs the hands in formation is incapable of accounting to itself for the origin, gradations, or the media of the process.

(*PP*, 504)

Perhaps because for Shelley language is inherently a product of volitional consciousness, it disguises the mysterious, non-volitional way in which he here sees the 'instinct and intuition' of conception working themselves out, in apparently oblique relation to the directing will of the artist. The potential greatness of conception momentarily deprives composition of any but a tangential significance. By transforming the previous image of Dante's words as 'pregnant with a lightning which has yet found no conductor' into the image of a work of art as 'a child in the mother's womb', Shelley finally literalizes his pervasive concern with 'conception' and expands it until it takes over the functions of composition or 'formation' altogether.

In the concluding paragraphs of the *Defence*, language retains the mainly privative status it assumes in the critical 'fading coal' paragraph –it provides a system of signs for marking the spaces between and the residual traces of those 'evanescent visitations of thought and feeling' which Shelley has come to see as the essence of poetry:

> [Poetry] is as it were the interpenetration of a diviner nature through our own; but its footsteps are like those of a wind over a sea, which the coming calm erases, and whose traces remain only as on the wrinkled sand which paves it.

(*PP*, 504)

Early in the *Defence*, Shelley had quoted Bacon in characterizing the 'similitudes or relations' apprehended through 'vitally metaphorical' language as 'the same footsteps of nature impressed upon the various subjects of the world'. Now those footsteps of poetic thought are erased as soon as they are 'impressed', leaving the conscious mind with nothing but 'traces' (Shelley's rhyme here, 'erases' / 'traces', beautifully traces his own thought) of their dream-like 'visitations'.

> And the beasts, and the birds, and the insects were drowned
> In an ocean of dreams without a sound
> Whose waves never mark, though they ever impress
> The light sand which paves it – Consciousness.

(*The Sensitive Plant*, 'Part First', 102–5)

At first the 'vitally metaphorical' language of poetry seemed capable to

Shelley of impressions which were simultaneously mental and graphic –
'it marks the before unapprehended relations of things and perpetuates
their apprehension.' But now the wind of the poet's 'evanescent
visitations' of thought, like the waves of dream in *The Sensitive Plant*,
impress but 'never mark', never imprint, the sea above or the sand
below. Even 'vitally metaphorical' language provides only 'traces' of
the fleeting steps of 'the original conception of the Poet'.[62]

There has been a gradual and persistent darkening of the poetic
process as Shelley imagines it in the latter part of the *Defence*, from
Dante's words as 'sparks' and 'burning atom[s] of inextinguishable
thought', to those same 'sparks' 'covered in the ashes of their birth', to
'the mind in creation . . . as a fading coal', to the 'feeble shadow' which
poetry affords of 'the original conception of the poet'. It is consistent
with this pattern that the metaphor of language as veil pervades the
closing paragraphs of the *Defence*. Perpetuating the 'before unapprehended relations of things', redeeming 'from decay the visitations of the
divinity in Man' (*PP*, 505), come to be identified with veiling them.
Shelley's figurative darkenings and obscurations are all the more
striking for the way in which they are woven through the glowing
optimism of his rhetorical texture as a whole:

> Poetry thus makes immortal all that is best and most beautiful in
> the world; it arrests the vanishing apparitions which haunt the
> interlunations of life, and veiling them or in language or in form
> sends them forth among mankind.
>
> (*PP*, 505)

The excited assurance with which this sentence begins and ends is
momentarily eclipsed by the shadowy, gloomy activity of 'veiling' the
'vanishing apparitions which haunt the interlunations of life' – those
dark intervals when even the reflected light of the moon is absent.
Because he consistently sees poetry from both an expressive and a
representational perspective, Shelley can insist that poetic language and
form are a veil and yet claim that poetry 'strips the veil of familiarity
from the world, and lays bare the naked and sleeping beauty, which is
the spirit of its forms (*PP*, 505). This sentence is the precise representational antithesis to Shelley's prior expressive characterization of
great poetry like Dante's: 'Veil after veil may be undrawn, and the
inmost naked beauty of the meaning never exposed.' Poetic language
reveals the world's 'naked and sleeping beauty' even as it inevitably but
provocatively conceals the poet's conception 'in its original purity'. In

the next paragraph Shelley draws the two perspectives together in a dramatic paradox:

> All things exist as they are perceived: at least in relation to the percipient. . . . poetry defeats the curse which binds us to be subjected to the accident of surrounding impressions. And whether it spreads its own figured curtain or withdraws life's dark veil from before the scene of things, it equally creates for us a being within our being.
>
> (PP, 505)

The division in Shelley's attitude towards language is nowhere more concentratedly and daringly revealed than in this doubling of the veil/curtain/vestment figure.[63] Language 'defeats the curse' of solipsistic subjectivity but is itself, to adapt Bacon's phrase, 'the second general curse'. It is a medium wholly created 'by that imperial faculty, whose throne is curtained within the invisible nature of man', yet it expresses the 'instinct and intuition of the poetical faculty' only by veiling them in 'its own figured curtain'. By hiding 'the inmost naked beauty of the meaning', that 'figured curtain' makes poetry an inexhaustible 'source of an unforeseen and an unconceived delight' for generations of readers. For the poet, however, the curtain of language transmits only a 'feeble shadow' of what he foresees and conceives.

IV

As I have been reading it, *A Defence of Poetry* is in part a defense against, and a resourceful but uncertain triumph over, the linguistic skepticism which pervades Shelley's other writing. His strongest confidence in language derives from exactly the same source as his deepest anxiety about it, from the man-made, arbitrary relation of thoughts and words which Locke had placed at the center of our understanding of what language is. Language in the *Defence* begins as a mirror and ends as a veil of the poet's thoughts. That veil reveals as well as conceals; it makes meaning infinite and inexhaustible for the reader by hiding the original conception of the poet; it gives articulate form to pure thought which would otherwise elude mortal perception. But in the end the veil of language remains as evidence of 'the limitedness of the poetical faculty', in spite of Shelley's wondrous capacity to make a virtue of that limitedness.

In its unstable and at times paradoxical effort to recognize both the peculiar strengths and the inherent limitations of the verbal medium, the *Defence* provides the fullest, most complex account we have of Shelley's attitude towards language. But Shelley was also capable of entertaining a different conception of what language might be, a more visionary and mythical conception which receives its ultimate articulation in the transformed Earth's soaring lyric in Act IV of *Prometheus Unbound*:

> Language is a perpetual Orphic song,
>   Which rules with Daedal harmony a throng
> Of thoughts and forms, which else senseless and shapeless
> were.

(415–17)

As Susan Hawk Brisman observes in her impressive study of the problem of voice in *Prometheus Unbound*, these lines assume a view of language quite distinct from that encountered in the *Defence*: 'Act IV will not let the reader confine the power of speech to the unifying and relational activities of the mind explored in *A Defence of Poetry*.'[64] Brisman sees in *Prometheus Unbound* 'a repeatedly renewed conflict about the nature of language'.[65] In her scheme there is, on the one hand, the 'Hermetic' idea of language – represented in the speeches of Mercury, the Furies, Jupiter and Prometheus himself in the early phases of the drama – 'an idea of language that separates thoughts from words and gives the former priority', that understands languages as 'reference' and as 'the ornament rather than the incarnation of the thought'. On the other hand there is the 'Promethean' idea of language which 'denies that thoughts have sense and shape without words', and which holds instead that 'speech creates, that is, gives sense and vitality to thought' and 'strives to bring word and world into being simultaneously'.[66] This 'Promethean' ideal is gradually enacted in the reformation of the title character and is celebrated in the last act. Brisman acknowledges the connections between her argument and the account of Shelley and language developed in Gerald Bruns's *Modern Poetry and the Idea of Language*, an account which also emphasizes *Prometheus Unbound*. Bruns begins with Shelley's skepticism about 'ordinary language' but distinguishes this attitude sharply from what he calls 'the *Logos* of Shelley', 'conceived as a transcendent synthesis of being, percept, and word'.[67] Part of Prometheus's liberation, Bruns claims, is 'precisely the liberation of man from ordinary speech', 'a transformation of human language into something approximating the language of the gods'.[68] According to Bruns, Shelley sees the language of poetry as participating in such a transformation and as mediating between ordinary language and this ideal of the *Logos*. Like Brisman, Bruns insists on Shelley's belief in the constitutive power of language over thought, and he compares Shelley's position to that of Wilhelm von Humboldt, for whom language 'is not an artifact of the spirit but the very form in which the life of the spirit is realized'; it 'does not simply articulate the already formed contents of man's interior' but 'is the activity by which man's inner life takes on form and meaning'.[69]

Bruns and Brisman have done much to illuminate Shelley's vision of an ideally transformed language in *Prometheus Unbound*. But to take their versions of that vision as the culmination of – or even as characteristic of – Shelley's thinking about language would be misleading. That Shelley imagines a future condition of language in which it will become 'a perpetual Orphic song' is an important reflection of what he wants language in the present to be; as he says at the end of the *Defence*, in a convergence of previously antithetical images, poets are 'the mirrors of the gigantic shadows which futurity casts upon the present' (*PP*, 508). But as a poet who must necessarily confront and write out of a situation in which language is at best a momentary rather than a 'perpetual Orphic song', Shelley has to do more than contemplate the shadows of a future linguistic utopia. The fact is that all poetry, including the visionary lyrics of *Prometheus Unbound* itself, has to be fashioned out of what Bruns calls 'ordinary language', with all its resources and limitations. This is a fact more fully addressed in the *Defence* than anywhere else in Shelley's writing.

In their efforts to describe Shelley's vision of a perfect language in terms drawn from or at least consistent with modern critical and linguistic theory, Bruns and Brisman sometimes misrepresent what he actually says. For instance, Bruns quotes the passage in the *Defence* where Shelley evokes the inherent tendency of language to decline from its original metaphorical vitality into a system of dead signs with stale associations, and comments: 'We can pass over the evident commonplace that languages die and need to be revitalized, in order to observe that the language of poetry constitutes for Shelley a way of seeing unity in diversity.'[70] But to 'pass over' what Bruns calls this 'evident commonplace' is to misapprehend Shelley's sense of the poet's critical relationship to the language he inherits; it is to fail to see what a poet must do to make language 'a way of seeing' – or as Shelley says, a

way of 'marking' – anything vital at all, including 'unity in diversity'.
Brisman, as we have seen, is aware that her version of the linguistic ideal
in *Prometheus Unbound* is at odds with what Shelley says about language
in the *Defence* (and in most of his other writing, one might add). But the
discrepancies are crucial and deserve more than a passing acknowledgement. 'Promethean voice', she says, 'is always reclaiming speech from a
language of reference, where words are assumed to have stronger
relations to the objects and thoughts they represent than to one
another.'[71] In the *Defence* language is always and primarily 'a language
of reference', in that it 'is arbitrarily produced by the imagination and
has relation to thoughts alone' (my emphasis; Shelley avoids 'reference'
and 'refer' and instead prefers 'relation' or 'representation'). This
assumption of an intrinsic representational or signifying function does
not prevent him from recognizing that there is an 'order in . . . words
. . . distinct from that of the objects and the impressions represented by
them', that 'Sounds as well as thoughts have relation both between each
other and towards that which they represent'. Poetic language is never
merely 'a language of reference'; but like all language, only with
greater intensity and delicacy, it refers or 'has relation to thoughts
alone', and it is not at all clear what it would mean in Shelleyan terms to
'reclaim' language from this essential condition or function. When
Brisman goes on to categorize as 'Hermetic' and therefore un-
Promethean 'an idea of language that separates thoughts from words
and gives the former priority', that sees language as 'the ornament
rather than the incarnation of the thought', she is offering a debased
characterization of the idea of language that prevails in the *Defence* and
throughout most of Shelley's poetry and prose. The substitution of
'ornament' for Shelley's images of 'mirror', 'shadow', 'vesture' and
'veil', and the appeal to the un-Shelleyan notion of language as the
'incarnation' of thought, are strong indications that the linguistic
alternatives she poses for *Prometheus Unbound* are inadequate for
understanding his basic attitude.

What about the claims for Shelley's belief in the power of language
to shape and constitute – not just to represent or signify – thought? The
passage from Act IV of *Prometheus Unbound* about language ruling 'a
throng / Of thoughts and forms, which else senseless and shapeless
were' (416–17) makes it clear that this belief is part of the poem's vision
of future linguistic perfection. But Asia's words in Act II, scene iv also
suggest that language had this constitutive power when it was first given
to man as a gift from Prometheus:

He gave man speech, and speech created thought,
Which is the measure of the Universe . . .

(72–3)

These passages pose a number of important questions. How does Shelley's sense of the power of language to create thought relate to the fundamental principle expressed in the *Defence*, that 'language is arbitrarily produced by the imagination and has relation to thoughts alone? What does Shelley's understanding of this power have in common with the eighteenth- and early nineteenth-century linguistic theory available to him? Is the power of language over thought always the benefit and blessing it appears to be from the mythical past and future perspectives of *Prometheus Unbound*?

We might begin to answer these questions by going back to Locke – Shelley seems to have done this himself on several occasions – and by noticing that there is an incipient sense of the constitutive power of language in Book III of the *Essay Concerning Human Understanding*. It is implicit in Locke's general conviction that human knowledge has 'so near a connexion with words, that unless their force and manner of Signification were first well observed, there could be very little said clearly and pertinently concerning Knowledge' (III.ix.21). And it becomes explicit in his analysis of complex ideas: 'it is in the power of Words, standing for the several *Ideas*, that make that Composition, to imprint complex *Ideas* in the Mind, which were never there before' (III.iv.12). Locke could speak of language in this way without denying his fundamental principle that words are made by the mind as arbitrary signs for pre-existent thoughts. As he says in a famous passage about the collection of simple ideas into complex ideas: 'Though therefore it be the Mind that makes the Collection, 'tis the Name which is, as it were the Knot, that ties them fast together' (III.v.10). For Locke names are the work of the mind, but they in turn are indispensable in enabling the mind to work.

This notion of a reciprocal interdependence between thought and language was taken up, given new emphasis and variously elaborated and refined by theorists of language in the course of the eighteenth century. The most significant step in extending Locke's view of the dependence of certain modes of thought on developments in language was taken by Condillac, who argued in his *Essai sur l'origine des connaissances humaines* (1746) that reflection becomes possible only when the mind learns to use natural signs such as emotive gestures and instinctive cries as the basis for forming artificial 'signs of institution'. In reflection, says Condillac, 'thinking becomes an art, and that art is the art of speaking.'[72] Condillac's greatly expanded sense of the constitutive function of language in his account of the interdependent progress of language and thought was influential on all the French theorists that followed him: Rousseau,[73] Diderot[74] and especially the group at the end and turn of the century known as the *idéologues*. Pierre Jean Georges Cabanis, one of this group, makes clear the line of development back through Condillac to Locke in his *Rapports du physique et du moral* (1796), which Shelley ordered from his bookseller in December 1812: 'Since Locke, one has suspected the influence of language on ideas: since Condillac, one knows that the progress of the human spirit depends, in large part, on the perfection of the language proper to each science.'[75] Condillac's theory anticipated the careful speculations of Adam Smith's *Considerations Concerning the First Formation of Languages* (1767), and the much more ambitious and far-reaching claims of Herder's *Essay on the Origin of Language* (1772).[76]

The notion that language is both created by and constitutive of thought was therefore a central feature of much eighteenth-century linguistic theory. Near the end of the century the tendency to emphasize the dependence of thought on language grew much stronger. Horne Tooke rightly felt himself to be announcing a new age of philological science when he claimed in *The Diversions of Purley* (1786–1805) that 'the greatest part of Mr. Locke's Essay, that is, all which relates to what he calls the composition, abstraction, complexity, generalization, relation, &c. of Ideas, does indeed merely concern *Language*.'[77] But this effort to understand the operations of mind as operations of language could still be either resisted outright or accepted, as Locke and even Condillac had accepted it, as one aspect of a relationship that needed to remain mutual, reciprocal. Monboddo had resisted the tendency outright in *The Origin and Progress of Language*. Although he thought that 'from the study of language, if it be properly conducted, the history of the human mind is best learned,'[78] he tenaciously affirmed the priority of human thought over language and argued that civilized language was not the result of a natural progression from primitive signs and cries 'but must have been the work of *artists*' (II.i.1).[79] Shelley himself resisted outright when he said in the *Speculations on Metaphysics*:

Logic, or the science of words must no longer be confounded with metaphysics or the science of facts. Words are the instruments of mind whose capacities it becomes the Metaphysician accurately to know, but they are not mind, nor are they portions of mind. The discoveries of Horne Tooke in philology do not, as he has asserted, throw light upon Metaphysics, they only render the instruments requisite to its perception more exact and accurate.

(*CW*, VII, 63)

This is early Shelley, with his traditional suspicion of language at its most extreme, but it nevertheless stands as an important contrast to the Shelley who would later sing of speech as creating and ruling thought. It also poses a serious challenge to any hypothesis about a Shelleyan 'Logos'.

Between the extremes of Horne Tooke's philological radicalism and Shelley's youthful metaphysical purism we can locate the shifting and divided attitude implied in the *Defence*: to the extent that 'language is arbitrarily produced by the imagination and has relation to thoughts alone,' thought has an undeniable if unpredictable priority over language; and to the extent that language, once created by the mind, has the power to mark 'the before unapprehended relations of things and perpetuates their apprehension', it becomes indispensable to and constitutive of thought. The richest evocation of this attitude in Shelley's poetry is Cythna's in *The Revolt of Islam*, as she tells Laon of her long isolated imprisonment in a cavern beside the sea:

'My mind became the book through which I grew
　　Wise in all human wisdom, and its cave,
Which like a mine I rifled through and through,
　　To me the keeping of its secrets gave. . . .

'And on the sand would I make signs to range
　　These woofs, as they were woven, of my thought;
Clear, elemental shapes, whose smallest change
　　A subtler language within language wrought. . . .'

(VII.3100–12)

Cythna's self-education depends upon her already possessing a language, a means by which her memory can record her mind's reflections on its own impressions and processes and thus become its own book. As her mind grows it also fashions a language partly its own – partly, because it is 'A subtler language *within language*' (my emphasis). Cythna's linguistic inventions are wrought through changes within the possibilities of language as she finds it.[80] They come into being through writing, moreover – through marking 'These woofs, as they were woven, of my thought' not just mentally, in memory, but graphically, 'on the sand'. Shelley comes to affirm a reciprocal interdependence of thought and language. Although in 1812, as we have seen, he argued against Godwin's view of the centrality of language to intellectual development, by 1817–18 he would have agreed with Godwin's claim in *An Enquiry Concerning Human Justice* that the mental power of 'Abstraction, which was necessary to the first existence of language, is again assisted in its operations by language.'[81] Notice that in recognizing the importance of language for certain operations of the mind, Godwin still insists on the originating priority of thought. This impulse remains consistently strong in Shelley's later writing. Even in *Prometheus Unbound*, with its exuberant and utopian celebrations of the power of speech to create thought, we must remember that in Shelley's version of the myth it was Prometheus – *forethought*, 'the type of the highest perfection of moral and intellectual nature' (*PP*, 133) – who 'gave man speech' in the first place.

We must also remember that if language in an ideally transformed world has the constitutive power to rule 'with Daedal harmony a throng / Of thoughts and forms', in the actual untransformed world that same power can imprison and tyrannize thought. This is part of what Prometheus comes to understand about his own performative curse; it is an aspect of 'the shadow of the truth' he sees in Act I:

> Names are there, Nature's sacred watchwords – they
> Were borne aloft in bright emblazonry.
> The nations thronged around, and cried aloud,
> As with one voice, 'Truth, liberty and love!'
> Suddenly fierce confusion fell from Heaven
> Among them – there was strife, deceit and fear;
> Tyrants rushed in, and did divide the spoil.
>
> (648–54)

Language as a repository of 'symbols of domination and imposture', as Shelley describes it in *A Philosophical View of Reform* (1819), or language as 'a perpetual Orphic song' – in both cases it is the power of language to constitute and rule thought that is at stake. As Richard Cronin observes, for Shelley a situation in which speech creates thought and 'the limits of thought are defined by the limits of language' is often 'a cause not for celebration but for dismay'.[82] Only in the paradoxical myth of an original 'infancy of society' when 'language itself is poetry' (paradoxical because Latin *infans* means 'unable to speak', as Shelley certainly knew), or in the complementary myth of an ideal future when 'Language is a perpetual Orphic song', is Shelley momentarily able to celebrate the power of words over thought.

In the world as he found it Shelley knew with Bacon that 'although we think we govern our words . . . yet certain it is that words, as a Tartar's bow, do shoot back upon the understanding of the wisest, and mightily entangle and pervert our judgment' (*The Advancement of Learning*, Book II). He knew with Wordsworth that 'Words are too awful an instrument for good and evil to be trifled with; they hold above all other external powers a dominion over our thoughts' (*Essay Upon Epitaphs* III). Language arbitrarily produced by the imagination can just as easily tyrannize over as prove 'plastic and obedient to the controul of that faculty of which it is the creation'. Only by constantly reclaiming the mind's precarious dominion over words, 'the instruments of its own creation' ('On Life', *PP*, 477), can the poet compose those 'traces' of 'original conception' into something approximating an 'image of life expressed in its eternal truth' (*PP*, 485).

II IMAGING THE OPERATIONS OF THE HUMAN MIND

What Shelley says about language in the *Defence* carries uncertain implications for his own poetic practice. The skepticism about language evident in some passages might be seen to invite a stylistic defeatism often associated with him: why bother to work deliberately and scrupulously with language, since even in the greatest poets it can only shadow, veil or trace 'the original conception of the poet'? Keats may have sensed such a disposition in Shelley when he charily admonished him to ' "load every rift" of your subject with ore. The thought of such discipline must fall like cold chains upon you, who perhaps never sat with your wings furl'd six Months together.'[1] But there is more than one way of working the rifts of composition; the shifting and divided attitude towards words traceable in the *Defence* need not be taken to imply a frenzied flight of stylistic despair. It can and often does lead towards a self-conscious effort to exploit what Shelley sees as the unique but imperfect relation between language and thought. Through stylistic gestures and rifts in which language calls attention to itself as an arbitrary product of the imagination, as a medium supremely conductive of yet resistant to the mental activity from which it derives, Shelley acknowledges its inherent limitations while extending its resources. It is this impulse that I want to begin to explore by looking at specific stylistic aims and practices informed by Shelley's conviction that 'language is arbitrarily produced by the imagination and has relation to thoughts alone'.

The prefaces and advertisements to Shelley's poems offer important instances in which the theoretical ideals and speculations of his essays and his actual poetic practice converge. In the Preface to *Prometheus Unbound* he announces one particular stylistic aim which corresponds more fully and complexly to the treatment of language in the *Defence* than anything else he ever said. It is fundamental to Shelley's writing as a whole, as well as to his ambitious and radical experiment in poetic drama:

> The imagery which I have employed will be found in many instances to have been drawn from the operations of the human mind, or from those external actions by which they are expressed. This is unusual in modern Poetry; although Dante and Shakespeare are full of instances of the same kind: Dante indeed more than any other poet and with greater success. But the Greek poets, as writers to whom no resource of awakening the sympathy of their contemporaries was unknown, were in the habitual use of this power, and it is the study of their works (since a higher merit would probably be denied me) to which I am willing that my readers should impute this singularity.
>
> (*PP*, 133)

Critics have frequently quoted and referred to this paragraph;[2] some have used it to gloss the mentalistic similes so characteristic of the writing in *Prometheus Unbound*:

> As suddenly
> Thou comest as the memory of a dream . . .
>
> (II.i.7–8)

But they have shown little inclination to brood over Shelley's perplexing initial formulation, or to imagine in much detail his exact sense of the precedents he cites for what he insists on calling a stylistic 'singularity'.

We customarily expect a poem's imagery to present sensory analogues or vehicles for the figurative expression of mental states and operations:

> Sudden a thought came like a full-blown rose,
> Flushing his brow, and in his pained heart
> Made purple riot . . .[3]
>
> (Keats, *The Eve of St. Agnes*, 136–8)

The assumed connection between imagery and sense experience is deep-rooted and long-standing. Dr Johnson's definition of verbal *imagery* – 'such descriptions as force the image of the thing described upon the mind' – is grounded in his primary definitions of *image* as

'Any corporeal representation', and of *imagery* as 'Sensible representations'. This assumption has continued to be pervasive in modern
criticism: 'images' are 'the vestigial representatives of sensations'
(Wellek and Warren, *Theory of Literature*);[4] '*imagery* refers to images
produced in the mind by language, whose words and statements may
refer to experiences which could produce physical perceptions . . . or to
the sense-impressions themselves' (*Princeton Encyclopedia of Poetry and
Poetics*).[5] In what we may take to be the most explicit form of 'imagery
. . . drawn from the operations of the human mind', Shelley reverses the
usual figurative function of imagery and makes a mental state or
operation the vehicle in a figure whose tenor is sensory and
physical:

> . . . her way was paved, and roofed above
> With flowers as soft as thoughts of budding love. . . .
>
> (*Epipsychidion*, 327–8)

'Budding' is there partly to remind us of a conventional figurative
situation (representing thoughts of love as budding flowers) which is
reversed or inverted in this passage. Similes such as this radically alter
the rhetorical and epistemological status of thought and feeling in
relation to experience of the physical world. They might be considered
an extreme instance of Ruskin's 'pathetic fallacy', one of the ways in
which that rhetorical convention undergoes 'a violent expanding', as
Josephine Miles puts it,[6] in Shelley's writing. But it is clear from
Shelley's calling this kind of imagery a 'singularity', and from his saying
that it 'is unusual in modern Poetry', that he has something different in
mind from the familiar forms of bestowing human emotion on nature in
late eighteenth- and nineteenth-century poetry. He does extend his
formulation to 'those external actions by which [the operations of the
human mind] are expressed' and thus includes as part of his stylistic aim
figures based upon traditional ways of relating the mental to the
physical. The stylistic consequences of the distinction Shelley observes
here – the interactions between the two kinds of mentally expressive
imagery he designates – are important and will need to be examined.
But it is his former claim that imagery may be drawn directly from
mental operations that makes the passage in Shelley's Preface so
disconcertingly audacious.

The term *imagery*, it has been said, 'is one of the most common in
modern criticism, and one of the most ambiguous'. Shelley's notion of
'imagery . . . drawn from the operations of the human mind' exposes

this ambiguity by challenging the term's commonly assumed reference to 'the objects and qualities of sense perception'.[7] *Imagery* is no more limited than imagination to the *picturable*, or even to the sensuous. He suggests that mental actions and processes may themselves be represented as imagery in poetry, subject of course to the arbitrary and imperfect conditions of the linguistic medium. Implicit in his prefatory formulation is the recognition that in both rhetorical and non-rhetorical usage, the words *image* and *imagery* constantly transgress the presumed boundary between the inner and the outer, the mental and the material. The Ellis *Concordance* shows that in his own poetry Shelley took full advantage of this semantic adaptability. He uses *image* to refer to 'a statue or figure', to the 'appearance' or 'form' of a thing, to a thing's 'pictured representation' or to its 'reflection, mirrored counterpart' – and also to 'an idea or conception of the mind':[8]

> What are the words which you would have me speak?
> I, who can feign no image in my mind
> Of that which has transformed me.
>
> (*The Cenci*, III.i.107–9)

Similarly, he uses *imagery* to refer to 'sculpted figures', to 'painting', to 'imitation' and 'representation' – and also to 'phantasms of the brain':

> tyrants would flee
> Like a dream's dim imagery.
>
> (*The Mask of Anarchy*, 211–12)

Shelley's prefatory comment on the verbal *imagery* of *Prometheus Unbound* may well be part of a more pervasive interest in the term's curious, and for him philosophically valuable, amphibiousness.

I

At a purely theoretical or conceptual level, 'imagery . . . drawn from the operations of the human mind' might be understood as an overt stylistic corollary to the metaphysical and linguistic speculations of Shelley's essays. The usual idea of metaphorical or figurative imagery takes for granted a dualism of mind and matter, thoughts and objects of sense; the principal function of imagery, from this perspective, is to give expression to mind and thought by means of verbal correspondences drawn from physical objects and sensations. This is precisely the perspective Shelley attacks in the essay 'On Life', when he rejects the 'shocking absurdities of the popular philosophy of mind and matter' in favor of 'the intellectual philosophy' represented most clearly and vigorously in Sir William Drummond's *Academical Questions*:

> Nothing exists but as it is perceived. The difference is merely nominal between those two classes of thoughts which are vulgarly distinguished by the names of ideas and of external objects. . . . By the word *things* is to be understood any object of thought, that is, any thought upon which any other thought is employed, with an apprehension of distinction. The relations of these remain unchanged.
>
> (*PP*, 477–8)

The linguistic consequences of this position are fully consistent with Shelley's claim in the *Defence* that 'language is arbitrarily produced by the Imagination and has relation to thoughts alone'. If thoughts alone may be said to exist, then it certainly follows that words can signify 'thoughts alone'. The Lockean view of verbal signification undergoes a strange transformation once Locke's common-sense faith in a realm of external material objects is abandoned. If language 'has relation to thoughts alone', figurative imagery consists of relations between terms signifying 'different classes of thought' – not to thoughts, ideas and feelings on the one hand, and to objects, material qualities and physical processes on the other.

In his essays Shelley implies that all imagery must be drawn from mental operations, either from the 'human mind' or from the 'one mind' of which each individual human mind is 'a portion' ('On Life', *PP*, 478). But putting the issue raised in the *Prometheus* Preface in these terms inevitably leads back to the discrepancy between pure philosophical ideals or principles and the exigencies and limitations of actual linguistic experience. A difference between our names for thoughts and external objects which is 'merely nominal' from the metaphysical perspective of the essay 'On Life' may become critically nominal in a poem which has to use ordinary human language to question and transfigure the assumptions built into that language, or to reimagine accepted relations among 'classes of thoughts'. Whatever Shelley's metaphysical convictions or aesthetic ideals may have been, he had to work with a language in which differences between mind and matter, internal feelings and externally caused sensations, are fundamental, unavoidable, undeniable. As a specific and self-conscious feature of Shelley's style, 'imagery . . . drawn from the operations of the human mind' functions in relation to and derives at least part of its expressive force from the philosophically 'vulgar' and delusive distinctions it is designed to destabilize, subvert and renovate. It is therefore misleading to think of this or any other aspect of Shelley's style as a technique for transcending the limitations of language. On Shelley's own terms, he has to accept and work within the imperfections of ordinary language in order to realize what he sees as language's most precious potential, its reciprocally generative relation to thought.

The degree to which an awareness of irreducible linguistic limitations impinges upon and complicates Shelley's impulse towards mentalistic imagery in *Prometheus Unbound* and elsewhere may be clarified by considering another question recurrent in post-Lockean linguistic theory. In the famous passage from Book III of the *Essay* which provided a foundation for eighteenth-century etymologists such as Charles de Brosses and Horne Tooke, Locke remarks

> how great a dependance our *Words* have on common sensible *Ideas*; and how those, which are made use of to stand for Actions and Notions quite removed from sense, *have their rise from thence, and from obvious sensible* Ideas *are transferred to more abstruse significations*, and made to stand for *Ideas* that come not under the cognizance of our senses; *v.g.* to *Imagine, Apprehend, Comprehend, Adhere, Conceive, Instill, Disgust, Disturbance, Tranquillity*, etc. are all Words taken from the Operations of sensible Things, and applied to certain Modes of Thinking. *Spirit*, in its primary signification, is Breath; *Angel*, a Messenger: And I doubt not, but if we could trace them to their sources, we should find, in all Languages, the names, which stand for Things that fall not under our Senses, to have had their first rise from sensible *Ideas*.[9]
>
> (III.i.5)

Locke here presents a serious challenge to any affirmation of a direct and immediate relation between 'operations of the human mind' and the words we use to name them. Even Monboddo, who in so many respects rejected the empiricist account of language developed by Locke's followers, openly acknowledges his agreement with Locke on this point. Savages, he says, have hardly any words to express the operations of mind. And in all languages, even those the most cultivated, the words of that kind are metaphors borrowed from the objects of sense. [Note] This, I think, is an observation of Mr Locke.[10]

(I.i.11)

there is a set of words, I believe, in all languages, which are metaphorical, but, for want of other words, are constantly used as proper, so that the metaphor is intirely overlooked. The words I mean are those expressing the operations of mind, which are commonly translations from bodily operations. Such are the words *reflect, ponder, ruminate,* and the like.[11]

(II.iv.4)

For both Monboddo and Locke, Shelley's idea of 'imagery . . . drawn from the operations of the human mind' might seem to involve a linguistic delusion, since the words we use to refer to such operations are themselves metaphorical images originally drawn not directly from mental processes themselves, but from our ideas of 'sensible things' and 'bodily operations'.

The etymological structure of Shelley's mentalistic images is an interesting issue, one very much worth returning to as part of a detailed reading of particular passages. For the moment, however, it should be noted that Shelley's stylistic ideal is less circumscribed by Locke's etymological perception than one might think – and not simply because he rejected the ontological distinction between 'sensible things' and 'operations of the human mind' upon which Locke's perception is based. First of all, Locke's apparent confidence that all our words for mental operations and categories could in time be traced back to 'sensible ideas' has not been borne out. Etymologists still trace the word *mind* back to ancient forms which seem to be only variants of the modern meaning (Latin *mens,* mind; Greek *menos,* rage; Sanskrit *mati,* thought).[12] *Think* and *thought* have similarly refused to reveal any origin in sensory metaphor. Secondly, the fact that most terms for mental operations are dormant sensory metaphors need not preclude their functioning as images 'drawn from the operations of the human mind', or – as Shelley goes on to say – 'from those external actions by which they are expressed'. Dugald Stewart speaks shrewdly to this point in arguing against the presumed philosophical significance of Horne Tooke's etymological studies:

This figurative language, with respect to mind, has been considered by some of our later metaphysicians, as a convincing proof, that the doctrine of its materiality is agreeable to general belief; and that the opposite hypothesis has originated in the blunder of confounding what is very minute with what is immaterial.

To me, I must confess, it appears to lead to a conclusion directly opposite. For, whence this disposition to attenuate and subtilize, to the very verge of existence, the atoms or elements supposed to produce the phenomena of thought and volition, but from the repugnance of the scheme of materialism to our natural apprehensions; and from a secret anxiety to guard against a literal interpretation of our metaphorical phraseology?[13]

('On the Tendency of Some Late Philological Speculations', 1810)

The very process by which writers apply figures derived from the material world to mental experience, Stewart suggests, may betoken acts of consciousness that defy materialist reduction. Stewart's remarks help us understand why the 'disposition to attenuate and subtilize' material accounts of mental phenomena 'to the very verge of existence' is so central to Shelley's metaphorical practice. It is part of his effort to make language 'vitally', not just dormantly, 'metaphorical' (*Defence*, PP, 482), 'to guard against a literal interpretation of our metaphorical phraseology', to show that it is the human mind that makes the metaphors by virtue of which we are able to reflect upon its operations.

Locke himself had argued in Book II of the *Essay* that even though the names of certain indispensable 'ideas of reflection' depend upon sensory metaphors, these ideas themselves derive not from sense experience but from 'reflection on the Operations of our Mind'. Locke's comment in Chapter xxi on how we derive and name ideas of power is particularly relevant to Shelley's announced stylistic aim in *Prometheus Unbound*:

if we will consider it attentively, Bodies, by our Senses, do not afford us so clear and distinct an *Idea* of *active Power*, as we have from reflection on the Operations of our Minds. . . . we find in our selves a *Power* to begin or forbear, continue or end several actions of our minds, and motions of our Bodies, barely by a thought or preference of the mind.[14]

(II.xxi.4–5)

Such is the difficulty of explaining, and giving clear notions of internal Actions by sounds, that I must here warn my Reader that *Ordering, Directing, Chusing, Preferring*, etc. which I have made use of, will not distinctly enough express *Volition*, unless he will reflect on what he himself does, when he *wills*[15]

(II.xxi.15)

The sensory origins of words, Locke seems here to suggest, may obscure rather than reveal the reflexive mental origins of the ideas they signify. Shelley's 'imagery . . . drawn from the operations of the human mind' recognizes and contends with this aspect of language by calling attention to it and by showing that the Lockean process in which 'words taken from the operations of sensible things' are 'applied to certain modes of thinking' is itself an 'operation of the human mind' which the language of poetry may display and explore figuratively, rather than take for granted.

II

As a transition to naming his great predecessors in 'imagery . . . drawn from the operations of the human mind', Shelley claims that such imagery 'is unusual in modern Poetry'. The word 'unusual' is tantalizingly unspecific – perhaps deliberately so, given Shelley's concern in the following paragraph of the Preface with 'the degree to which the study of contemporary writings may have tinged my composition', and with the impossibility 'that his [or any other writer's] language and tone of thought may not have been modified by the study of the productions of those extraordinary intellects' of his own era (*PP*, 133–4).[16] Although evidence is slim that Blake was in Shelley's mind as a contemporary who shared an interest in the 'unusual' mental imagery of *Prometheus Unbound*, there are passages in the prophetic poems which come closer than anything else in Romantic poetry to the 'language and tone of thought' of Shelley's drama. Orc breaks free of his chains at the beginning of *America: A Prophecy* (1793) in similes which anticipate Shelley's reversal of the usual relation between the psychical and the physical:

Silent as despairing love, and strong as jealousy,
The hairy shoulders rend the links; free are the wrists of fire . . .[17]

(Preludium, 21–2)

The liberating power of those 'wrists of fire' is imaged near the end of the poem in Blake's version of mentalistic metaphor rather than simile:

> The doors of marriage are open, and the Priests in rustling scales
> Rush into reptile coverts, hiding from the fires of Orc,
> That play around the golden roofs *in wreaths of fierce desire*,
> Leaving the females naked and glowing with the lusts of
> youth.
>
> (Pl. 15, 19–22; my emphasis)

Writing such as this throws into relief the circular structure and function of images 'drawn from the operations of the human mind' in allegorical poetry. Since Orc is Blake's figurative embodiment of 'fierce desire', saying that Orc's fires 'play around the golden roofs in wreaths of fierce desire' offers as metaphorical vehicle an explicit naming of what the reader already understands as part of the poem's allegorical subject or tenor.

For a comparable effect in Shelley, consider the following sequence of similes spoken by the Chorus of Spirits in Act I of *Prometheus Unbound*:

> As the birds within the wind,
>   As the fish within the wave,
> As the thoughts of man's own mind
>   Float through all above the grave,
> We make there, our liquid lair,
> Voyaging cloudlike and unpent
> Through the boundless element –
>
> (683–9)

In the references to 'birds' and 'fish' and to 'Voyaging cloudlike', the Spirits proceed figuratively by comparing the psychical and immaterial – in this instance themselves – to the physical and material. But with the third simile, the Spirits compare themselves to what they in fact are – 'the thoughts of man's own mind'. Wimsatt's perception about the way in which tenor and vehicle in Romantic nature imagery frequently derive from the same act or field or imaginative perception would seem to apply even more definitively to Romantic allegorical imagery, at least to the mental allegory of Blake and Shelley.[18] They extend and complicate the usual process of allegorical personification (in which thoughts might be presented as floating, or desire as burning) until it turns around on itself in a figurative cycle which destabilizes and seems to dissolve conventional distinctions between the mental and the material, even between tenor and vehicle.

An interest in what might be described as 'imagery . . . drawn from the operations of the human mind' is also conspicuous in Coleridge and Wordsworth, although in them such imagery is less extravagant than in Blake and Shelley and remains more closely tied to what Shelley calls 'those external actions by which [mental operations] are expressed'. Reading the *Biographia Literaria* in late 1817, the year before he started work on *Prometheus Unbound*, Shelley would have found Coleridge countering Wordsworth's primitivist inclinations in the 1800 Preface with an affirmation close to his own linguistic ideals:

> The best part of human language, properly so called, is derived from reflections on the acts of the mind itself. It is formed by a voluntary appropriation of fixed symbols to internal acts, to processes and results of imagination.[19]

Wordsworth had worked out his own commitment to language 'derived from reflection on the acts of the mind itself' in his Preface to the *Poems* of 1815. There, in anticipation of his analysis of metaphorical *hanging* in passages from Vergil, Shakespeare and Milton (Wordsworth's own poetry is full of instances that turn upon literal or figurative hanging), he argues:

> Imagination . . . has no reference to images that are merely a faithful copy, existing in the mind, of absent external objects; but is a word of higher import, denoting operations of the mind upon those objects, and processes of creation and composition.[20]

The significant phrase here is 'upon those objects': 'operations of the mind upon those objects' implies a continuing reference to a realm external to the mind and distinguishes what Wordsworth says from Shelley's notion that imagery may be drawn 'from the operations of the human mind' *tout court*. Even as he celebrates images that are not 'merely a faithful copy . . . of absent external objects', Wordsworth hangs on to those objects and to the actual, recollected or imagined activity of perceiving them through the senses. When Milton envisions Satan flying 'far off' as 'at Sea a Fleet descried / *Hangs* in the clouds' (II.636–7), he does so, Wordsworth says, 'both for the gratification of the mind in contemplating the image itself, and in reference to the motion and appearance of the sublime object to which it is compared'. What Wordsworth admires is imagery drawn from the operations of the human mind as it interacts through the senses with objects in some way external to it. Even 'when the light of sense / Goes out' (1805 *Prelude*, VI.534–6), it is 'flashes' of that light 'that have shewn to us / The invisible world'.[21]

The more radical figurative inversions of mind and matter frequent in Shelley and Blake occur only rarely, and to quite different effect, in Wordsworth's poetry. There appear to be two instances in the fourth verse paragraph of *Tintern Abbey*:

> I cannot paint
> What then I was. The sounding cataract
> Haunted me like a passion: the tall rock,
> The mountain, and the deep and gloomy wood,
> Their colours and their forms, were then to me
> An appetite; a feeling and a love,
> That had no need of a remoter charm,
> By thought supplied, nor any interest
> Unborrowed from the eye. –[22]

(75–83)

Strangely, these images 'drawn from the operations of the human mind' ('Haunted me like a passion', 'were then to me / An appetite; a feeling and a love') characterize a former state of 'dizzy raptures' (85) when the imagination was more intimately tied to the senses, less dependent upon the reflective contribution 'of a remoter charm, / By thought supplied'. It is in recollecting the immediate and ambivalently intense reciprocity between landscape and mind of his former experience that Wordsworth momentarily allows 'passion' and 'appetite' to assume such strange figurative prominence. But the strangeness is carefully placed and controlled. The extreme metaphorical identification is counterbalanced by a stylistic circumspection – the verb 'Haunted' bridges and explains the comparison of 'sounding cataract' to 'passion'; the OED cites Wordsworth's use of 'appetite' in line 81 as a belated survival of one of its older meanings, 'the object of desire or longing'. At the end of the verse paragraph one feels that the mature Wordsworth is not just 'well pleased' but more pleased

>   to recognise
> In nature and the language of the sense
> The anchor of my purest thoughts . . .

(107–9)

Both medial and terminal crises in *The Prelude* might be said to move towards, but in different ways to back off from, Shelleyan or Blakean inversions of the usual figurative relationship between 'operations of the human mind' and physical or sensory phenomena. In Book VI the features of the landscape in the Ravine of the Gondo, paradoxically motionless and full of dizzy motion,

> Were all like workings of one mind, the features
> Of the same face, blossoms upon one tree,
> Characters of the great apocalypse,
> The types and symbols of eternity,
> Of first, and last, and midst, and without end.

(1805; VI.568–72)

Wordsworth's peroration turns upon an initial recognition that the natural landscape is *like* a mind – the divine mind that originally created it, perhaps, but also the individual human mind that recreates in perceiving it. Yet the full force of the first term in Wordsworth's great compound simile is muted by the natural and Biblical terms that follow and partly absorb it. In the analogous moment near the end of *The Prelude*, as Wordsworth recalls the 'meditation' provoked by 'the scene' revealed to him from Mount Snowdon, the simile of Book VI gives way to even more complexly cautious rhetoric:

>   . . . it appeared to me
> The perfect image of a mighty mind. . . .

(1805; XIII.68–9)

The 'perfect image' *of* 'a mighty mind' appeared (and reappears in memory) *to* Wordsworth's mind, conveying as it unfolds verbally the 'operations' of both. But that 'image' has its origins and remains located in a 'scene' – or in the 1850 text, a 'vision' – that 'Nature there / Exhibited' (1805; XIII.74–5). It is deeply characteristic of Wordsworth to insist that imaginative language depends upon images which do not merely copy external objects but denote instead 'operations of the mind upon those objects' – and yet to resist language which gives 'operations of the mind' a radical figurative priority, even in moments which recognize the mind's 'strength / Of usurpation' (1805; VI.532–3).

III

'Imagery . . . drawn from the operations of the human mind, or from those external actions by which they are expressed' may not have been as 'unusual in Modern poetry' as Shelley's Preface would have us believe, but it is none the less important that he names as his stylistic predecessors not Blake, Coleridge and Wordsworth, but Dante, Shakespeare and 'the Greek poets'. His claim that Dante employs such imagery 'more than any other poet and with greater success' hardly seems surprising, especially given the secondary emphasis of the stylistic principle as Shelley articulates it. Nowhere is imagery that expresses mental states or operations through both allegorical and non-allegorical 'external actions' more continuously and powerfully present than in the language of the *Divine Comedy*. Shelley began reading Dante in April 1818, about six months before starting work on *Prometheus*. He may be remembering one of Dante's similes in the *Prometheus* Preface itself when he refers to the 'spirit' of contemporary poets as 'the uncommunicated lightning of their own minds' and when he goes on to claim that 'the cloud of mind is discharging its collected lightning' (*PP*, 134):

> Come foco di nube si diserra
>   per dilatarsi sì che non vi cape,
>   e fuor di sua natura in giù s'attera,
> la mente mia così . . .[23]
>
> (Paradiso XXIII.40–3)

> [Like to the fire,
> That, in a cloud imprison'd, doth break out
> Expansive, so that from its womb enlarged,
> It falleth against nature to the ground;
> Thus . . . my soul . . .]

Such Dantean imagery is conspicuous and familiar. But trying to imagine Shelley's way of responding to it turns out to be instructive and revealing about both poets.

A close look at the passages Shelley marked or annotated in his copy of the *Divine Comedy*[24] calls into question the view, enunciated by T.S. Eliot and widely accepted among modern readers, that the peculiar force of Dante's similes derives from their relatively simple, unmetaphorical sensory concreteness, above all from their power 'to make us see more *definitely*'.[25] Some similes marked by Shelley, such as this one depicting the revival of Dante's spirits when he hears about Beatrice's appeal to Vergil, do seem to function mainly as Eliot says:

Quali fioretti dal notturno gelo
   chinati e chiusi, poi che 'l sol li 'mbianca,
    si drizzan tutti aperti in loro stelo,
tal me fec'io di mia virtude stanca . . .

                              (*Inferno* II.127–30)

[As florets, by the frosty air of night
Bent down and closed, when day has blanch'd their leaves,
Rise all unfolded on their spiry stems;
So was my fainting vigor new restored . . .]

The past participle 'chinati' might be thought to carry some inherent metaphorical coloring of a light and delicate kind – the word means 'bowed', 'drooping' as well as 'inclined', 'lowered', and the reflexive form can mean 'bowed down in submission' – but there is no real divergence here from the literal idiom. Consider another simile, however, also marked by Shelley, elaborating an earlier moment of revival and relief:

E come quei che con lena affannata,
   uscito fuor del pelago a la riva,
    si volge a l'acqua perigliosa e guata,
così l'animo mio, ch'ancor fuggiva,
   si volse a retro a rimirar lo passo
    che non lasciò già mai persona viva.

                               (*Inferno* I.22–7)

[And as a man, with difficult short breath,
Forespent with toiling, 'scaped from sea to shore,
Turns to the perilous wide waste, and stands
At gaze; e'en so my spirit, that yet fail'd,

Struggling with terror, turn'd to view the straits
That none hath passed and lived.]

This simile gives us something to see, but its more significant function is to make the reader participate in an act of seeing, an act in which literal and spiritual sight become indistinguishable in Dante's language. The act of literal seeing condensed into the verb 'guata' at the end of the simile's first term is extended in the verb 'rimirar' in the second term and emphasized by the parallelism of 'si volge' and 'si volse'. But it is Dante's 'spirit' (or more properly 'mind', since Dante uses 'animo', not 'anima'), not his eyes, which 'turn'd to view the straits'. The passage confirms the observation C.P. Brand makes in commenting on Shelley's reference to Dante in the *Prometheus* Preface: 'both poets employ images in which mental or spiritual and material phenomena are curiously mingled.'[26]

Eye and sight imagery is pervasive in the *Divine Comedy*, but it is illuminating to notice which instances of such imagery caught Shelley's eye and mind as he read. He seems to have been struck by some of the lines leading up to Dante's meeting with Brunetto Latini in Canto xv of the *Inferno*:

. . . incontrammo d'anime una schiera
  che venian lungo l'argine, e ciascuna
  ci riguardava come suol da sera
guardare uno altro sotto nuova luna;
  e sì ver' noi aguzzavan le ciglia
  come 'l vecchio sartor fa ne la cruna.

(16–21)

    [. . . we met
A troop of spirits, who came beside the pier.
  They each one eyed us, as at eventide
One eyes another under a new moon;
And toward us sharpen'd their sight, as keen
As an old tailor at his needle's eye.]

Eliot, following Matthew Arnold, picked out the second simile here – the old tailor squinting at his needle – to illustrate Dante's direct, unmetaphorical comparisons: 'The purpose of this type of simile is solely to make us see more *definitely* the scene which Dante has put before us . . . the simile . . . is merely to make you see more clearly how the people looked, and is explanatory.'[27] Eliot's phrase 'how the people looked' is tellingly ambiguous, and Dante's language is anything but unmetaphorical, especially in the Cary translation ('sharpen'd their sight', 'at his needle's eye'). Yet this simile does seem simple and homespun compared to the first simile, which is the one Shelley bracketed in his copy: 'They each one eyed us, as at eventide / One eyes another under a new moon.' These 'external actions' (to use Shelley's term) of looking and being looked at in a mysteriously beautiful but deceptive light evoke with precise and moving obliqueness, as James J. Wilhelm has argued, the homoerotic world and sensibility of 'Ser Brunetto' (xv.30), whom Dante addresses with such reverent compassion.[28] It is the kind of passage that only a reader peculiarly alert to the full range of Dante's resources for imaging the acts and dispositions of the human mind would have singled out.[29]

Shelley's sense of what is distinctive in Dante's writing is much closer to the view Hazlitt expresses in his introductory essay 'On Poetry in General' (1818) than to Eliot's or Arnold's:

> His mind lends its own power to objects which it contemplates, instead of borrowing it from them. . . . He does not place before us the objects by which the emotion has been created; but he seizes on the attention, by shewing us the effect they produce on his feelings. . . . Dante's great power is in combining internal feelings with external objects.[30]

This account of the mind mingling with and ultimately dominating or determining its objects in Dante's poetry, which interestingly echoes some of Hazlitt's earlier remarks on Wordsworth,[31] is confirmed in many of the passages to which Shelley was attracted. It is confirmed in Dante's idiosyncratic use of synaesthetic imagery, which always implies the activity of a mind combining and transposing different kinds of sensory phenomena, and which Glenn O'Malley has shown to have been a source for Shelley's use of 'negative intersense analogy' in *The Triumph of Life*:[32]

mi ripigneva là dove 'l sol tace.

(*Inferno* i.60)

[Impell'd me where the sun in silence rests.]

Io venni in loco d'ogne luce muto . . .

(*Inferno* v.28)

[Into a place I came
Where light was silent all.]

  'And the fair shape waned in the coming light
As veil by veil the silent splendour drops
  From Lucifer . . .'

(The Triumph of Life, 412–14)

As he read Dante, Shelley marked instances where the language dramatizes a still more explicit fusion of the physical with the psychical. In the following tercet from Canto VI of the *Inferno*, Dante and Vergil walk over the shades of the Gluttonous:

Noi passavam su per l'ombre che adona
  la greve pioggia, e ponavam le piante
  sovra lor vanità che par persona.

(34–6)

[We, o'er the shades thrown prostrate by the brunt
Of the heavy tempest passing, set our feet
Upon their emptiness, that substance seemed.]

The effect of the passage, as Shelley would have seen, depends in part on allegorical punning in which material and moral meanings converge in a single word: 'vanità' literally means 'emptiness', 'hollowness' (Latin *vanus*) as well as 'vanity'. Dante achieves a similar effect through the verb 'tremare' in a tercet Shelley marked in Canto IV:

Quivi, secondo che per ascoltare,
  non avea pianto mai che di sospiri
  che l'aura etterna facevan tremare;

(25–7)

[Here, as mine ear could note, no plaint was heard
Except of sighs, that made the eternal air
Tremble. . . .]

Everything about this image depends on hearing and feeling, rather than seeing. 'Tremare' is the key: it names a physical action so closely linked with feeling that both seem to be transferred simultaneously and endlessly from the Limbo-dwellers' sighs to the 'eternal air' which is their medium. A different form of the same verb is the pivot of another image bracketed in Shelley's text, one which is only a step away from

the figurative reversals of mind and matter in *Prometheus Unbound*.
Vergil tells Dante how a great rock came crashing down into the lower
depths of Hell when Christ descended into Limbo:

> da tutte parti l'alta valle feda
>   tremò sì, ch'i' pensai che l'universo
>   sentisse amor . . .

(XII.40–2)

> [Such trembling seized the deep concave and foul,
> I thought the universe was thrill'd with love . . .]

Dante's image of the physical universe trembling with love undergoes
extended lyric elaboration in Acts III and IV of *Prometheus Unbound*.
Earth responds to the kiss of the liberated Prometheus in language
which translates what Vergil says into eroticized geology:

> I hear – I feel –
> Thy lips are on me, and their touch runs down
> Even to the adamantine central gloom
> Along these marble nerves . . .

(III.iii.84–7)

The image of love transmitted 'Along these marble nerves' is not just an
isolated cosmic conceit: it recalls Earth's reference in Act I to her 'stony
veins' within which 'Joy ran' when Prometheus was born; it also
anticipates and supports Earth's rapturous description later in Act III,
scene iii of the statues in the temple dedicated to Prometheus:

> And populous most with living imagery –
> Praxitelean shapes, whose marble smiles
> Fill the hushed air with everlasting love.

(164–6)

Shelley's efforts to create his own kind of 'living imagery' in these
instances were very likely inspired, at least in part, by what Hazlitt
called 'Dante's great power . . . in combining internal feelings with
external objects'.

IV

In characterizing what he saw as the literal directness of Dante's similes,
Eliot contrasted him to Shakespeare. But Shelley saw in them both a

shared mastery over 'imagery . . . drawn from the operations of the human mind'. His claim that such imagery is important in Shakespeare may be substantiated by familiar instances:

You sulph'rous and thought-executing fires . . .[33]

(*King Lear*, III.ii.4)

Haste me to know't, that I, with wings as swift
As meditation or the thoughts of love,
May sweep to my revenge.

(*Hamlet*, I.v.29–31)

Hamlet's simile is doubly ironic: because 'meditation', especially for Hamlet, refuses to twin itself in swiftness with 'thoughts of love', and because neither the swiftness of 'meditation' nor of 'thoughts' guarantees the swiftness of revenge. Intervening between Hamlet's metaphorical 'wings' and their extension in 'May sweep to my revenge', the simile enacts verbally a schism in him between 'operations of the human mind' and 'those external actions by which they are expressed.' Shelley uses virtually the same image in Act IV of *Prometheus Unbound*, but the context gives it a very different function:

CHORUS OF HOURS
Whence come ye so wild and so fleet,
For sandals of lightning are on your feet
And your wings are soft and swift as thought,
And your eyes are as Love which is veiled not?
CHORUS OF SPIRITS
We come from the mind
Of human kind . . .

(89–94)

In Shelley the simile 'as swift as thought' meets no resistance from a contrasting realm of 'external actions', as it does in Shakespeare. Instead, it anticipates the identity of and is swiftly confirmed by the voices it addresses and describes. 'Your wings are as swift as thought.' 'Indeed, we are thought.' The comparison with Shakespeare raises a question to which we will need to return: what happens to images that derive their force from inversions of the usual figurative relationship between mind and matter in passages where mind is all that matters?

In Shakespeare as in Dante, explicit comparison of material to mental

phenomena is much less frequent than is imagery that respects and
seems to preserve our customary ways of relating these two realms
while suggesting their mysterious interdependence or interpenetration.
Claudio's contemplation of death in *Measure for Measure*, echoed by
Shelley in the last act of *The Cenci* and elsewhere in his poetry, is full of
such imagery. The following passage, which does not figure in Leavis's
well-known attack on the use Shelley makes of the speech,[34] is
indicative of the kind of imagery Shelley was drawn to in
Shakespeare:

> To be imprisoned in the viewless winds,
> And blown with restless violence round about
> The pendent world . . .
>
> (III.i.123–5)

Claudio is desperately straining to adapt what he knows of physical
suffering – particularly his own actual imprisonment, which he refers to
again six lines later – to the fate of a condemned spirit. But while bodily
existence might be imprisoned *by* the wind, to be imprisoned *in* the
wind is to enter a state verging on the disembodied, on becoming a
spiritus in the rudimentary senses of that word. 'Viewless', meaning
'incapable of being seen', emphasizes the incorporeal power of these
winds, as Shelley certainly recognized when he echoed Shakespeare's
phrase in *Mont Blanc*:[35]

> For the very spirit fails,
> Driven like a homeless cloud from steep to steep
> That vanishes among the viewless gales!
>
> (57–9)

And may Shakespeare's 'viewless' not also mean 'unable to see, blind'
(like 'my sightless view' in Sonnet 43, rather than like Macbeth's
'sightless couriers of the air', I.vii.22), thus anticipating the 'restless
violence' with which Claudio imagines being 'blown . . . about / The
pendent world'? 'Viewless winds' would then become a demonic
version of the correspondent breeze, a *spiritus* at once invisible and
unseeing, immaterial and blindly chaotic, which imprisons by
absorbing Claudio's once 'delighted spirit' (III.i.120). The passage
refuses us any clear distinction between imagery drawn from operations
of the human body and imagery drawn from operations of the human
mind.

The influence of Shakespeare's imagery is apparent throughout *The*

Cenci – not just in specific borrowings and echoes, the importance of which has often been misconstrued, but in the total orientation of Shelley's writing. He certainly has Shakespeare in mind in the Preface, as he adjusts the *Prometheus Unbound* ideal of imagery 'drawn from the operations of the human mind' to the demands of a drama in which the human minds in question are those of historical characters represented 'as they probably were'.

> In a dramatic composition the imagery and the passion should interpenetrate one another, the former being reserved simply for the full development and illustration of the latter. Imagination is as the immortal God which should assume flesh for the redemption of mortal passion. It is thus that the most remote and the most familiar imagery may alike be fit for dramatic purposes when employed in the illustration of strong feeling, which raises what is low, and levels to the apprehension what is lofty, casting over all the shadow of its own greatness.
>
> (*PP*, 241)

The metaphor of language incarnating or embodying thought does not come naturally to Shelley. But in the more explicitly proximate form of a simile ('Imagination is as the immortal God which should assume flesh') it does serve here as an elaboration of the central notion of interpenetration. 'Imagery' and 'passion', language and mental action, are reciprocally dependent in dramatic writing; the former are validated by and in turn *illustrate* (bring to light) the shadowy power of the latter.

Such is the ideal of the dramatic poet. But Shelley's Preface also demonstrates what for him is an unusually practical sense of his audience, and in the preceding paragraph he singles out one speech, 'Beatrice's description of the chasm appointed for her father's murder', where the remoteness of the imagery might be thought to violate the audience's sense of dramatic propriety. The speech is modelled not on Shakespeare but, as Shelley's own note acknowledges, on Calderon's *Purgatorio de San Patricio*, a play which in Shelley's view displays 'specimens of the very highest dramatic power, approaching Shakespeare, and in his character' (*Letters* II, 105). Shelley's worry about his audience's response is revealing, since the speech represents a striking attempt to adapt the mentalistic figures of *Prometheus Unbound* to a very different kind of dramatic writing:

                                    But I remember
Two miles on this side of the fort, the road
Crosses a deep ravine; 'tis rough and narrow,
And winds with short turns down the precipice;
And in its depth there is a mighty rock,
Which has, from unimaginable years,
Sustained itself with terror and with toil
Over a gulph, and with the agony
With which it clings seems slowly coming down;
Even as a wretched soul hour after hour,
Clings to the mass of life; yet clinging, leans;
And leaning, makes more dark the dread abyss
In which it fears to fall: beneath this crag
Huge as despair, as if in weariness,
The melancholy mountain yawns . . . below,
You hear but see not an impetuous torrent
Raging among the caverns, and a bridge
Crosses the chasm; and high above there grow,
With intersecting trunks, from crag to crag,
Cedars, and yews, and pines; whose tangled hair
Is matted in one solid roof of shade
By the dark ivy's twine. At noon day here
'Tis twilight, and at sunset blackest night.

                                    (III.i.243–65)

This speech, as Stuart Curran has shown, is anything but an intrusion of
what Shelley calls 'mere poetry', of 'detached simile' and 'isolated
description'.[36] The images fuse Beatrice's state of mind moments after
the incestuous rape with the wild landscape she regards both in
recollection and anticipation, and they are intricately linked with the
play's recurrent patterns of imagery. The basis for the mental imagery is
there in Calderon, but Shelley develops and extends it in ways which
suggest a determination to avoid the charges of indulgent lyricism he
anticipates in the Preface.

   The initial image of the 'mighty rock' in lines 247–51 follows
Calderon closely:

¿No ves esse peñasco, que parece
que se está sustentando con trabajo,
y con el ansia misma que padece,
ha tantos siglos que se viene abaxo?[37]

[Don't you see that great rock, that seems to be sustaining itself
with labor, and with the very anguish that it suffers has for so
many centuries been coming down?]

Calderon works here entirely in extravagant humanizing metaphor: the
rock is implicitly like a struggling, anguished human being. In
extending the figure for another three and a half lines, however, Shelley
turns it into a simile, as if he wanted to justify Calderon's baroque
conceit by making explicit its relevance to Beatrice. The result is a
curiously dizzying interpenetration of 'imagery' and 'passion', for
within the simile the landscape tenor of the original metaphor becomes
a landscape vehicle for Beatrice's despair:

Even as a wretched soul hour after hour,
Clings to the mass of life; yet clinging, leans;
And leaning, makes more dark the dread abyss
In which it fears to fall . . .

Shelley similarly elaborates the next such image he borrows from
Calderon, but this time in anticipation of its explicit appearance. 'The
melancholy mountain yawns' (257) directly translates the Spanish, 'el
monte melancólico bosteza'. But where Calderon's clause is preceded
by a grotesque image of the chasm as a mouth, Shelley's is preceded by
two similes which gloss 'melancholy' and 'yawns' respectively:

Huge as despair, as if in weariness. . . .

In both this and the previous instance, Shelley's figurative elaborations
are the very opposite of 'detached similes'. Although the vertiginous
circularity of landscape and human emotion does call attention to itself
as a verbal or stylistic eccentricity, the pressure behind these
elaborations, one senses, comes from a sometimes obsessive determination to make the imagery he takes from Calderon 'interpenetrate'
and 'illustrate' the 'passion' of his character. Fortunately, the pressure at
this point in the play may also be felt to come from Beatrice herself, as
she shapes 'the chasm appointed for her father's murder' more and
more intently into an extended image of her own mind.

V

In a notebook entry initially focused on Shakespeare and originally
conceived as part of the *Cenci* Preface, Shelley gives us one of the most

specific indications we have of why he names 'the Greek poets' in the *Prometheus* Preface as his most important models for imagery 'drawn from the operations of the human mind, or from those external actions by which they are expressed'. Shelley follows a quotation from Shakespeare's Sonnet 111 and a reference to Aeschylus's *Agamemnon* with a line from Sophocles' *Oedipus Rex*: πολλὰς δ'ὁδοὺς ελθόντα φροντίδος πλάνοις.[38]   He offers this translation and commentary:

> 'Coming to many paths in the wanderings of careful thought' [. And the words ὁδους & πλαναι had not been used as now they have been so long less in a metaphorical than an absolute sense, as to lose all outline & distinctness, as we say 'Ways & means' & wanderings for 'error & confusion' but they meant literally paths or roads such as we tread with our feet, & wanderings such as a man makes when he loses himself in a desart, or roams from city to city, as Oedipus the speaker of this verse was destined to wander, blind & askin[g] Charity. What a picture does this line suggest of the mind as a wilderness of intricate paths, wide as the universe which is here made its symbol, a world within a world – which he, who seeks some Knowledge with respect to what he ought to do, searches throughout, as he would search the external wilderness for some valued thing which was hidden from him upon its surface.

Like the image of the mind as a cave, the image of 'the mind as a wilderness of intricate paths' was important to Shelley, particularly in *Prometheus Unbound* and in the other poetry he wrote during its composition:

> FOURTH SPIRIT
> On a Poet's lips I slept
> Dreaming like a love-adept
> In the sound his breathing kept;
> Nor seeks nor finds he mortal blisses
> But feeds on the aerial kisses
> Of shapes that haunt thought's wildernesses.
> (*Prometheus Unbound*, 1.737–42)

> He wanders, like a day-appearing dream
>   Through the dim wildernesses of the mind . . .[39]
> ('Fragment: A Wanderer', 1–2)

But this image is only implicit in the line from Sophocles, and what enables Shelley to sense its latent force there is his sensitivity to dead or dormant metaphor, his awareness that the true metaphorical potential of words depends on our remaining in touch with their literal as well as their figurative meanings.[40] It is this awareness that underlies Shelley's warning in the *Defence*: 'vitally metaphorical' words 'become, through time, signs for portions or classes of thoughts instead of pictures of integral thoughts; and then if no new poets should arise to create afresh the associations which have been thus disorganized, language will be dead to all the nobler purposes of human intercourse' (*PP*, 482).

Shelley's notebook commentary is an exercise in creating afresh the associations which may have become 'disorganized' – deprived of their prior lifelike interrelationship – for Sophocles' modern reader. Sophocles' line uses 'external actions' metaphorically to express 'operations of the human mind', but so habituated are we to speaking of the 'ways' and the 'wanderings' of our minds that we are likely to miss the force of ὁδοὺς and πλάνοις. Shelley originally translated the former word as 'ways' but crossed it out and substituted 'paths' to bring out the simple but powerful figurative sense of the Greek.[41] He would have been alert to the physical meaning of πλάνοις from Sophocles' own literal use of it in *Oedipus at Colonus* (1114), and from Prometheus's oracular words to Io in Aeschylus's *Prometheus Bound*:

σοὶ πρῶτον,'Ιοῖ, πολύδονον πλάνην φράσω,
ἣν ἐγγράφου σὺ μνήμοσιν δέλτοις φρενῶν.[42]

(788–9)

[First to you, Io, I shall tell the tale
of your sad wandering, rich in groans – inscribe
the story in the tablets of your mind.]

In *Oedipus the King* the figurative force of πλάνοις is crucial; from Oedipus's early speech it is echoed at the turning point in the play, when he hears from Jocasta how Laius was killed:

οἷόν μ᾽ ἀκούσαντ᾽ ἀρτίως ἔχει, γύναι,
ψυκῆς πλάνημα κἀνακίνησις φρενῶν.[43]

(726–7)

[O dear Jocasta,
as I hear this from you, there comes upon me
a wandering of the soul – I could go mad.]

Much as οδους underscores the literal sense of πλάνοις in the first speech, so the unusual noun κἀνακίνησις (a 'moving to and fro', by extension 'a stirring up') helps activate the literal sense of the familiar noun πλάνημα ('wandering') in the second. In his own poetry Shelley often works 'to create afresh the associations' of 'wandering thought' in ways which indicate why this metaphor mattered to him in Sophocles. In *Queen Mab* Ahasuerus, the Wandering Jew, appears as a 'phantasmal portraiture / Of wandering human thought' (VII. 274–5); in *Mont Blanc* the speaker imagines 'One legion of wild thoughts, whose wandering wings / Now float above thy darkness, and now rest . . .' (41–2).

Buxton Forman complained that in quoting (with some modifications) Shelley's notebook entry in her own note on *Prometheus Unbound*, 'Mary Shelley does not seem to have seen that the main part, that about Sophocles, had any connexion with the *Cenci* preface or with the so-called Note on Shakespeare.'[44] But Mary Shelley's instinct in this case was sound; like Neville Rogers, she recognized that 'What Shelley says about Sophocles is very close to what he reveals obliquely of himself when commenting in the Preface to *Prometheus Unbound* upon its imagery':[45]

> Most popular poets clothe the ideal with familiar and sensible imagery. Shelley loved to idealize the real – to gift the mechanism of the material universe with a soul and a voice, and to bestow such also on the most delicate and abstract emotions and thoughts of the mind. Sophocles was his great master in this species of imagery.
>
> (*PW*, 272)

Mary Shelley does blur Shelley's distinction between imagery 'drawn from the operations of the human mind' and imagery drawn 'from those external actions by which they are expressed'. Shelley praises Sophocles for the latter, for the way in which he figures Oedipus's mental turmoil as the 'external action' of wandering through many paths. But Mary Shelley introduces the notebook entry as if it expressed admiration for Sophocles' mastery of the former. For her, 'idealizing the real' appears to mean primarily animation through personification, and without the distinction conveyed by Shelley's 'or', she slides in mid-sentence from 'the mechanism of the material universe' to 'the most delicate and abstract emotions and thoughts of the mind' as realities 'idealized' through the imagery of Sophocles and Shelley. Yet in certain respects this confusion is not entirely false to Shelley's way of

using and of writing about what may well have been for him a single
'species of imagery'. In *Prometheus Unbound* images referring directly to
mental states or processes often merge, as we have seen, with images
referring to expressive 'external actions'. In the *Preface* Shelley speaks in
the singular of a 'kind' of imagery, of 'this power' and 'this singularity'.
For a writer who believed that the 'difference . . . between those two
classes of thoughts which are vulgarly distinguished by the names of
ideas and external objects' is 'merely nominal', the kind of image in
which Sophocles pictures 'the mind as a wilderness of intricate paths'
might be seen to differ only in its nominal or verbal structure from the
kind of image in which Shelley compares an avalanche to the
accumulation and release of thought 'in Heaven-defying minds'
(*Prometheus Unbound* II.iii.36–42).

Aeschylus may have been even more important to Shelley than
Sophocles in providing models for imaging 'the operations of the
human mind'. The passage from the *Agamemnon* that Shelley apparently
singles out for praise in his notebook 'excursus' – the stately sequence
of familiar similes with which Clytemnestra greets her husband's return
(896–902) – offers little indication of Aeschylus's influence in this
regard.[46] But consider this much earlier passage, which begins with a
version of Sophocles' metaphor of mental pathways (ὁδώσαντα means
'put on the way', 'guided'), from the chorus's nervous paean to
Zeus,

> τὸν φρονεῖν βροτοὺς ὁδώ-
> σαντα, τὸν πάθει μάθος
> θέντα κυρίως ἔχειν·
> στάζει δ᾽ ἔν θ᾽ ὕπνῳ πρὸ καρδίας
> μνησιπήμων πόνος·

(176–80)

> [who guided men to think,
> who has laid it down that wisdom
> comes alone through suffering.
> Still there drips in sleep against the heart
> grief of memory.]

Since στάζει commonly and literally refers to the dripping of blood, its
transference here to the relentless subconscious action of painful
memory makes the familiar substitution of heart (καρδίας) for
emotions throb with an unexpected figurative life. Memory, sleep, and

the pathways of the mind fuse again in a later choral antistrophe evoking Menelaus's loss of Helen:

ὀνειρόφαντοι δὲ πενθήμονες
πάρεισι δόξαι θέρου-
σαι χάριν ματαίαν.
μάταν γάρ, εὖτ᾽ ἂν ἐσθλά τις δοκῶν ὁρᾷ,
παραλλάξασα διὰ χερῶν
βέβακεν ὄψις οὐ μεθύστερον
πτεροῖς ὀπαδοῦς᾽ ὕπνου κελεύθοις.

(420-6)

[Shining in dreams the sorrowful
memories pass; they bring him
vain delights only.
It is vain, to dream and to see splendours,
and the image slipping from the arms' embrace
escapes, not to return again,
on wings drifting down the ways of sleep.]

Even if this passage is not deliberately echoed in *Alastor* ('for ever lost, / In the wide pathless desart of dim sleep, / That beautiful shape', 209–11), it certainly must have struck Shelley when he reread the *Agamemnon* in the summer of 1817 (*Mary Shelley's Journal*, 83). He might have been struck too by the Chorus's description of its terrible forebodings as Agamemnon enters the palace:

σπλάγχνα δ᾽ οὔτοι ματᾴζει
πρὸς ἐνδίκοις φρεσὶν τελεσφόροις
δίναις κυκώμενον κέαρ.

(995-7)

[Surely this is not fantasy,
Surely it is real, this whirl of drifts
that spin the stricken heart.]

Such extended metaphorical expressions of psychical process are a conspicuous stylistic feature of the *Agamemnon* and of other late plays of Aeschylus.[47] They are more boldly figurative and extravagantly lyrical than comparable moments in Sophocles, and they suggest why Shelley thinks of 'the choruses of Aeschylus' in the *Defence* when he wants to exemplify the timeless power of 'the highest poetry' (*PP*, 483).

One other instance of mental imagery in Greek poetry deserves attention; it comes from a text which Shelley worked with in great detail, and which differs sharply in style and tone from the passages of Aeschylus and Sophocles we have just looked at. The Homeric *Hymn to Hermes*, a playful account of the wily and unscrupulous god's exploits as a child, was recast by Shelley into ottava rima and is his most successful translation from the Greek. He elaborates the original with considerable freedom (580 lines of Greek text becomes 772 lines in Shelley's English version), but the translation is close enough to let us see Shelley responding directly to details of imagery. Early in the poem the infant Hermes' precocious cunning in fashioning a lyre from a tortoise shell is presented in a double simile:

ὡς δ᾽ ὁπότ᾽ ὠκὺ νόημα διὰ στέρνοιο περήσῃ
ἀνέρος, ὅν τε θαμειαὶ ἐπιστρωφῶσι μέριμναι,
ἢ ὅτε δινηθῶσιν ἀπ᾽ ὀφθαλμῶν ἀμαρυγαί,
ὡς ἅμ᾽ ἔπος τε καὶ ἔργον ἐμήδετο κύδιμος Ἑρμῆς.[48]

(43–6)

[As a swift thought darts through the heart of a man
when thronging cares haunt him, or as
bright glances flash through the eye, so
glorious Hermes planned both thought and deed at once.]

The simile is dissonant and enigmatic in its circular movement from 'operations of the human mind' to 'those external actions by which they are expressed', then back again to mental operations. It begins by establishing a comparison between dissimilar acts of thought, setting the young god's carefree ingenuity in perversely ironic parallel to human suffering. The simile's second image offers a physical gesture which could apply to 'a man when thronging cares haunt him' (his eyes light up with momentary hope), but which seems apter for Hermes' self-delighting scheming. Shelley's expansion of the simile goes beyond the obligations of merely filling out his ottava rima stanza and demonstrates a bold attempt to contend with the difficulties and elaborate the suggestiveness of the original:

Not swifter a swift thought of woe or weal
  Darts through the tumult of a human breast
Which thronging cares annoy – not swifter wheel
  The flashes of its torture and unrest
Out of the dizzy eyes – than Maia's son

All that he did devise hath featly done.

(51–6)

Shelley intensifies the moral and psychological contrast between
vehicle and tenor. By twice adding negative internal comparatives
('Not swifter', 'not swifter') and by spelling out and linking the content
of human thought in each case ('of woe or weal', 'of its torture and
unrest'), he integrates the simile's double vehicle and makes the second
image as overtly mental as the first. In defiance of the disjunctive ἤ
which introduces the second image in the Greek, he fashions the flashes
from the eyes into 'external actions' expressive of the thoughts that pass
through a tormented human breast. And as Timothy Webb has shown,
he seizes upon the figure of circular movement contained in the
verb δινηθῶσιν (literally 'swirl around' or 'eddy'; cf. δίναις, 'spin', in
line 997 of the *Agamemnon* quoted above) and opens out its
suggestiveness as a metaphor for mental action, first by translating it as
'wheel' and then by extending it in 'dizzy eyes'.[49] Shelley's translation
may be said to impose a new and alien sense of psychical coherence on
this enigmatic simile, but in doing so it reveals metaphorical
connections between internal and external action latent in the Greek
text. In this case the violet may not flourish in the crucible of
translation, but it is artificially exfoliated with determined figurative
resourcefulness.

VI

Shelley wrote to Godwin (11 December 1817):

> I am formed, – if for anything not in common with the herd of
> mankind – to apprehend minute & remote distinctions of feeling
> whether relative to external nature, or the living beings which
> surround us, & to communicate the conceptions which result from
> considering the moral or the material universe as a whole.

(*Letters*, I, 557).

Whatever one may think of its accuracy, this is an important self-
characterization. The fullest articulation we have of a corresponding
stylistic ideal is what Shelley says about imagery in the *Prometheus*
Preface. In its broader implications, that ideal either embraces or
conditions every aspect of his writing. Before tracing some of those
broader implications as they reveal themselves in characteristic features

of his style, I want to look once again at the most explicit form of
Shelley's imagery . . . drawn from the operations of the human mind ' –
the similes comparing physical to psychical experience.

It would be wrong-headed to say that all such similes are successful in
Shelley simply because they challenge customary assumptions about
figuring the relation of mind to matter, just as it would be wrong-
headed to reject them out of hand as being inherently vague and
question-begging. But what does make for success or failure in
Shelley's mentalistic similes? Several criteria have been suggested by
the similes of his designated predecessors: psychical vehicles are given
definition and specificity by larger narrative or dramatic pressures;
immediate figurative contexts place similes that reverse the expected
relation of thought to matter or sensation in revealing relationship to
conventionally organized similes or tropes; tenors referring to the
material world or to physical experience are intricately linked to
psychical vehicles through what Shelley himself speaks of as
interpenetrating images of matter and mind, or through dormant but
arousable etymological metaphor within the simile. Three sequences
from *Prometheus Unbound* will allow us to evaluate Shelley's success in
realizing the expressive potential of this kind of reversed or inverted
simile.

Questioning the Furies who come to torment him in Act I,
Prometheus himself seems to realize that these agents of Jupiter may
also be projections of his own capacity for hate and revenge:

> Horrible forms,
> What and who are ye? Never yet there came
> Phantasms so foul through monster-teeming Hell
> From the all-miscreative brain of Jove;
> Whilst I behold such execrable shapes,
> Methinks I grow like what I contemplate
> And laugh and stare in loathsome sympathy.[50]

(445–51)

For their part, the Furies define themselves as a function of
Prometheus's way of conceiving of them:

> THIRD FURY
> Thou think'st we will live through thee, one by one,
> Like animal life; and though we can obscure not
> The soul which burns within, that we will dwell
> Beside it, like a vain loud multitude

Vexing the self-content of wisest men –
That we will be dread thought beneath thy brain
And foul desire round thine astonished heart
And blood within thy labyrinthine veins
Crawling like agony.
    PROMETHEUS
              Why, ye are thus now . . .

                         (483–92)

In the line he shares metrically with this Fury, Prometheus verifies her verbal account of his tormented experience as a present, not future, reality. (Present and future are curiously collapsed in the Fury's speech, since the future verbs 'will live', 'will dwell', and 'will be' all depend grammatically on the present 'Thou think'st'). That account mocks the very impulse to image mental experience in physical terms, and yet dramatizes a relentless invasion of the spirit by physical pain. As Prometheus imagines them, and thus as they imagine themselves, the Furies are psychical phenomena ('dread thought', 'foul desire'), and yet they surround the core of Prometheus's psyche in a sequence of grotesquely spatial and anatomical adverbial phrases: 'Beside it [the soul]', 'beneath thy brain', 'round thine astonished heart'. This sequence completes itself in a figurative movement that at once confirms and reverses the preceding convergences of mental and physical life: as the Furies finally enter and become one with Prometheus's body ('And blood within thy labyrinthine veins'), the concluding simile suggests that they do so as a mental force, 'Crawling like agony'.[51] Yet 'agony' names a condition of conflict or struggle that can be physical as well as psychical. So while the simile 'Crawling like agony' may at first seem to reverse the bodily emphasis of the Fury's initial simile ('we will live through thee . . . / Like animal life'), it also draws that emphasis out. And through its etymological roots in the idea of a public confrontation or contest, 'agony' reaches back to the external public aspect of the Fury's partly internalized second simile ('like a vain loud multitude / Vexing the self-content of wisest men') and links it to Prometheus's more fully internalized reworking of it in his reply:

Yet am I king over myself, and rule
The torturing and conflicting throngs within
As Jove rules you when Hell grows mutinous.

                         (492–4)

'Crawling like agony' gains additional power when we read it as a figurative inversion, and thus also an extension, of the way in which Prometheus imaged his suffering in his opening speech:

> Ah me! alas, pain, pain ever, for ever!
>
> The crawling glaciers pierce me with the spears
> Of their moon-freezing chrystals . . .   (I.30–2)

Shelley's writing in the exchange between Prometheus and the Fury insists on presenting mental torment as physical and physical torment as mental – on treating the difference between mental and physical torment, one might say, as 'merely nominal' ('On Life', *PP*, 477). Such writing makes extreme demands on the reader's ability and willingness to follow its convoluted figurative movement. In this case, however, his compositional eccentricities are demonstrably and coherently rooted in his experiment in psychical allegory.

Mentalistic similes are used to quite different effect in Asia's apostrophe to spring at the beginning of Act II:

> From all the blasts of Heaven thou hast descended –
> Yes, like a spirit, like a thought which makes
> Unwonted tears throng to the horny eyes
> And beatings haunt the desolated heart
> Which should have learnt repose, – thou hast descended
> Cradled in tempests; thou dost wake, O Spring!
> O child of many winds! As suddenly
> Thou comest as the memory of a dream
> Which now is sad because it hath been sweet;
> Like genius, or like joy which riseth up
> As from the earth, clothing with golden clouds
> The desart of our life. . . .   (II.i.1–12)

The boldness with which Asia's similes articulate natural seasonal regeneration as psychical regeneration is a demonstration of what Panthea has just called 'her transforming presence' (I.832). The figurative energy latent in her first simile, 'like a spirit', is fanned into life by the surrounding wind imagery ('the blasts of heaven', 'Cradled in tempests', 'child of many winds').[52] That simile is part of a descending action which reverses itself into a rising action at the end of the sequence, grammar and imagery conspiring to suggest a cyclical process in nature and in thought:

> . . . thou hast descended –
> Yes, like a spirit, like a thought . . .
> Like genius, or like joy which riseth up . . .

In a characteristic Shelleyan maneuver, the last of these similes contains within it another simile – the vehicle of one figure becomes the tenor of a subsequent figure – which in this instance completes the cyclical movement of the passage by returning to the imagery of physical nature with which it began:

> . . . or like joy which riseth up
> As from the earth, clothing with golden clouds
> The desart of our life.

The internal similes in Asia's address are characteristic in another way: they compare a natural phenomenon to the intellectual or emotional effect it produces in the mind of the speaker. Such similes always risk seeming either reductive or tautological. Shelley contends with that risk successfully here and turns it into an expressive resource by making the thoughts to which spring gives rise in Asia's mind, and to which she compares its arrival, thoughts of spring's absence as well as of its presence. Spring descends 'like a thought' in a 'desolated heart' which has all but forgotten what spring was like; it comes 'as suddenly', and as sadly, 'as the memory of a dream' of sweetness past. Shelley creates and sustains a necessary difference between the seasonal and psychical terms of his comparisons, even as those comparisons express the seasonal and the psychical as transformations of each other.

Later in Act II, as she and Panthea approach the volcanic abode of Demogorgon, Asia describes another kind of descent associated with spring:

> Hark! the rushing snow!
> The sun-awakened avalanche! whose mass,
> Thrice sifted by the storm, had gathered there
> Flake after flake, in Heaven-defying minds
> As thought by thought is piled, till some great truth
> Is loosened, and the nations echo round
> Shaken to their roots: as do the mountains now.
>
> (II.iii.36–42)

Donald Reiman's note is apt:

> This simile is one of the best examples of the reversal of imagery

that Shelley mentions in the fourth paragraph of the Preface, for here an external natural event (the avalanche, 36–38) is compared to a figure 'drawn from the operations of the human mind' – in this case, the slow growth of new concepts in Heaven-defying minds until there is an intellectual revolution.

(PP, 169)

One might go on to notice just how Shelley prepares for and complicates the 'reversal of imagery' Reiman describes. The massive weight of the avalanche is miraculously etherealized by its having been 'sun-awakened', 'thrice sifted', and 'gathered there / Flake after flake'. Shelley suggests momentarily that the avalanche may actually be a psychical event 'in heaven-defying minds' through the syntactic inversion that postpones announcing the simile with 'As' until the following line. The inversion is not necessitated by the meter, and one would expect 'Flake after flake' to be followed immediately by the figurative and syntactic parallelism of 'As thought by thought'. Once oriented within the simile's references to mental action, the reader may be disoriented again by verbs which express that mental action in terms individually and sequentially appropriate to the 'external natural event': 'piled', 'loosened', 'echo round', 'Shaken to their roots' (the 'great truth' is radical). Even more disorienting is the way in which the simile circles back on itself. 'As do the mountains now' can be read as a second simile folded within the first, representing as figurative vehicle an echo of the original tenor. Or, giving 'now' its full force, it can be read as a temporal clause conveying simultaneous natural and mental actions: while the mountains echo the rushing snow, nations are responding to 'some great truth'.

An uncertainty about whether to take 'as' in a comparative or temporal sense emerges elsewhere in *Prometheus Unbound*:

And lovely apparitions dim at first
Then radiant – as the mind, arising bright
From the embrace of beauty (whence the forms
Of which these are the phantoms) casts on them
The gathered rays which are reality –
Shall visit us . . .

(III.iii.49–54)

. . . swift shapes and sounds which grow
More fair and soft as man grows wise and kind . . .

(III.iii.60–1)

Such indeterminacy in Shelley's similes doubles the stylistic process of drawing together 'external actions' and 'operations of the human mind' into a perceptual continuum. The resulting disorientation is part of any reader's experience of the poem, and for some, no account of Shelley's figurative principles and practices can adequately compensate for the toll that disorientation takes on their sympathy and patience. Yet a writer who insists that 'All things exist as they are perceived' (the 'as' in this very sentence from the *Defence* may mean both 'in the manner or form in which' and 'while', 'in so far as') can teach us a good deal about our habitual dependence upon distinguishing thoughts and things. Whether we believe that the difference between 'ideas' and 'external objects' is 'merely nominal' or not ('On Life', *PP*, 477), Shelley's extreme figurative crossings and restructurings of those differences challenge us to read with an expanded sense of how the mind finds or makes meaning in a world which is always, to some degree, the mind's own place.

III REFLEXIVE IMAGERY

'But even with so limited an instrument as the short-circuited comparison, he could do great things' – William Empson concludes his remarks on Shelley in *Seven Types of Ambiguity*[1] with this curiously qualified compliment, which he illustrates with two lines from *The Triumph of Life*:

> And others mournfully within the gloom
>
> Of their own shadow walked, and called it death . . .
>
> (58–9)

Although Empson calls attention here to a prominent verbal pattern in Shelley's writing, he does not go on to elucidate the 'great things' Shelley does with it, and the gist of his remarks on these 'short-circuited comparisons' – what he earlier calls 'self-inwoven similes' – is negative. He sees them as products of hasty, unpremeditated composition: 'when not being able to think of a comparison fast enough he compares the thing to a vaguer or more abstract notion of itself, or points out that it is its own nature, or that it sustains itself by supporting itself.' My contention in this chapter will be that while Shelley's reflexive imagery (to broaden the terminology) does present special critical difficulties, it is not, as Empson implies, an inherently limited stylistic mannerism with no particular expressive function. It is, on the contrary, a characteristic form of Shelley's imagery 'drawn from the operations of the human mind', one which he uses to articulate some of his deepest poetic concerns.

I use the term 'reflexive' to refer to locutions in which an object or action is compared, implicitly or explicitly, to an aspect of itself, or is said to act upon or under the conditions of an aspect of itself. Such locutions call unusual attention to the act of mind they presuppose in the writer and provoke in the reader, an act of mind in which something is perceived as both one thing and more than one thing, as both itself and something other than itself. Reflexive images often include or appear in connection with references to literal physical reflection (or shadow, as above in *The Triumph of Life*), and when they do they may appeal strongly and teasingly to the visual imagination. But the basis of the reflexive image *per se* is grammatical and syntactical; the signifying function of a phrase or clause turns back on itself, and its doing so marks an 'operation of the human mind' that couples analysis or division (as an aspect is separated from the idea to which it belongs) with synthesis or reunion (as the separated or divided aspect is re-identified with that same idea):

> One seat was vacant in the midst, a throne,
>   Reared on a pyramid like sculptured flame,
> Distinct with circling steps which rested on
>   Their own deep fire . . .
>
>   (*The Revolt of Islam*, i.613–16)

'Deep fire' is simultaneously separate from 'circling steps' and thus capable of becoming the grammatical object of the phrase 'rested on', and inseparable from 'circling steps', since what the steps rest on is an aspect of themselves. In the case of 'the self-inwoven simile', a subcategory of reflexive imagery which is in fact less frequent in Shelley's writing than Empson implies, the separation of idea and aspect is even more conspicuously a result of the mind's ability to perceive relational difference within sameness and identity:

> He has invented lying words and modes,
> Empty and vain as his own coreless heart . . .
>
>   (*Queen Mab*, iv.232–3)

The punning paradox of 'coreless heart' ('heartless heart', as Hamlet might have said)[2] brings to a sharp conclusion this line's turn of language and thought. Shelley's reflexive images may be thought of as extremely condensed (but not necessarily 'short-circuited') versions of the figurative situation analyzed by Wimsatt in 'The structure of Romantic nature imagery', where tenor and vehicle 'are wrought in a parallel process out of the same material'.[3]

The resources of reflexive imagery have been displayed with brilliant resourcefulness by Christopher Ricks in an essay entitled ' "It's own resemblance" '.[4] The essay takes its title from Marvell's 'The Garden', and it is Marvell and his seventeenth-century contemporaries who are seen to demonstrate most fully the figure's 'range of mood, intent, and form'. But Ricks also finds the distinctive qualities of reflexive imagery in varying degrees of realization in a series of later examples – in Pope; in Dickens, Meredith and Clough; in Proust; and – most interestingly among the twentieth-century examples he offers, as the Shelley of *An Address to the Irish People* would have seen – in Seamus Heaney and other recent Ulster poets. Ricks's comments about Shelley himself will be considered later in some detail. What his essay enables us to recognize here at the outset is that reflexive imagery is not nearly 'so limited an instrument' as Empson held it to be, and that the 'great things' any writer can do with it turn upon the figure's peculiar capacity to suggest both the creative power and the limitations of the imagination.

I

Reflexive imagery is recurrent throughout Shelley's poetry, from *Queen Mab* to *The Triumph of Life*. But the place to begin an exploration of its fundamental importance for him is *Alastor*. No poem of Shelley's is more thoroughly inwoven with this figure, and as Wasserman's account of the poem's epistemological and psychological substructure suggests, it performs a central function:

> In a deficient and 'false' – that is, inconstant – world . . . there remains . . . only . . . a subject with the capacity of being its own object. . . . the solitary mind is driven to project itself as its own narcissistic object. . . .
> His [the wandering poet's] mind requires an infinite subject as its object, an 'intelligence similar to itself' . . . when the mind refuses to limit itself to any finite being it has no choice but to envision its own object . . . The act is reflexive and has no completing object but itself.[5]

One of the difficulties of writing about poetic reflexiveness, as Wasserman's prose demonstrates, is that it is impossible to do so without echoing the poet's own reflexive language ('when the mind refuses to limit itself to any finite being it has no choice but to envision its own object'). This very difficulty should make us aware, however, of a rudimentary connection between the situation Wasserman describes and the language that situation elicits from both poet and critic. The 'short-circuited comparisons', 'self-inwoven similes', and other reflexive locutions in *Alastor* are intrinsic to Shelley's ambivalent exploration of solipsism, radical idealism and imaginative self-sufficiency. They often ask to be read as verbal simulacra of the process of reflexive imaginative projection which Wasserman, following Shelley's own preface, defines as the poem's central concern.

Wasserman traces in *Alastor* a complex dialectical relationship between the narrator's passionate but troubled nature-worship and the wandering poet's equally passionate but solipsistic quest after a reality that lies outside nature, a quest which becomes a desire for union with the self's ideal reflection. Reflexive imagery functions on one level within this dialectic of attitudes by enacting verbally the process through which the wandering poet's imagination projects the self as other. In the first major crisis of the poem the poet dreams erotically (and autoerotically) of a maiden whose 'voice was like the voice of his own soul / Heard in the calm of thought' (153–4):

> at the sound he turned,
> And saw by the warm light of their own life
> Her glowing limbs beneath the sinuous veil . . .
>
> (174–6)

Here the reflexive image appears not in a simile or comparison but in an involuted adverbial phrase analogous in grammatical structure to the passage from *The Triumph of Life* quoted by Empson ('within the gloom of their own shadow'). The point of saying that the wandering poet sees the dream-maiden's limbs 'by the warm light of their own life' is, I think, that the very same power is responsible for the life of those limbs and for the fact of their being 'seen' – namely, the protagonist's imagination. The 'light' with which the dream-maiden's limbs 'glow' comes from the mind which creates and perceives them; the reflexive locution signals a self-inclosed psychical experience. What might at first appear to be vague and gratuitous erotic intensification turns out to serve a distinct expressive purpose. Even the words 'warm' and 'glowing' suggest the way in which qualities of the dreamer's fervid imagination have been transferred to the projected self-reflection.

A related but more difficult reflexive image occurs some ten lines earlier in this section of *Alastor*:

> wild numbers then
> She raised, with voice stifled in tremulous sobs
> Subdued by its own pathos.
>
> (163–5)

Shelley here evokes an emotional intensity so extreme that it checks or inhibits the verbal outpouring it inspires. This stifling of expression, which itself produces a kind of music ('tremulous sobs'), may in turn heighten the intensity. But the reflexive phrase 'subdued by its own pathos' also suggests the degree to which the dreamer's mind is determining the nature of what it projects. We understand the pathos of the dream-maiden's song as a projection of the wandering poet's own dilemma, and the reflexive image intimates a transference, from the mind of the dreamer to the projected image of the self as sexual other, of desire which intensifies itself by frustrating its own expression. What the poet envisions is his own desire turning back on itself.

The wandering poet projects himself as another person in dream; he also projects this self into an 'external' world that threatens otherwise to become dead and meaningless. What he sees in nature – in a wandering stream, for instance – is an image of his own mind, which in turn becomes the 'type' of that natural image:

Thou imagest my life. Thy darksome stillness,
Thy dazzling waves, thy loud and hollow gulphs,
Thy searchless fountain, and invisible course
Have each their type in me.

(505–8)

Some of Shelley's reflexive images may be said to imitate verbally this impulse of the mind to invest nature with its own reflexive activity. Having emerged from a devastating vacancy after his erotic dream, the protagonist sets out in a small boat upon waters which image his life in a sequence of threatening vortical tempests. He is almost swallowed up in a vast whirlpool, at the center of which

was left,
Reflecting, yet distorting every cloud,
A pool of treacherous and tremendous calm.

(384–6)

He momentarily escapes from this whirlpool only to find himself upon 'a placid stream' that conducts him to a 'calm' like that at the center of the whirlpool. The stream flows into a cave where it is

closed by meeting banks, whose yellow flowers
For ever gaze on their own drooping eyes,
Reflected in the crystal calm.

(406–8)

Here the reflexive locution reinforces an image of literal reflection; together they give appropriate verbal form to the state of involuted consciousness into which the questing, alienated mind has driven itself. There are other instances in Shelley's poetry of eyes looking at their own reflected image, when the activity of reflection duplicates the act of looking. A passage from *The Sensitive Plant* makes it clear that the unnamed yellow flowers in the *Alastor* passage are narcissi:

> Then the pied wind-flowers and the tulip tall,
> And narcissi, the fairest among them all
> Who gaze on their eyes in the stream's recess,
> Till they die of their own dear loveliness . . .
>
> ('Part First', 17–20)

The Narcissus myth is paradigmatic in *Alastor*: the flowers gazing 'on their own drooping eyes / Reflected in the crystal calm' are recapitulative emblems of the protagonist himself when, just prior to his partly autoerotic dream, 'Beside a sparkling rivulet he stretched / His languid limbs' (148–9).

The reflected narcissi also anticipate the poem's second major crisis, where reflexive imagery and imagery of literal reflection again come together in a reciprocally intensifying way. The wandering poet comes upon 'a well' whose 'translucent wave' (458) is also a 'liquid mirror' (462) that 'images all the woven boughs above':

> Hither the Poet came. His eyes beheld
> Their own wan light through the reflected lines
> Of his thin hair . . .
>
> (469–71)

Grammatically this reflexive image is more condensed, more nearly 'short-circuited', than any of the previous examples: 'their own wan light' is connected to the verb 'beheld' as a direct object, not as an adverbial phrase or simile. The reference to the wandering poet's 'thin hair', itself a sign of his premature physical wasting and alienation from bodily life, dramatizes the impression here of the act of looking finding itself duplicated in the process of reflection. He looks through the hair fallen over his eyes to see his eyes looking back at him 'through the reflected lines / Of his thin hair'. At this critical moment in the narrative, the patterns of reflective and reflexive imagery are taken to bizarre extremes in Shelley's attempt to find a stylistic equivalent for the mind's involuted descent into the depths of a relentless and distorted self-consciousness.

The wandering poet is associated throughout the poem with the moon. Its reflected light, further removed from its source as it is reflected again in water on earth, images his emptiness as he emerges from the death-like trance that concludes his dream:

> His wan eyes
> Gaze on the empty scene as vacantly
> As ocean's moon looks on the moon in heaven.
>
> (200–2)

As the poet's life ebbs away at the end of the narrative, Shelley brings this lunar configuration to impressive culmination in an extended parallel between the setting of the moon and the dying of reflexive consciousness. The poet looks out from a desolate mountain precipice upon the crescent moon sinking below the horizon and once again sees his own eyes duplicated by the moon, this time by the still visible tips of its horns. It is impossible to determine whether the 'two lessening points of light' that 'alone / Gleamed through the darkness' (634–5) belong to the poet or to the moon he looks at. Finally, as the 'minutest ray' of moonlight is 'quenched':

> the pulse yet lingered in his heart.
> It paused – it fluttered. But when the heaven remained
> Utterly black, the murky shades involved
> An image, silent, cold, and motionless,
> As their own voiceless earth and vacant air.
>
> (658–62)

The word 'image' has echoed through *Alastor* as part of the poem's ambiguous merging of introspective and projective vision. Now in death the wandering poet has become an 'image', and in one sense has finally and ironically succeeded in uniting himself with the projected self for which he has quested. The 'image' in line 661 is described in a reflexive simile curiously different from Empson's 'self-inwoven simile', in which something is compared to an aspect of itself. The 'voiceless earth and vacant air' belong to the 'murky shades' but are compared to the 'image' those shades 'involve', not to the shades themselves. The simile is one step removed from the completely 'self-inwoven simile', but the effect is to show that in death the wandering poet has become merely an 'image' indistinguishable from the lightless, lifeless void which surrounds and 'involves' him. And at this moment it can no longer be the protagonist who invests the world he perceives with the reflexive activity of his own mind. The narration of his death forces us to acknowledge a larger sphere of perception which includes or 'involves' the wandering poet as an object of its own reflexive perception.

All the images of reflection and reflexiveness in *Alastor* have to be read, ultimately, on a second interpretive level, as products of the narrator's imagination; they are part of his way of articulating the wandering poet's experience. So while these images serve within the narrator's story to evoke his protagonist's self-reflexive quest, they also convey the narrator's own capacity for and tendency towards such reflexiveness. He cannot describe the life of the poet whom he reveres but whose imaginative orientation initially seems to be different from his own without retracing and re-enacting the very compulsion that underlies that poet's tragedy. When the poet's dead body becomes the tenor of a reflexive simile, the reader has no choice but to relocate the ultimate fictional source of the poem's reflexiveness within the narrator. Shelley has given *Alastor* a rhetorical structure which is itself reflexive, self-infolded.

Having made this adjustment in rhetorical perspective, we should return to the narrator's framing comments at the beginning of the poem and look at an anticipatory instance there of the reflexive image. The invocation to the 'Mother of this unfathomable world' has been taken as evidence of the narrator's Wordsworthian commitment to the natural world rather than to a transcendent ideal. Yet what he recalls there is his as yet unsuccessful attempt to charm nature into yielding her deepest secrets:

> In lone and silent hours,
> When night makes a weird sound of its own stillness,
> Like an inspired and desperate alchymist
> Staking his very life on some dark hope,
> Have I mixed awful talk and asking looks . . .
>
> (29–33)

The spirit of this is more Coleridgean than Wordsworthian: the idea of night making 'a weird sound of its own stillness' – of a silence so extreme that for the watchful, self-haunted mind it takes on the force of sound – may well have been borrowed from *Frost at Midnight*:

> 'Tis calm indeed! so calm, that it disturbs
> And vexes meditation with its strange

And extreme silentness.[6]

(8–10)

By reworking Coleridge's idea into a reflexive image, Shelley shows the narrator, at a moment when he recalls being threatened with alienation and solitude much like that which overwhelms the wandering poet, anticipating the kind of language he will use obsessively in narrating the quest of his protagonist. From the beginning such verbal patterns suggest that the narrator is more like than different from the dead poet he eulogizes, that he contains within himself the potential for reflexive despair which, as he seems to recognize at the end, is the real subject of his 'solemn song' (19). So he concludes that song by turning poetry against itself in an image which reflexively negates the efficacy of imagery:

> Let not high verse, mourning the memory
> Of that which is no more, or painting's woe
> Or sculpture, speak in feeble imagery
> Their own cold powers.

(707–10)

Alastor may be called a radically 'self-reflexive' poem in the sense in which Daniel Hughes has used that term to refer to poems which are 'about poetry and the poetic process'.[7] What Shelley presents in *Alastor* is one poetic consciousness (the narrator) gradually coming to terms with and recognizing the depth of his attachment to another poetic consciousness (the wandering poet). By the end of the poem the otherness of the wandering poet has all but disappeared in the narrator's realization that his own 'dark hope' (32) has 'fled' with the protagonist (695–9). It is possible, then, that the wandering poet is not another poet at all, but the projection of a submerged impulse in the narrator's own mind. The wandering poet may be seen as the narrator's deeper self projected as spectral other, much as the dream-maiden could be understood as the wandering poet's deeper self projected as other. When we read the poem this way, the entire elegiac narrative becomes a symbolic fiction in which the wandering poet, the dream vision and the landscape function as projections of the narrator's troubled psyche. The images of reflection and self-reflexiveness convey his capacity to become what he represents his protagonist as being, a disillusioned pantheist whose alienation from natural life becomes increasingly solipsistic, and finally self-annihilating.

II

In the Preface to *Alastor* Shelley says with an air of philosophical detachment that the poem 'may be considered as allegorical of one of the most interesting situations of the human mind' (*PP*, 69). That situation was interesting to many of Shelley's predecessors and contemporaries as well, though none of them pursued it with his relentlessness. In these writers the 'situation' of imaginative self-projection and self-destruction often assumes verbal shapes instructively related to the patterns we have been tracing in *Alastor*.

When Thomas Weiskel says that desire in *Alastor* and in Romantic poetry generally is 'fundamentally narcissistic',[8] he is emphasizing a dilemma to which Shelley's poem itself gives unmistakable prominence, and he is insisting that our understanding of it ought to include more than disgust or condescending pity. Ovid's narrator is neither disgusted by nor condescending towards the Narcissus of the *Metamorphoses*. He is instead transfixed (like Narcissus himself) by what he sees in his narrative:

> adstupet ipse sibi vultuque inmotus eodem
> haeret . . .[9]   (III.418–19)

> [He looks in speechless wonder at himself and
> hangs there motionless in the same expression.]

Unlike Narcissus, however, the narrator is anything but speechless; his elaborate rhetorical patterning mimics a situation full of both poetic opportunity and human pathos:

> cunctaque miratur, quibus est mirabilis ipse :
> se cupit imprudens et, qui probat, ipse probatur,
> dumque petit, petitur . . .
>
>   (III.424–6)

> [all things . . . he admires for which he is himself admired. Unwittingly he desires himself; he praises, and is himself what he praises; and while he seeks, is sought . . .]

In establishing the rhetoric of overt narcissism, Ovid combines reflexive syntax with the echoing of one verb form by another ('miratur'/ 'mirabilis', 'probat'/'probatur', 'petit'/'petitur'). This pattern of deviated verbal repetition is elaborated mythologically in the account

of the nymph Echo, whose fate in the narrative provides an aural counterpart to Narcissus's tragic captivation by visual self-duplication.[10]

Later writers interested in going beyond a mere thematic reference
or allusion to the Narcissus episode in the *Metamorphoses* often look back
to and adapt Ovid's stylistic maneuvers. In Shakespeare's *Venus and
Adonis*, an erotically desperate Venus taunts Adonis with the charge of
Narcissus-like self-love:

> 'Is thine own heart to thine own face affected?
> Can thy right hand seize love upon thy left?
> Then woo thyself, be of thyself rejected;
> Steal thine own freedom, and complain on theft.
>   Narcissus so himself himself forsook,
>   And died to kiss his shadow in the brook.'
>
> (157–62)

The Ovidian patterns of reflexive syntax and verbal doubling play
throughout the stanza and converge with sarcastic wit in the
penultimate line, where reflexive pronouns are brought, as it were, face
to face (or, given the double suggestiveness of the verb, back to back):
'Narcissus so himself himself forsook'. The structure of the line is a
rhetorical diagram of what it says – Narcissus lost himself in his desire
to unite with that self's delusive duplication. When Milton's Eve recalls
almost losing herself in the same way, her language echoes Ovid's
verbal mirroring and echoing but not his reflexive syntax, because she
did not recognize the beautiful shape as her own. The passage is full of
Shelleyan anticipations:

>   I thither went
> With unexperienc't thought, and laid me down
> On the green bank, to look into the clear
> Smooth Lake, that to me seemed another Sky.
> As I bent down to look, just opposite,
> A Shape within the wat'ry gleam appear'd
> Bending to look on me, I started back,
> It started back, but pleas'd I soon return'd,
> Pleas'd it return'd as soon with answering looks
> Of sympathy and love . . .[11]
>
> (IV.456–65)

It was Adam, Eve recalls, who introduced her to reflexive self-consciousness and language: 'What there thou seest fair creature is thyself' (IV.468). But he did so in order to transform Eve's naive narcissism into another, less solipsistic mode of uniting with one's own image and of reproducing oneself:

> hee
> Whose image thou art, him thou shalt enjoy
> Inseparably thine, to him shalt bear
> Multitudes like thyself . . .
>
> (IV.471–4)

> Part of my Soul I seek thee, and thee claim
> My other half . . .
>
> (IV.487–8)

Milton can insist that the fruit of narcissistic self-love is self-destruction and yet recognize that love in its proper and higher forms incorporates and transfigures, rather than cancels, self-love. There is a reflexive dimension to Adam's love of Eve, as there is to God's love of them both: 'in his own Image hee / Created thee, in the Image of God / Express' (VII.526–8).

: If Eve's potential narcissism is the arrested and distorted version of an impulse which also finds noble and virtuous expression in *Paradise Lost*, then the same might be said of Satan's. His vaunt of solipsistic self-sufficiency contains what must be the most familiar reflexive image in the language:

> The mind is its own place, and in itself
> Can make a Heav'n of Hell, a Hell of Heav'n.
>
> (I.254–5)

It is a commonplace that Satan's vaunt was given new moral, psychological and epistemological meaning by the Romantics. And not just by Blake and Shelley – there are pivotal moments verging on Satanic reflexiveness in Wordsworth and Coleridge as well:

> The mind beneath such banners militant
> Thinks not of spoils or trophies, nor of ought
> That may attest its prowess, blest in thoughts
> That are their own perfection and reward –
>
> (1805 *Prelude*, VI.543–6)

O Lady! we receive but what we give,
And in our life alone does Nature live.

(Dejection: An Ode, 47–8)

In the *Defence* Shelley explicitly connects Satan's lines with a variation on his favorite maxim from the 'intellectual philosophy': 'All things exist as they are perceived: at least in relation to the percipient. "The mind is its own place, and of itself can make a heaven of hell, a hell of heaven" ' (*PP*, 505). Shelley's misquotation – 'of itself' for 'in itself' – intensifies Satan's claim that the mind provides both the substance and the location of the world it inhabits. For Shelley, Satan's words epitomize an essentially skeptical epistemological position, a 'curse' which poetry simultaneously expresses and overcomes:

> But poetry defeats the curse which binds us to be subjected to the accident of surrounding impressions. And whether it spreads its own figured curtain or withdraws life's dark veil from before the scene of things, it equally creates for us a being within our being.
>
> (*PP*, 505)

One of the ways in which poetry 'defeats the curse' of the mind's being 'its own place' is by spreading 'its own figured curtain' – that is, by re-enacting the mind's necessarily reflexive condition in a verbal artifact.[12] The mind 'defeats' its 'curse' by repeating and articulating it at a higher level of self-consciousness (as Prometheus does through the Phantasm of Jupiter), by fashioning an inevitably approximate image of its own operations in language. The movement in Shelley's passage from Satan's 'The mind is its own place' to poetry's creating 'for us a being within our being' revises an analogous movement in *Paradise Lost*: the vaunt of the fallen archangel in Book I is transvalued in Michael's consoling advice to fallen man in Book XII:[13]

> then wilt thou not be loath
> To leave this Paradise, but shalt possess
> A paradise within thee, happier far.
>
> (585–7)

Shelley knew that Satanic self-environing, like narcissistic self-love, is a powerful force in Milton because it is allied as well as opposed to 'the ways of God to men'.

Shelley and his contemporaries recognized that in its narcissistic and Satanic modes the reflexive imagination is a doubly enthralling force, fascinating but also imprisoning. Wordsworth is at once overjoyed and disturbed at the beginning of *The Prelude* to find that the 'corresponding mild creative breeze' he 'felt within' as a response to nature's 'gentle breeze' has become self-generating, that it

> is become
> A tempest, a redundant energy,
> Vexing its own creation.
>
> (1805; I.45–7)

The vexations of another kind of self-reflexiveness prove to be productively unsettling in Book IV, when Wordsworth compares himself as autobiographer to a man looking into the depths of 'a still water' from 'a slow-moving boat':

> Yet often is perplexed, and cannot part
> The shadow from the substance, rocks and sky,
> Mountains and clouds, from that which is indeed
> The region, and the things which there abide
> In their true dwelling; now is crossed by gleam
> Of his own image, by a sunbeam now,
> And motions that are sent he knows not whence,
> impediments that make his task more sweet . . .[14]
>
> (1805; IV.254—61)

Wordsworth is perplexed but also delighted by the mind's tendency to project its own identity into a scene already complicated by reflections from beyond the self. De Quincey is haunted by a more extreme and delusive form of such reflexive projection, for in his dreams the entire scene carries the distorted image of the dreamer's mind:

> To my architecture succeeded dreams of lakes – and silvery expanses of water: – these haunted me so much, that I feared (though possibly it will appear ludicrous to a medical man) that some dropsical state or tendency of the brain might thus be making itself (to use a metaphysical word) *objective*; and the sentient organ *project* itself as its own object. –[15]

But De Quincey knew how to take poetic advantage of as well as philosophize about the situation he recalls; this account of his watery dreams continues with that remarkable passage in which 'translucent lakes, shining like mirrors . . . became seas and oceans', and 'my mind tossed – and surged with the ocean'.

Byron's mind tosses and surges in a similarly reflexive relation to nature in Canto III of *Childe Harold's Pilgrimage*, written when Byron was being dosed by Shelley 'with Wordsworth physic even to nausea'.[16] Early in the canto Byron reintroduces Harold, 'The wandering outlaw of his own dark mind' (III.20),[17] and holds out the prospect that having 'thought / Too long and darkly, till my brain became, / In its own eddy boiling and o'erwrought' (III.55–7), he and Harold may be able to escape their reflexive predicament by asking nature to bear the burden:

> Like the Chaldean, he could watch the stars,
> Till he had peopled them with beings bright
> As their own beams . . .
>
> (III.118—20)

The stars have aroused Harold's imagination to create beings whose brightness is measured by the stars they inhabit: for a moment the balance and reciprocity between the creative imagination and the external natural beauty which activates it seem to offer a way out of the mind's struggle to 'find / A life within itself' (III.107–8). But the reflexive syntax of 'beings bright / As their own beams' suggests that in such star-gazing the mind is still its own place. Again and again in Canto III Byron turns his mind outward to nature only to find, as Wordsworth did with different consequences, the mind's habits and passions reflected back at him:

> Lake Leman woos me with its crystal face,
> The mirror where the stars and mountains view
> The stillness of their aspect in each trace
> Its clear depth yields of their far height and hue:
> There is too much of man here . . .
>
> (III.644–8)

Byron's way finally is not to escape from, but to accept and to find an artistic shape for, the predicament which links him to 'the self-torturing sophist, wild Rousseau' (III.725).[18] For him as for Napoleon, the absence of self-projection will only make him self-consuming,

> as a flame unfed, which runs to waste
> With its own flickering, or a sword laid by
> Which eats into itself, and rusts ingloriously.
>
> (III.394–6)

Like Byron, Shelley was capable of turning reflexive imagery back not only upon himself but upon contemporaries whom he thought were alienated and isolated by the very power and independence of their imaginations. Thus the reflexiveness of Byron's imagination is simultaneously described and verbally enacted in the Preface to *Julian and Maddalo*: 'His ambition preys upon itself, for want of objects which it can consider worthy of exertion.' The same is true in the poem itself, when Julian takes up the reflexive image again and combines it with an image of visual reflection:

> The sense that he was greater than his kind
> Had struck, methinks, his eagle spirit blind
> By gazing on its own exceeding light.
>
> (50–2)

Shelley reworks this image, altering the tone and subsidiary associations, in the lines on Coleridge in the 'Letter to Maria Gisborne'. He repeats both the idea of the eagle and the pun on 'exceeding' ('of surpassing value or quality', but also 'excessive'):

> You will see Coleridge – he who sits obscure
> In the exceeding lustre and the pure
> Intense irradiation of a mind
> Which, with its own internal lightning blind,
> Flags wearily through darkness and despair –
> A cloud-encircled meteor of the air,
> A hooded eagle among blinking owls. –
>
> (202–8)

Byron is the eagle who, instead of flying towards the sun in a process of aspiring self-renewal, preys upon himself and is blinded by the superiority of his own talents; Coleridge is the eagle paradoxically hooded, encircled, into obscurity by the 'intense irradiation' and 'internal lightning' of his own mental powers. Both, Shelley suggests, are caught up in their own versions of the central dilemma of *Alastor*, imprisoned within the self and driven to search despairingly for completion through self-reflection and self-projection.

Shelley's finest assessment of the reflexive dilemma he saw in his contemporaries as well as in himself comes in his satirical account of Wordsworth's poetic decline, *Peter Bell the Third*. Hazlitt wrote of the author of *The Excursion*:

He may be said to create his own materials; his thoughts are his real subject. . . . He sees all things in himself. . . . The power of his mind preys upon itself. It is as if there were nothing but himself and the universe. He lives in the busy solitude of his own heart.[19]

Shelley agreed, but in terms more intricately ambivalent, and more evidently tinged with self-criticism:

> All things that Peter saw and felt
>   Had a peculiar aspect to him;
> And when they came within the belt
> Of his own nature, seemed to melt
>   Like cloud to cloud, into him.
>
> And so the outward world uniting
>   To that within him, he became
> Considerably uninviting
> To those, who meditation slighting,
>   Were moulded in a different frame.

(273–82)

>   . . . thus
>   His virtue, like our own, was built
> Too much on that indignant fuss
> Hypocrite Pride stirs up in us
>   To bully one another's guilt.
>
> He had a mind which was somehow
>   At once circumference and centre
> Of all he might or feel or know;
> Nothing went ever out, although
>   Something did ever enter.
>
> He had as much imagination
>   As a pint-pot: – he never could
> Fancy another situation,
> From which to dart his contemplation,
>   Than that wherein he stood.
>
> Yet his was individual mind,
>   And new created all he saw

In a new manner, and refined
Those new creations, and combined
   Them, by a master-spirit's law.

(288–307)

This is shrewd criticism from a poet who cared intensely about
Wordsworth, who read him with at least as much sympathy as
antipathy.[20] Leavis was right to observe that

> Shelley . . . had turned upon Wordsworth the critical scrutiny
> which one poet turns upon another who can help him – whose
> problems bear on his own. For a poet in such a case the
> recognition of affinities is at the same time the realization of
> differences.[21]

Wordsworth's problem in these stanzas of *Peter Bell the Third* – his 'Sin',
as Part the Fourth is called – is that his mind is essentially, powerfully,
self-centered and self-referring. That this is indeed a problem that bears
upon Shelley's own should be apparent to anyone who has read *Alastor*.
It is internally apparent as well in Shelley's more than merely strategic
confession that 'His virtue, like our own' was too often built upon
proud indignation, and in his applying to Peter's all-encompassing mind
the same metaphor which he later applies to poetry itself in its highest
form:

> He had a mind which was somehow
>   At once circumference and centre
> Of all he might or feel or know . . .

(293–5)

> Poetry is indeed something divine. It is at once the centre and
> circumference of knowledge . . .

(*A Defence of Poetry, PP*, 503)

If Peter 'had as much imagination / As a pint-pot', it was not because his
writing gave expression to the common 'curse' that 'All things exist as
they are perceived', that 'the mind is its own place', but because he
accepted that 'curse' with such unvarying and undeflected autobiographical seriousness. The reflexive power of Wordsworth's mind
was, in Shelley's view, too narrowly and mundanely focused. Yet
constriction of imagination in this sense does not preclude, and may
even intensify, the creative vitality of that 'individual' reflexive
power, for

       though unimaginative,
   An apprehension clear, intense,
Of his mind's work, had made alive
The things it wrought on; I believe
   Wakening a sort of thought in sense.

                                        (308–12)

III

After *Alastor* reflexive imagery continues to be a recurrent figure in Shelley's poetry and appears in a wide variety of lyrical and narrative contexts. Empson's view that the figure became a kind of habit with Shelley, a consequence of his so often being 'too helplessly excited by one thing at a time',[22] has yet to be considered with respect to the later poetry. I want to move on to the two major works from which Empson's own examples are drawn (*Prometheus Unbound* and *The Triumph of Life*), and to a third which he does not mention (*The Cenci*), by way of *The Revolt of Islam*, the least read – for quite understandable reasons – of Shelley's ambitious poetic undertakings.

Reflexive imagery is fundamentally ambivalent in *The Revolt of Islam*; the states of consciousness – especially political consciousness – it signals may be either auspicious or inauspicious, benign or malign. Consider the imagery of self-illumination. In Canto I the narrator is led into a vast temple of prophetic vision where 'long and labyrinthine aisles' appear 'more bright / With their own radiance than the Heaven of Day' (597–8). But in Canto V, when Laon approaches the tyrant Othman, he finds him 'Upon the footstool of his golden throne, / Which, starred with sunny gems, in its own lustre shone' (1897–8). Throughout the poem, as so often in Shelley's later poetry, political oppression is imaged reflexively, suggesting that to an important degree it is, at least passively, self-imposed. In Canto II Laon remembers how the citizens of his native Argolis had allowed 'one Power' to gain 'supreme control / Over their will by their own weakness lent' (732–3); in Canto V he appeals to his followers to show mercy towards their former oppressors, since 'to avenge misdeed / On the misdoer, doth but Misery feed / With her own broken heart' (1813–15).

In Canto X the forces of counter-revolution brutally regain control and leave the populace prey to disease and famine:

> Many saw
> Their own lean image everywhere, it went
> A ghastlier self beside them, till the awe
> Of the dread sight to self-destruction sent
> Those shrieking victims . . .

(3982–6)

Whether suicide is provoked by seeing one's own emaciated shadow or by seeing one's starving fellow citizens is left horrifyingly indeterminate. Related indeterminacies of reference and implication appear in instances where forces of political regeneration or liberation are imaged reflexively. An old hermit revives Laon's spirits in Canto IV by telling him how Cythna has inspired her people to try to conquer Othman's soldiers by sympathy rather than by force:

> . . . the multitude
> Surrounding them, with words of human love,
> Seek from their own decay their stubborn minds to move.

(1645–7)

'From their own decay' can appropriately refer either to the social and physical condition of the 'multitude', or to the moral condition of the soldiers who oppress them. In Canto V Laon returns to Argolis and leads the people to victory over Othman and his army. There is a night of rejoicing, and the canto comes to a close with this couplet:

> The multitudes went homeward, to their rest,
> Which that delightful day with its own shadow blessed.

(2333–4)

'With its own shadow' at first seems merely intensive, a way of emphasizing the point that the end of a day of victory and celebration brings an additional reward of peaceful rest. But the reflexive syntax also enhances an ominous undertone in that last line, a suggestion that even this glorious day is shadowed by the suffering that has and is to come.

Reflexive images in *The Revolt of Islam* lack the intensely developed psychological context they have in *Alastor*, and rarely are they articulated with the finesse of Shelley's later writing at its best. But one can see Shelley working towards an expanded sense of the figure's possibilities in this poem – particularly in Cythna's narrative of her imprisonment, release and return to Argolis in Cantos VII and VIII. Extending what he took to be the epistemological and educational implications of the 'intellectual philosophy', Shelley has Cythna describe her isolated confinement in a seaside cave as an extreme symbolic enactment of the essential reflexive condition of mind. ' "We live in our own world" ', she says (VII.3091), in words that recall Satan's 'The mind is its own place':

'My mind became the book through which I grew
   Wise in all human wisdom, and its cave,
Which like a mine I rifled through and through,
   To me the keeping of its secrets gave –
   One mind, the type of all, the moveless wave
Whose calm reflects all moving things that are . . .'
(VII.3100–5)

Cythna's mind becomes its own book and teacher, generates its own 'subtler language within language' (VII.3112). Like the wandering poet in *Alastor*, but with an access to consciousness other than her own that he never achieves, she sustains herself with her own visionary love-songs:

     – and sweet melodies
  Of love, in that lorn solitude I caught
From mine own voice in dream, when thy dear eyes
Shone through my sleep, and did that utterance harmonize.[23]
(VII.3114–17)

In learning to rely on the self-sustaining power of mind, however, Cythna also learns to mistrust the mind's tendency to project itself as a god-like 'Power' separate from and superior to the human imagination. When an earthquake shatters her cavern-prison and she is rescued by a passing ship, she upbraids the mariners for their superstitious belief in a personified deity:

' "What is that Power? Ye mock yourselves, and give
   A human heart to what ye cannot know:
As if the cause of life could think and live . . ." '
(VIII.3235–7)

' "What is that Power? Some moon-struck sophist stood
   Watching the shade from his own soul upthrown
Fill Heaven and darken Earth, and in such mood
   The Form he saw and worshipped was his own,

His likeness in the world's vast mirror shown . . ." '

(VIII.3244–8)

Cythna gives new force to the Miltonic adjective 'moon-struck' as she imagines the sophist lost in a lunacy of unselfconscious reflection, projecting his own 'likeness' as an object of worship. What makes her attack on this false form of reflexive projection so striking is the way in which it echoes her previous appeal to the mariners' self-reliance:

' "What dream ye? Your own hands have built an home,
    Even for yourselves on a beloved shore." '

(VIII.3226–7)

' "Is this your care? Ye toil for your own good –
    Ye feel and think – has some immortal power
Such purposes?" '

(VIII.3231–3)

The reflexive impulse weaves its way ambivalently in and out of Cythna's narrative, showing itself now as self-reliance and self-sufficiency, now as self-deception and mere selfishness. She concludes her speech to the mariners by urging them to 'know thyself' and yet to recognize and shun 'the dark idolatry of self' (VIII.3388, 3390).

That 'One mind, the type of all' to which Cythna gains access by studying herself in *The Revolt of Islam* (VII.3104) becomes the center of Shelley's metaphysical allegory in *Prometheus Unbound*. Here again, but with greater figurative daring and cogency than in the earlier work, reflexive imagery articulates the mind's capacity for self-imprisonment and self-liberation. Wasserman's reading of Act I is particularly powerful in its analysis of the fundamental thematic reflexiveness in Shelley's handling of the Prometheus myth. Commenting on the repetition of Prometheus's curse by the Phantasm of Jupiter, Wasserman asks us

> to recognize this as the actual identification of the execrating Prometheus with Jupiter, the god he made in his own image. Not only does the audience watch the Phantasm uttering Prometheus' curse against him of whom it is the phantom; it also observes Prometheus facing his own former self in Jupiter's ghost.[24]

That such self-confrontation is a necessary and critical phase in Prometheus's liberation is indicated analogically and prophetically in the Earth's response to her immortal son's plea that the curse against Jupiter be 'recalled' (I.59):

PROMETHEUS
But mine own words, I pray, deny me not.

THE EARTH
They shall be told. – Ere Babylon was dust,
The Magus Zoroaster, my dead child,
Met his own image walking in the garden.
That apparition, sole of men, he saw.[25]

(I.190–4)

When the Earth tells Prometheus later in the same speech to 'Call at will / Thine own ghost, or the ghost of Jupiter' (I.210–11), her ambiguous syntactic alternation allows for the reflexive identification of Prometheus with his self-created tormenter ('I gave all / He has, and in return he chains me here,' I.381–2).

Confronting his former self in the Phantasm of Jupiter completes this phase of the movement within Prometheus from hatred to pity ('I wish no living thing to suffer pain,' I.305). But pity alone is not enough. Prometheus's curse is not recalled just to be revoked; the words repeated by the Phantasm also contain the verbal pattern through which Prometheus will reclaim power for himself on behalf of mankind and mortal existence. When he cursed Jupiter, Prometheus had reminded him that 'O'er all things but thyself I gave thee power, / And my own will' (I.273–4), words which again establish a reciprocal identification as well as a distinction between oppressor and oppressed. Prometheus reserved to himself a power which he denied Jupiter but which hatred had prevented him from fully realizing. In the course of Act I he reclaims this power by freeing himself from the constrictions of hate. Rhetorically, as he responds to the taunts of the Furies, he re-recalls those critical words and frees them from the context of his curse:

Yet am I king over myself, and rule
The torturing and conflicting throngs within
As Jove rules you when Hell grows mutinous.

(I.492–4)

The process by which Prometheus's original defiant assertion of autonomy is recalled and transformed into its fullest political realization comes to completion at the end of Act III, where the Spirit of the Hour extends that autonomy, and the stylistic motif which has become its signature, to man '– the King / Over himself; just, gentle, wise – but man' (III.iv.196–7).[26]

As Empson recognized, however, not all the 'self-inwoven' figures in *Prometheus Unbound* bear such immediate relation to the poem's central mythic and psychical action, nor are they always as internally coherent as the instances we have just been looking at. The figure pervades the lyric celebration of Act IV; it is no accident that all the examples queried by Empson come from this part of the poem. Shelley could be uneven in exploiting this stylistic resource in moments of extravagant visionary intensity. Consider Panthea's description of the regenerated earth and the attendant spirit asleep within its 'Ten thousand orbs involving and involved' (IV.241):

> . . . they whirl
> Over each other with a thousand motions
> Upon a thousand sightless axles spinning
> And with the force of self-destroying swiftness,
> Intensely, slowly, solemnly roll on –
> Kindling with mingled sounds, and many tones,
> Intelligible words and music wild. –
> With mighty whirl the multitudinous Orb
> Grinds the bright brook into an azure mist
> Of elemental subtlety, like light,
> And the wild odour of the forest flowers,
> The music of the living grass and air,
> The emerald light of leaf-entangled beams
> Round its intense, yet self-conflicting speed,
> Seem kneaded into one aerial mass
> Which drowns the sense. Within the Orb itself,
> Pillowed upon its alabaster arms
> Like to a child o'erwearied with sweet toil,
> On its own folded wings and wavy hair
> The Spirit of the Earth is laid asleep,
> And you can see its little lips are moving
> Amid the changing light of their own smiles
> Like one who talks of what he loves in dream –
>
> (IV.246—68)

The images of 'self-destroying swiftness' and 'intense, yet self-conflicting speed' are both cogently precise in their evocation of whirling concentric spheres off-setting and counter-balancing each other's motions as together, in a paradoxical 'whirlwind harmony', they 'slowly, solemnly roll on'. But the infant Spirit of the Earth sleeping calmly at the center of all this spinning movement is presented in gratuitously reflexive terms. Empson comments on the redundancy of the simile in line 268 ('The last comparison is merely a statement of what he is');[27] he might also have complained about the triviality of the Spirit's lying 'On its own folded wings and wavy hair', and about the awkwardness of 'Amid the changing light of their own smiles'. This last image is troubling not because it lacks a discernible expressive function: Panthea sees the Spirit of the Earth here in a way that recalls Asia's response to Panthea's prophetic dream-vision of a liberated Prometheus in Act II.

> There is a change: beyond their inmost depth
> I see a shade – a shape – 'tis He, arrayed
> In the soft light of his own smiles . . .

(II.i.119–21)

Like Prometheus in Act II, the Spirit of the Earth in Act IV appears in an illumination generated internally by love and radiated from within, not from an external source.[28] But the problem with the Act IV image arises because of the odd plurals in 'their own smiles' (why not 'its own smiles', or 'his own smiles'?). 'Their' has its antecedent in the plural 'lips' of line 266, but the reader has to struggle with the distracting thought of each individual lip forming its own smile on the way to seeing that Shelley is referring to 'smiles' as separate, repeated actions. The image in Act IV is not carefully composed, and if many of Shelley's reflexive images were articulated with this kind of looseness, one would be inclined to agree with Empson that the figure had become a bad habit.

But elsewhere in Act IV Shelley shows that reflexive imagery is not habitually a resource he takes for granted. The first speech uttered by the Earth after Panthea's long rhapsodic introduction culminates in one of the poem's most compelling 'self-inwoven similes':

> The joy, the triumph, the delight, the madness,
> The boundless, overflowing bursting gladness,
> The vaporous exultation, not to be confined!
>   Ha! ha! the animation of delight
>   Which wraps me, like an atmosphere of light,

And bears me as a cloud is borne by its own wind!

(IV.319–24)

The commentators who have shown us the specificity and precision of
Shelley's meteorological knowledge would be right to point out here
that in thunderstorms clouds are actually moved about by their own
internally generated turbulence.[29] Shelley uses the simile's meteorological energy to animate an otherwise vapid 'vaporous exultation', and
to invigorate the metaphorical life of 'an atmosphere of light'. But the
simile is effective in other ways as well, as we may see by comparing it
to an earlier version of itself from *The Revolt of Islam*. Laon remembers
how he persisted in his cause despite being separated from Cythna:

> Doth the cloud perish, when the beams are fled
>   Which steeped its skirts in gold? or, dark and lone,
>   Doth it not through the paths of night unknown,
> On outspread wings of its own wind upborne
>   Pour rain upon the earth?

(IV.1686–90)

The effect of this melodramatic cloud and wind image is wonderfully
enhanced in *Prometheus Unbound* by its new dramatic context: the
lightness and ebullience the Earth feels in realizing its recently acquired
freedom give the simile of the cloud, with its implied contrast to the
massive weight and solidity we normally associate with the Earth, a
witty appropriateness. The main point of the reflexive simile is to
convey the Earth's participation in the self-generated freedom and
power realized by Prometheus – a freedom and power that come from
within, like the wind in line 324, and initially depend on no external
source. Reflexive images continue to display this fundamental
condition of mind and experience right through to the end of the poem.
In its antiphonal song with the Moon, the Earth celebrates the
renovated human condition by elaborating once again the idea of man
as 'King / Over himself':

> Man, one harmonious Soul of many a soul
> Whose nature is its own divine controul . . .

(IV.400–1)

Then there is Demogorgon's concluding exhortation about what must
be done if oppressive evil should ever regain power:

> To defy Power which seems Omnipotent;
> To love, and bear; to hope, till Hope creates

From its own wreck the thing it contemplates . . .

(IV.572–4)

The rhyme here –'creates' and 'contemplates' reinforce each other conceptually as well as phonetically – complements the reflexive syntactic figure; together they give memorable shape to the ideal of a self-liberating and self-sustaining psychical potential.

While *Prometheus Unbound* contains Shelley's most positive exaltation of the reflexive imagination, the poem also recognizes that the same mental capacity can be negative and destructive.[30] Prometheus replies to Mercury's request that he divulge the 'secret known / To thee and to none else of living things' (I.371–2) by denouncing Jupiter's perversion of the very principle which will enable Prometheus to liberate himself and mankind:

> Evil minds
> Change good to their own nature.

(I.380–1)

These Satanic words could serve as an epigraph for *The Cenci*, which Shelley wrote between Acts I–III and Act IV of *Prometheus Unbound*. One of the many ways in which *The Cenci* inverts the vision of human potential expressed in *Prometheus Unbound* is in its articulation of the mind's power to know itself and to make the world over in its own image. Orsino's soliloquy at the end of Act II both anatomizes and enacts the reflexive imagination in its Cencian shape:

> It fortunately serves my close designs
> That 'tis a trick of this same family
> To analyse their own and other minds.
> Such self-anatomy shall teach the will
> Dangerous secrets: for it tempts our powers,
> Knowing what must be thought, and may be done,
> Into the depth of darkest purposes:
> So Cenci fell into the pit; even I,
> Since Beatrice unveiled me to myself,
> And made me shrink from what I cannot shun,
> Shew a poor figure to my own esteem,
> To which I grow half reconciled.

(II.ii.107–18)

This 'trick' of infectious 'self-anatomy' and self-corruption is pervasive in *The Cenci*; a father's rape of his own daughter, a perversion of the positive incestuous bond between brother and sister which figures significantly in other of Shelley's poems, is only one of its many manifestations. What makes this pattern of behavior so disturbing is that it springs from the same capacity of mind to become conscious of its own operations and impulses which Shelley elsewhere celebrates – in the Preface to *The Cenci* itself, for instance:

> The highest moral purpose aimed at in the highest species of the drama, is the teaching of the human heart, through its sympathies and antipathies, the knowledge of itself.[31]
>
> (*PP*, 240)

The sharp distinction between 'self-anatomy' and 'self-knowledge' developed by Wasserman in his reading of *The Cenci* has its usefulness,[32] but it obscures the mental dynamic which Shelley's dramatic characters share with his ideal dramatic audience (or which Jupiter shares with Prometheus). Cencian 'self-anatomy', like Promethean self-knowledge, is often represented in circular figures. Internally *The Cenci* offers no escape from the circle of negative reflexiveness; corrupt self-consciousness can finally only reconfigure itself as self-destruction:

> And we are left, as scorpions ringed with fire,
> What should we do but strike ourselves to death?
>
> (II.ii.70–1)

'The line circumscribed by the agonized scorpion's self-destruction is enclosed by a second circle, the wall of fire representing destructive experience' – Stuart Curran's comment shows why he sees this figure as emblematic of Shelley's vision of a world in which 'evil is the only force . . . good, transferred into action, into force, as a deterrent to evil, becomes evil.'[33] As Prometheus says, 'Evil minds / Change good to their own nature'.

The deep-lying ambivalence of Shelley's reflexive imagery is nowhere more powerfully evident than in *The Triumph of Life*, the other major poem from which Empson draws his examples of this characteristic figure. The opening lines signal the importance of the reflexive pattern through what appears to be a propitious personification:

> Swift as a spirit hastening to his task
>   Of glory and of good, the Sun sprang forth
> Rejoicing in his splendour . . .[34]
>
> (1–3)

But 'splendour' in *The Triumph* is only intermittently and briefly cause for rejoicing; within his 'waking dream' (42) the narrator soon encounters 'a cold glare, intenser than the noon / But icy cold' which 'obscured with [   ] light / The Sun as he the stars' (77–9). The course of this strange new light appears in a reflexive figure which itself 'obscures', by recalling and transforming, the opening image of the sun's joyous 'splendour':

> So came a chariot on the silent storm
> Of its own rushing splendour . . .
>
> (86–7)

The internal dynamics of this particular image are striking: the initial paradox of 'silent storm', which at first appears to be contradicted by the strong aural force of 'rushing', is eventually validated as that aural force is absorbed into the wholly visual effect of 'splendour'. 'Silent storm' and 'rushing splendour' stand in chiastic synaesthetic relation to each other. Empson juxtaposes these lines with a second passage from much later in Rousseau's inset narrative:

> 'I among the multitude
> Was swept; me sweetest flowers delayed not long,
> Me not the shadow nor the solitude,
>
> 'Me not the falling stream's Lethean song,
> Me, not the phantom of that early form
> Which moved upon its motion.'
>
> (460–5)

Although Empson does not make it clear that the 'early Form' of this second passage is not the chariot of Life referred to in the first, his juxtaposition is none the less suggestive: the 'shape all light' envisioned by Rousseau moves with the same kind of self-sustaining motion as the chariot of Life, in whose 'coming light' that 'fair shape waned' (412). This connection is anticipated, and linked with the sun's rising movement at the beginning of the poem, through a contrasting reflexive figure in Rousseau's account of 'that early form's' first appearance:

> ' . . . there stood
>
> 'Amid the sun, as he amid the blaze

Of his own glory, on the vibrating
Floor of the fountain, paved with flashing rays,

'A shape all light . . .'

(348–52)

Rousseau's 'shape' may be nothing more than an idealized reflection of
the sun's 'flashing rays' at a moment of illusory stasis. Like the narrator's
perception of the sun, Rousseau's perception of the 'shape all light' is
paradoxically 'obscured' by the intense glare of a force whose
movement duplicates and mocks both sun and 'shape'. The interlocking
reflexive images provide one of the means by which Shelley suggests a
complexly infolded and parallel relationship between Rousseau's
experience and that of the narrator.

Empson comments directly on only one part of this sequence of
images: about 'the phantom of that early form / Which moved upon its
motion' he says, 'The *Form* is its own justification; it sustains itself, like
God, by the fact that it exists.' This comment is actually more
appropriate to the previous passage in which Life's chariot appears 'in
the silent storm / Of its own rushing splendour', since Life is
triumphant in Shelley's poem simply 'by the fact that it exists', and in
many respects it does assume the role of God in its self-sustaining and
relentless omnipotence. But Empson is right to question the apparently
tautological redundancy of 'moved upon its motion'. Whether logically
and verbally pointless, as he argues, or somehow strangely expressive,
the phrase pushes the reflexive figure to an extreme. In *Epipsychidion* the
speaker refers to Emily as 'a tender /Reflection of the eternal Moon of
Love / Under whose motions life's dull billows move' (117–19), but the
absence of a reflexive relation here between 'motions' and 'moves' only
accentuates by comparison the excessive involution of the later image.[35]
What this image is meant to convey, I would suggest, is Rousseau's
attenuated memory of the 'shape all light's' increasingly faint and
finally negative corporeal presence. Even when 'that early form' first
appeared to him, its spectral movements seemed barely to register on
the natural world:

'– the fierce splendour
Fell from her as she moved under the mass

'Of the deep cavern, and with palms so tender
Their tread broke not the mirror of its billow,

Glided along the river . . .'

(359–63)

'As one enamoured is upborne in dream
  O'er lily-paven lakes mid silver mist
To wondrous music, so this shape might seem

  'Partly to tread the waves with feet which kist
The dancing foam, partly to glide along
  The airs that roughened the moist amethyst . . .'

(367–72)

When the 'new Vision' of Life's chariot 'Burst' upon his sight and made 'that early form' the 'phantom' which Rousseau remembers in lines 464–5, this 'phantom' moves even more spectrally over and through the 'wilderness' of experience:

  'So knew I in that light's severe excess
The presence of that shape which on the stream
  Moved, as I moved along the wilderness,

'More dimly than a day appearing dream,
  The ghost of a forgotten form of sleep,
A light from Heaven whose half extinguished beam

  'Through the sick day in which we wake to weep
Glimmers, forever sought, forever lost. –
  So did that shape its obscure tenour keep

'Beside my path, as silent as a ghost . . .'

(424–33)

A moving shape whose 'tenour' has become as 'obscure' as this might plausibly be remembered as having attained a mode of 'presence' (425) so infinitely remote from immediacy ('The ghost of a forgotten form of sleep') that there is nothing left that it can 'move[ ] upon' but 'its [own] motion'. To say so, however, is to turn language back on itself so severely and completely that its signifying function momentarily stalls or breaks down. At such a moment we may recall that shortly after he began speaking to the narrator, Rousseau wearily paused 'like one who with the weight / Of his own words is staggered' (196–7).

But language need not stagger in enacting the burden of reflexive

consciousness, as Empson implies in praising the 'great things' Shelley does
with reflexive imagery in the narrator's opening vision of Life's victims. In
the passage Empson cites, the reader is asked to envision the experience of
simultaneously casting a shadow and walking 'within' its 'gloom':

> And others mournfully within the gloom
>
> Of their own shadow walked, and called it death . . .
>
> (58–9)

'Death', says the Earth in *Prometheus Unbound*, 'is the veil which those
who live call Life' (III.iii.113). What those who live call 'death', Shelley
suggests, is the fear of physical nonexistence, the 'shadow' of our
consciousness of physical existence. That this idea of death is a product
of the defeated, earthbound imagination is conveyed in a reflexive
image which gives us the metaphorical reverse or 'negative' of those
positive visions of beings or objects seen in their own light in *Prometheus
Unbound*: Asia's vision of Prometheus 'arrayed / In the soft light of his
own smiles' (II.i.120–1); Earth's description of the cavern to which
Prometheus and Asia will retire, surrounded by 'bright, golden globes /
Of fruit, suspended in their own green heaven' (III.iii.139–40).[36] The
image from *The Triumph of Life* involves a double psychic perspective
reminiscent of *Alastor*: the image is implicitly expressive of the
narrator's perception as well as explicitly expressive of the perception
of those among Life's followers who have seen their own shadow and
'called it death'. The narrator sees what the mourners do not – that what
they call death is only the shadow cast by their mortal form of existence,
by their bodies. Here again Shelley articulates the force of the reflexive
image by taking precise advantage of internal semantic relationships.
'Gloom', positioned emphatically at the end of the line, is itself an
image 'drawn from the operations of the human mind' and operates
here in a double sense: its original meaning, 'sadness', links it behind to
'mournfully'; the figurative meaning given it by Milton, 'darkness',
links it forward to 'shadow'. The double sense of 'shadow' ('image cast
by a body intercepting light' but also 'spectral form, phantasm', as in the
'shades' of Hell) links it behind to the physical meaning of 'gloom' and
forward to 'death'. The phrase 'and called it death' calls forth the latent
mental or spiritual senses of 'gloom' and 'shadow' and provides an
ironic stylistic analogue to the way in which the mourners mistake an
image of their own corporeality for death. Death is not the eclipsing of

bodily existence, we are left to infer, but rather the mind's experience of sadness and torment – 'the veil which those who live call Life'.

IV

Christopher Ricks acknowledges that Shelley's reflexive images are more often capable of 'serious functions' than Empson allows – but he finds them too relentlessly serious when measured against Marvell's exemplary balance and fusion of wit and pathos:

> it remains true, and is to my mind a grave limitation even of the best such images in Shelley, that their tone is obdurately self-enclosed, impervious to – though not invulnerable to – wit and humour. There is a self-gratification, an ease of continuity, in Shelley's use of the word 'mournfully' [in line 58 of *The Triumph of Life*], too at home with 'gloom' and 'shadow' and 'death'. . . . Whereas Marvell's word 'mournful' has a various play of light against the surrounding words 'Shines' and 'Light', achieving a fluctuant iridescence:

> But gazing back upon the skies,
>   Shines with a mournful Light;
>   Like its own Tear.[37]

('On a Drop of Dew', 11–13)

There is nothing in Shelley quite so brilliantly and teasingly compact as this Marvellian equivalent in words of an optical illusion. But are Shelley's reflexive images as 'obdurately self-enclosed', as 'impervious to . . . wit and humour', as Ricks says? Shelley was capable on occasion of being witty and humorous about a number of things – including his own tendency to take himself seriously. He concludes the bemusedly ironic self-portrait in the preface to *Julian and Maddalo* with the sentence, 'Julian is rather serious.' Without denying the prevailingly serious tone and import of reflexive images in Shelley's poetry, it is possible to see that some of them do indicate an openness to Marvell's kind of intellectual playfulness, that they do not all depend on a 'disjunction of the figure's mystery from all possibility of wit and humour'.[38]

The Witch of Atlas contains an extended, self-delighting display of the imagination's ability to project itself as other and to invest a fictional natural setting with its own reflexive operations. The cavern where the

Witch is born and lives in the early stanzas is as thoroughly infused with reflexive iridescence as any Shelleyan setting. Before the Witch is 'conceived', as we have seen, her mother, 'one of the Atlantides', 'lay enfolden /In the warm shadow of her loveliness' (60–1). In this condition of receptive reflexive warmth the sun 'kissed her with his beams' (62), and the result is an *aura seminalis* that eventually becomes the Witch herself:

> A lovely lady garmented in light
>   From her own beauty . . .

(81–2)

This image is recapitulated near the end of the poem, when the Witch passes through the world of sleeping mortals:

> And all the forms in which those spirits lay
>   Were to her sight like the diaphanous
> Veils, in which those sweet ladies oft array
>   Their delicate limbs, who would conceal from us
> Only their scorn of all concealment: they
>   Move in the light of their own beauty thus.
> But these and all now lay with sleep upon them
> And little thought a Witch was looking on them.

(561–8)

The poem is filled with such instances of the reflexive imagination at play, with what G. Wilson Knight called 'that queer business of using one's imaginative experience to create something surprising to oneself'.[39] The reflexive ambience of the Witch and the cave where she dwells envelops the natural creatures drawn by her voice:

> Then the sly serpent, in the golden flame
>   Of his own volumes intervolved . . .

(91–2)

The way in which 'volumes' gets taken up phonetically and etymologically in the Miltonic coinage 'intervolved' (the Latin source of both is *volvere*, 'to roll') rolls this reflexive clause into a witty iconic conclusion. Everything in the Witch's presence becomes self-illuminating. Among the things with which her cave is stored are

> Carved lamps and chalices and phials which shone
>   In their own golden beams –

(205–6)

These reflexive figures take on a larger importance if we read the poem allegorically and, following Yeats's suggestion, see the Witch's cave as 'the mind looking inward upon itself'.[40] But the cave is open to the world outside it, and the imagery which evokes 'the mind looking inward upon itself' in this poem is open to the playful, whimsical possibilities of a situation which Shelley elsewhere regards with high epistemological seriousness.

The Witch of Atlas was written in the summer of 1820, the year in which Shelley began to enjoy the congenial stimulus of what would become his 'Pisan Circle'. Other poems of that year contain reflexive figures which are even more broadly and conspicuously open to possibilities of wit and humor. In the Letter to Maria Gisborne, Shelley anticipates having the Witch of Atlas's cave 'stored with scrolls of strange device, / The works of some Saturnian Archimage' (185–6) with a self-portrait in which he puckishly casts himself as Spenser's arch-magician:

> And here like some weird Archimage sit I,
> Plotting dark spells, and devilish enginery,
> The self-impelling steam-wheels of the mind
> Which pump up oaths from clergymen, and grind
> The gentle spirit of our meek reviews
> Into a powdery foam of salt abuse,
> Ruffling the ocean of their self-content –
> I sit – and smile or sigh as is my bent . . .
>
> (106–13)

'The self-impelling steam-wheels of the mind', which produce salty antidotes to the grave reviewers' 'self-content', may sound like deliberate self-parody to a reader who recalls some of the images of imaginative freedom in Prometheus Unbound ('The vaporous exultation, not to be confined', IV.321). There is an undeniable impulse towards amused self-parody in Oedipus Tyrannus; or Swellfoot the Tyrant, Shelley's grotesquely comic satire on the divorce trial of Queen Caroline. Here is Purganax, Chief of the Council of Wizards (his name is a literal Greek translation of an Anglo-Italian pun on 'Castlereagh', 'castle-king'), as he contemplates the growing rebellion of the 'Swinish Multitude':

> The future looks as black as death, a cloud,
> Dark as the frown of Hell, hangs over it –
> The troops grow mutinous – the revenue fails –

> There's something rotten in us – for the level
> Of the State slopes, its very bases topple,
> The boldest turn their backs upon themselves!
>
> (I.i.96–101)

Turning one's back upon oneself is as impossible to visualize as Marvells' drop of dew becoming in its own tear. Later in this first scene Dakry, Shelley's impersonation of Eldon, the Lord Chancellor who had refused Shelley custody of his children, tells how he 'made a long / Harangue (all words) to the assembled Swine' (326–7);

> – and then I wept
> With the pathos of my own eloquence,
> And every tear turned to a mill-stone, which
> Brained many a gaping Pig . . .
>
> (I.i.332–3)

This is nothing less than a reworking of the dream-maiden's voice in *Alastor*, 'stifled in tremulous sobs / Subdued by its own pathos' (164–5). The macabre humor of the later passage, one feels, arises partly from Shelley's momentary displacement of his own bitter personal resentment.

Perhaps the closest Shelley comes in the poems of 1820 to the poised urbanity and tonal complexity of Marvell's reflexive images is at the end of 'The Cloud':

> I change, but I cannot die –
> For after the rain, when with never a stain
>   The pavilion of Heaven is bare,
> And the winds and sunbeams, with their convex gleams,
>   Build up the blue dome of Air –
> I silently laugh at my own cenotaph,
>   And out of the caverns of rain,
> Like a child from the womb, like a ghost from the tomb,
>   I arise, and unbuild it again. –
>
> (76–84)

The reflexive image here delightfully predicts the paradox of the cloud's affirming its mutable existence by 'unbuilding' a structure of refracted light in 'bare' and empty space. The cloud knows that a cenotaph is, literally, an 'empty tomb'; that is why it can laugh at the 'blue dome of air' as a monument to its momentary disappearance. The internal rhyme, 'laugh'/'cenotaph', points up the way in which the line gestures towards something grave while executing a brilliantly reflexive pirouette.

V

'Nought is but that which feels itself to be' – Ahasuerus's perorative line in *Hellas* (785) may stand as a reminder that reflexive patterns of language would have come instinctively and inevitably (though not unthinkingly) to a writer inclined to see self-conscious thought as the 'radical base' of existence.[41] Such patterns have also come inevitably to later writers who cared deeply enough about Shelley to characterize his poetry in its own terms. Here is Browning in 1852:

> with the primal elements of humanity he has to do; and he digs where he stands, – preferring to seek them in his own soul as the nearest reflex of that absolute Mind, according to the intuitions of which he desires to perceive and speak.
>
> Such was the spheric poetical faculty of Shelley, as its own self-sufficing central light . . . reveals it.[42]

And Yeats in 1932, backing off from the intensity of his earlier admiration for and sense of identification with Shelley:

> Shelley's art shows that he was an unconverted man though certainly a visionary, what people call 'psychic'; his landscapes are vaporised and generalised by his purpose, his spirits have not the separated existence even of those that in *Manfred* curse and yet have 'sweet melancholy' voices. He was the tyrant of his own being.[43]

And Carlos Baker:

> It is a limited and partial, and therefore misrepresentative view of Shelley which sees him only as Ariel. . . . For Shelley, like Prospero in the mantle of invisibility, or like the poet in his own lyric, 'The Skylark', was often hidden in the very light of his own thought; a manipulator of large conceptions whose fundamental operations no one quite understood.[44]

And Stephen Spender:

> Shelley frequently has images of objects or persons dissolving in

the intensity of their own radiance, and this may serve as a metaphor of what sometimes happens in his own poetry.[45]

Each of these critical assessments uses Shelley's characteristic verbal figure to articulate an impulse or situation fundamental to his entire poetic career. What makes this critical instinct doubly just is that the figure, with its range of associated impulses and situations, is also fundamental to Shelley's own endeavors as a critic. Throughout *A Defence of Poetry*, as we have seen, seminal formulations are cast in reflexive shapes.[46]

In the *Defence*, however, as in the rest of Shelley's writing, reflexive thinking and writing stand, sometimes unsteadily, beside fierce denunciations of selfishness, that 'dark idolatry of self' condemned in *The Revolt of Islam* (VIII. 3390).

> Poetry, and the principle of Self, of which money is the visible incarnation, are the God and the Mammon of the world.
>
> (*PP*, 503)

Byron called Shelley 'the *best* and least selfish man I ever knew'; Mary Shelley, Trelawny and others made this judgement part of the Shelley myth.[47] But Shelley's writing and his life continually make us aware that generous, altruistic self-projection and self-sacrifice may be only deceptively antithetical to those manifestations of 'the principle of Self' that Shelley hated. (The relation of his life to his writing in this regard will be one of the main concerns of the last chapter.) Shelley came to see with increasing dismay that the mind's reflexive powers make possible, but also limit and vex, the self's relations with the world and with other people.

> The great secret of morals is Love; or a going out of our own nature, and an identification of ourselves with the beautiful which exists in thought, action, or person, not our own. A man, to be greatly good, must imagine intensely and comprehensively; he must put himself in the place of another and of many others; the pains and pleasures of his species must become his own.
>
> (*PP*, 487–8)

For every movement 'out of our own nature' towards 'another' in this passage, there is a movement back towards the self: the phrase that concludes the first sentence, 'not our own', is eventually countered by the phrase that concludes the second, 'must become his own' (the shift from plural to singular is significant). Shelley's writing enacts this circle of subjectivity with boldness and originality by demonstrating the degree to which it is both a blessing and a curse – a blessing discoverable by poetry in the very fabric of the language, a curse that poetry can only partially and momentarily defeat by spreading 'its own figured curtain' (*PP*, 505).

IV EVANESCENCE: MELTING, DISSOLVING, ERASING

Imagining 'the mind in creation . . . as a fading coal' comes in *A Defence of Poetry* as the culmination of Shelley's agitated sense of the ineluctable discrepancy between 'conception' and 'composition', between the activity of thought and the conditions of verbal articulation. Yet even as he acknowledges what he goes on to call 'a limitedness of the poetical faculty itself', Shelley elaborates a pattern of articulation recurrent in his own poetry.

> We are aware of evanescent visitations of thought and feeling sometimes associated with place or person, sometimes regarding our own mind alone, and always arising unforeseen and departing unbidden, but elevating and delightful beyond all expression: so that even in the desire and the regret they leave, there cannot but be pleasure, participating as it does in the nature of its object. It is as it were the interpenetration of a diviner nature through our own; but its footsteps are like those of a wind over a sea, which the coming calm erases, and whose traces remain only as on the wrinkled sand which paves it. . . . Poets are not only subject to these experiences as spirits of the most refined organization, but they can colour all that they combine with the evanescent hues of this etherial world. . . . Poetry thus makes immortal all that is best and most beautiful in the world; it arrests the vanishing apparitions which haunt the interlunations of life, and veiling them or in language or in form sends them forth among mankind, bearing sweet news of kindred joy to those with whom their sisters abide – abide, because there is no portal of expression from the caverns of the spirit which they inhabit into the universe of

things. Poetry redeems from decay the visitations of the divinity in man.

(PP, 504–5)

Evanescence or 'fading' or 'decay' becomes for Shelley an intrinsic feature of the mind's most precious experiences. The value of such experiences, he suggests, is as much a function of 'the desire and the regret they leave' as it is of any initial immediacy or fullness of presence.

What is the special relation of poetry to such evanescence? Shelley offers a double and in some respects paradoxical answer to this question. On the one hand the poet is able to reflect the mind's evanescent moments of experience by articulating them in figurative language which is analogously evanescent: 'they can colour all that they combine with the evanescent hues of this etherial world.' Sometimes Shelley writes as if the production of 'vitally metaphorical' language entails its own inherent principle of evanescence,[1] regardless of whether it refers to transient experiences external to itself or not:

> Poetry enlarges the circumference of the imagination by replenishing it with thoughts of ever new delight, which have the power of attracting and assimilating to their own nature all other thoughts, and *which form new intervals and interstices whose void for ever craves fresh food.*

(PP, 488; my emphasis)

On the other hand, the language of poetry 'arrests the vanishing apparitions' Shelley values so highly, and thus inevitably – and at least momentarily, until the process of reading begins – violates or veils (Shelley's word) the transience intrinsic to such moments. How can poetry 'redeem[ ] from decay the visitations of the divinity in man' without being false to Shelley's conviction that an experience of decay, a consciousness of the void or vacancy these 'visitations' always leave behind, is part of what makes them seem divine? Can Shelley's powerful sense of the poem as text or artifact ever fully accommodate his even more powerful sense of the poem as experience?

The opening stanza of the *Hymn to Intellectual Beauty*, with its conspicuous verbal anticipations of the passage from the *Defence* we have been looking at, provides a familiar basis for beginning to answer these questions:

The awful shadow of some unseen Power

Floats though unseen amongst us, – visiting
This various world with as inconstant wing
As summer winds that creep from flower to flower. –
Like moonbeams that behind some piny mountain shower,
    It visits with inconstant glance
    Each human heart and countenance;
Like hues and harmonies of evening, –
    Like clouds in starlight widely spread, –
    Like memory of music fled, –
    Like aught that for its grace may be
Dear, and yet dearer for its mystery.

                                                    (1–12)

It is not just the references to 'the evanescent hues of this etherial world' that create the experience of evanescence in this passage – nor is it the repetition of such words as 'unseen', 'visiting' ('visits'), 'inconstant', nor the compounding of ideas of inconstancy and absence in the 'shadow of some unseen Power', 'inconstant glance', and 'memory of music fled'. What is most arresting about the stanza is the way in which its entire figurative progression enacts the vanishing of an impalpable 'Power' named in the first three lines. The sequence of similes begins tenuously enough with the inconstant 'summer winds' and the 'moonbeams' visible only from behind 'some piny mountain', and then becomes increasingly attenuated until the very act of comparison exhausts itself and collapses. 'Like aught' ends the movement with a precisely judged and felt refusal of specificity, with an emptiness which is simultaneously a plenitude to the desiring imagination.[2] Shelley 'arrests' the experience of 'evanescent visitations' by giving that experience a distinct and reproducible verbal shape: the delicate aptness of the rhyme ('visiting' / 'inconstant wing'; 'glance' / 'countenance') and management of syntax and line length enforce a strong sense of the stanza's formal integrity. But to read the stanza and submit ourselves to the attenuating flux of its figurative movements is to become conscious that a 'vanishing apparition' has been arrested by the poem's language only so that it may be released into motion again through the act of reading.

    Such at least is one way of understanding Shelley's project of writing verse which arrests and yet re-enacts the mind's evanescent access to power or beauty. The language of poetry proceeds from and returns us to the elusive flow of experience, even as it assumes a form that stands over against that flow. What the *Defence* shows, however, is that Shelley is as likely to be anxious as confident about the tension between what we might crudely term experiential and formal impulses in the poetic process. He might well have admired Robert Frost's cunning submissiveness to the evanescence of composition in 'The Figure a Poem Makes', but he never achieves Frost's kind of confidence, what Richard Poirier calls his 'truly marvelous poise':[3]

> originality need be no more than the freshness of a poem run in the way I have described: from delight to wisdom. The figure is the same as for love. Like a piece of ice on a hot stove the poem must ride on its own melting.

The analogy between poetry and love and the reflexive image are both very Shelleyan. Frost wittily transforms Shelley's fading coal into melting ice, domesticates the heat of inspiration in the figure of a hot stove, and locates the action of fading or melting in the poem itself. His simile, even more than Shelley's, suggests certain dissolution, a situation even less susceptible of being 'arrested'. But this makes his insistence that 'the poem must *ride* on its own melting' – must somehow buoy itself up through its own subsiding – all the more confident. Only a poet of great self-assurance could risk making a poem this vulnerable through his way of imagining it.

That Shelley's feelings for this situation were less assured is evident in an 1817 fragment:

My thoughts arise and fade in solitude,
    The verse that would invest them melts away
    Like moonlight in the heaven of spreading day:
How beautiful they were, how firm they stood,
Flecking the starry sky like woven pearl!

(PW, 549)

These lines present a puzzling compositional *occupatio* and are surprisingly and instructively hard to think about. The first three lines may be read as a present-tense recollection of a prior failure to arrest 'vanishing apparitions' – but the present tense also invites us to read them self-referentially, as an enactment of that very failure: the verse that 'would invest' the speaker's fading thoughts rides on its own melting just long enough to leave these traces of itself before it 'melts away'. The shift to past tense in line 4 confirms the illusion of looking back on an experience no longer present to us, even though the verses articulating that melting away stand there before us on the page. From this past perspective the speaker does succeed in arresting the 'thoughts' of line 1 retrospectively – 'How beautiful they were, how firm they stood'. The simile with which the fragment ends – 'like woven pearl' – casts them into an idealized, highly wrought artifact. These lines begin by trying to enact or trace the process of vanishing and conclude by trying to fix the memory of an original articulate intuition.

The actions of arising and fading (or fading and arising) appear often in Shelley's poems, and almost always, as Daniel Hughes has argued in 'Kindling and dwindling: the poetic process in Shelley',[4] they bear a reflexive relation to the poem in which they appear. Hughes emphasizes the moment of arising, initiation, ignition in the 'poetic process' and accordingly focuses on the word *kindle* and its variants as they function in Shelley's writing:

> Whether the word points to sexual awakening, to intellection, to revolution, or to the mystical presence of hypostatized Beauty, it has one constant function: the stirring and sustaining of the poetic process in the poem –evanescent, unstable, death-set as soon as it is born.[5]

My concern in this chapter is partly to complement Hughes's fine study by looking at a different but closely related set of images – those of melting, dissolving and erasing. I want to look at these figurative patterns as distinctive instances of imagery 'drawn from the operations of the human mind, or from those external actions by which they are expressed'. Like Hughes, I want to consider the ways in which such imagery may be self-referring and figure forth its own mode of being. My own emphasis will fall on Shelley's ways of imaging the process of dwindling, on his effort to arrest moments of experience as they move towards that absence or emptiness which is the condition of desire and regret.

I

Shelley's language of melting and dissolving often does more than register what Wordsworth calls 'Fallings from us, vanishings'.[6] It may also represent the merging of one substance with another, or transformations from one mode of existence to another. These senses are sometimes superimposed on one another, particularly when Shelley wants to register liminal or transitional states of being and consciousness. The speaker in *Queen Mab* describes the Fairy Queen as she is about to descend from her chariot:

> The Fairy's frame was slight, yon fibrous cloud
> That catches but the palest tinge of even,
> And which the straining eye can hardly seize
> When melting into eastern twilight's shadow,
> Were scarce so thin, so slight; but the fair star
> That gems the glittering coronet of morn,
> Sheds not a light so mild, so powerful,
> As that which, bursting from the Fairy's form,
> Spread a purpureal halo round the scene . . .
>
> (i.94-102)

Is it the 'cloud', the 'palest tinge of even', the 'straining eye', or all three which are here experienced as 'melting into eastern twilight's shadow'? The uncertain reference is an appropriate part of this effort to catch the uncatchable. The effect of melting momentarily gives way to the new image of the gem-like star, but it reappears when the 'palest tinge of even' is recapitulated in the 'purpureal halo' created by the light which that star 'Sheds'. The total effect the passage creates is of an evanescence prolonged or sustained through transformation, through the melting or diffusion of form into vapor, of vapor into color, of color into light.

Shelley reworked this imagery in a much discussed sequence of stanzas in 'To a Skylark', where the intransitive verb 'melts' initiates a complex movement of vanishing and transmutation:

> The pale purple even
>   Melts around thy flight,
> Like a star of Heaven
>   In the broad day-light
> Thou art unseen, – but yet I hear thy shrill delight,
>
> Keen as are the arrows
>   Of that silver sphere,
> Whose intense lamp narrows
>   In the white dawn clear
> Until we hardly see –we feel that it is there.
>
> All the earth and air
>   With thy voice is loud,

> As when Night is bare
>   From one lonely cloud
> The moon rains out her beams – and Heaven is overflowed.
>
> What thou art we know not;
>   What is most like thee?
> From rainbow clouds there flow not
>   Drops so bright to see
> As from thy presence showers a rain of melody.
>
> (16–35)

Much of the critical controversy surrounding this passage has had to do
with a kind of melting which is more than just evanescence or
disappearance.[7] Shelley's grammar is itself ambiguously molten, as
Empson has pointed out.[8] 'Melts' initially refers to the 'pale purple
even', not to the soaring bird, and 'Melts around thy flight' may either
suggest that the brilliant energy of the skylark's flight ('Like a cloud of
fire', 8) melts the surrounding atmosphere, or that sky and skylark
simultaneously melt away together and into each other. When the 'star
of Heaven' simile is introduced in line 18, the reader may think
momentarily that the first of these ideas is being confirmed, that the
skylark is being set off against the waning light and color of evening like
a star that grows brighter and brighter as the sky darkens. As the stanza
continues, however, we discover that the grammatical subject has
shifted from 'even' to 'Thou' after the comma in line 17, and that the star
to which the skylark is compared is itself melting 'In the broad day-
light'. The action of fading into growing darkness merges imper-
ceptibly with the apparently contrasting action of fading 'into the light
of common day'. Yet even as the skylark is vanishing from sight it
remains present through sound – sound imaged as if it were the product
of melting, as an interfusion of light and liquid:

> The moon rains out her beams – and Heaven is overflowed.
>
> From rainbow clouds there flow not
>   Drops so bright to see
> As from thy presence showers a rain of melody.

This capacity of the skylark to melt synaesthetically into its own song,
and into the poet's song, is one of the poem's sustaining figures. It has
been anticipated in the liquid imagery of the opening stanzas ('Pourest
thy full heart', 'Thou dost float and run'), and it is repeated in the poet's

concluding request: 'Such harmonious madness / From my lips would flow . . .' The way in which the poem's language arrests the melting of the skylark's presence through its own acts of grammatical and figurative melting is part of the larger rhetorical scheme through which the speaker defines both his access to and separation from the beautiful energy he longs for.

Shelley's references to 'dissolving' show even more emphatically his affinity for moments which may be said to turn upon the question of whether something disappears when it transforms itself or is transformed into something else. Here is an image from the 'Stanzas written in Dejection, December 1818, – Near Naples':

> I see the waves upon the shore
> Like light dissolved in star-showers, thrown . . .
>
> (12–13)

These lines offer the synaesthetic image of light dissolved in water, but also of light dissolved into a shower of light, as in a shower of meteors (the OED cites Shelley's passage as the earliest example of the phrase 'star-showers'). In either case the effect is of a transient, momentary display of light on the verge of extinction – an effect accentuated by the emphatic positioning of the rhyme-word 'thrown' after the pause-inducing comma. These lines mark a critical transition in the poem, from the dazzling vitality of the opening scene to the speaker's depressive isolation ('thrown', which gives the literal meaning of *dejected*, forms a couplet with 'I sit upon the sands alone'). The image of 'light dissolved in star-showers' grows out of the opening impression of the sun shining brilliantly in 'The purple noon's transparent might', and yet spins away from that impression as it anticipates the speaker's desire to

> weep away the life of care
> Which I have borne and yet must bear
> Till Death like Sleep might steal on me,
> And I might feel in the warm air
> My cheek grow cold, and hear the Sea
> Breathe o'er my dying brain its last monotony.
>
> (31–6)

The double action of dissolving – of verging on extinction, of merging with and being suspended in another medium – permeates these lines, as it does the speaker's concluding reference to

> this day which, when the Sun
> Shall on its stainless glory set,
> Will linger though enjoyed, like joy in Memory yet.

(43–5)

In 'Stanzas written in Dejection' light is dissolved in water or into itself; elsewhere in Shelley light is frequently a solvent for some other substance, as in *The Witch of Atlas*:

> Men scarcely know how beautiful fire is –
> Each flame of it is as a precious stone
> Dissolved in ever moving light, and this
> Belongs to each and all who gaze upon.

(259–62)

Walter Pater would idealize 'the passage and dissolution of impressions, images, sensations . . . – that continual vanishing away, that strange, perpetual weaving and unweaving of ourselves', in the image of burning with a 'hard, gemlike flame'.[9] But Shelley's image for 'that continual vanishing away' is an 'ever moving' flame, the preciousness of which depends upon its having dissolved what is hard and gemlike into an intensity as fluctuant as perception itself. A stable, unchanging, inert beauty becomes more beautiful, more desirable, as it is destabilized and made to participate in the drama of temporal experience.

The language of dissolving figures recurrently in Shelley's accounts of imaginative, emotional or sexual climax, sometimes with the additional complication that it seems to function in both its transitive and intransitive senses simultaneously. In *Alastor* the wandering poet reaches out to embrace the 'veiled maid' in his dream:

> . . . she drew back a while,
> Then, yielding to the irresistible joy,
> With frantic gesture and short breathless cry
> Folded his frame in her dissolving arms.

(184–7)

The maiden's arms are 'dissolving' in a double sense that condenses the reflexive relationship of dream-image to dreamer: they momentarily dissolve the figure of the dreamer even as they themselves are 'dissolving'. Both are 'swallowed up' together as

sleep,
Like a dark flood suspended in its course,
Rolled back its impulse on his vacant brain.

(189–91)

In Canto I of *The Revolt of Islam* the woman who guides the narrator into
the poem's visionary environment tells how 'A wingèd youth' once
appeared to her in dream:

'a wild dissolving bliss
Over my frame he breathed, approaching near,
And bent his eyes of kindling tenderness
Near mine, and on my lips impressed a lingering kiss. –'

(501–4)

The 'bliss' of this dream was at once 'kindling' and 'dissolving': it
lingered just long enough to dissolve her into receptive desire and to
arouse her deepest impulses; then it underwent its own dissolution:

' "A Spirit loves thee, mortal maiden,
How wilt thou prove thy worth?" Then joy and sleep
Together fled . . .'

(505–7)

Later in this opening canto the narrator follows the woman into a 'vast
hall' which images the entire cosmos:

soon as the Woman came
Into that hall, she shrieked the Spirit's name
And fell; and vanished slowly from the sight.
Darkness arose from her dissolving frame,
Which gathering, filled that dome of woven light,
Blotting its spherèd stars with supernatural night.

(616–21)

Her 'dissolving frame' dissolves everything around it in the darkness of
its own vanishing, creating a mysteriously substantial void or vacancy
from which the figures of Laon and Cythna gradually emerge to
recount their own histories. Yet even as darkness gives way to light and
hero and heroine come into focus, the figurative action of dissolving
persists: when Cythna first appears in the canto's final stanza, we see her
in 'Glances of soul-dissolving glory' (664).
When Shelley says of those 'evanescent visitations' in *The Defence*

that 'even in the desire and the regret they leave, there cannot but be pleasure, participating as it does in the nature of its object,' he suggests a way of understanding why the language of dissolving in his poetry sometimes oscillates from what the mind perceives to the mind itself and back again. The memory of having dissolved, or of having been dissolved, becomes a sign of the mind's participative, even constitutive, relation to the 'vanishing apparitions' it holds most dear. Or the 'dissolving' of thought may anticipate or prefigure the waning of an apparition, even as it signals that apparition's presence. Consider the following lines from Shelley's translation of the scene of Matilda gathering flowers from Canto XXVIII of Dante's *Purgatorio*:

> And then appeared to me, even like a thing
> Which suddenly for blank astonishment
> Dissolves all other thought,
>
> A solitary woman . . . [10]

(37–40)

There is nothing in the Italian that corresponds to Shelley's adjective 'blank'; and Dante's verb 'disvia', as the Cary translation tries to convey, means not 'dissolves' but 'leads astray' or 'drives away':

> e là m'apparve, sì com'elli appare
>   subitamente cosa che disvia
>   per maraviglia tutto altro pensare,
> una donna soletta . . .
>
>   [and there,
> As object, rising suddenly to view,
> That from our bosom every thought beside
> With the rare marvel chases, I beheld
> A lady all alone . . .]

Dante's Matilda turns out to be not a 'vanishing apparition' but the friend and attendant of Beatrice who guides him into her divine presence and through the final phase of his purgatorial experience. But her initial appearance is mysterious, uncertain, and this is precisely the moment Shelley seizes upon and emphasizes in his translation. As the 'solitary woman' 'dissolves' the poet's thoughts into 'blank astonishment', she provokes him to think of her as a figure on the point of vanishing:

> like Proserpine
> Thou seemest to my fancy, singing here
> And gathering flowers, at that time when
> She lost the spring and Ceres her . . . more dear.

(48–51)

It is significant that Shelley's translation should leave off at just this point. One can see why Dante's episode would come to provide a model for the appearance and disappearance of Rousseau's 'shape all light' in *The Triumph of Life*. Given Shelley's translation, the relation of Dante's *Purgatorio* passage to Rousseau's narration may not be so antithetical or 'parodic' after all.[11]

II

Shelley's concern with the volatility of perception and intuition – and either directly or implicitly with the poetic process – finds expression not just in individual images of melting and dissolving, but also in sequences of images that move through the entire cycle of physical transformation: freezing, melting or dissolving, evaporation, condensation. Here is the transition from the first to the second stanza of one of Shelley's relatively early lyrics about music, 'To Constantia' (1817–18):

> My heart is quivering like a flame;
> As morning dew, that in the sunbeam dies,
> I am dissolved in these consuming extacies.
>
> I have no life, Constantia, but in thee;
> Whilst, like the world-surrounding air, thy song
> Flows on, and fills all things with melody:
> Now is thy voice a tempest, swift and strong,
> On which, as one in trance upborne,
> Secure o'er woods and waves I sweep
> Rejoicing, like a cloud of morn.

(9–18)

At the end of the first stanza the speaker figuratively dies and is 'dissolved', evaporated like 'morning dew' by the heat of his own excitement ('quivering like a flame'), only to gain new figurative life in the second stanza when he condenses again (at a higher level) into a 'cloud of morn', swept along on the stream of song. The progression of images beautifully spans the stanza break; one might even see the space between stanzas as enhancing our sense of the momentary dissolving or vanishing. It may be there, between stanzas, that the 'evanescent visitation' is 'arrested'.

Image sequences such as this doubtless owe a good deal to Shelley's irrepressible fascination with chemistry, meteorology and other scientific and pseudo-scientific lore. But it is their stylistic function and formal integrity, not their referential basis, that now need attention. A meteorological understanding of 'The Cloud', Shelley's sportive exercise in disappearance and transmutation, only goes part of the way towards answering the questions Donald Davie raised about the poem's diction and 'conduct and development of . . . metaphor'.[12] The first two stanzas both end in dissolving. The cloud delights in dissolving, transforming and reconstituting itself; in the first stanza it congeals into hail and then, in its liquid state, melts that hail:

> I wield the flail of the lashing hail,
>> And whiten the green plains under,
> And then again I dissolve it in rain,
>> And laugh as I pass in thunder.
>
> (9–12)

Implicitly the cloud cannot dissolve the hail without dissolving itself – it is always dissolving transitively and intransitively at the same time. In the second stanza, the focus of Davie's scrutiny, the grammatical subject of 'dissolving' is not the cloud but the lightning that acts as its 'pilot':

> Over Earth and Ocean, with gentle motion,
>> This pilot is guiding me,
> Lured by the love of the genii that move
>> In the depths of the purple sea;
> Over the rills, and the crags, and the hills,
>> Over the lakes and the plains,
> Wherever he dream, under mountain or stream,
>> The Spirit he loves remains;
> And I all the while bask in Heaven's blue smile,
>> Whilst he is dissolving in rains.
>
> (21–30)

Davie thought it 'lunacy' for Shelley to say that the lightning is 'dissolving in rains'.[13] But what better way to suggest metaphorically the dispersal of electricity into the surrounding atmosphere of a thunderstorm, and at the same time to extend the conceit, drawn from natural philosophy, of the lightning's desire to join the antithetically charged 'Spirit he loves' in its own preferred medium? If the cloud itself can 'bask' (literally 'bathe') 'in Heaven's blue smile', then surely lightning can be said to dissolve and mingle with 'the genii that move / In the depths of the purple sea'.

The celebration of an identity founded upon continual evanescence and metamorphosis links 'The Cloud' to *The Witch of Atlas*, which was written the same year (1820).[14] The Witch herself is conceived through a process delicately suspended between metaphor and meterology. Her mother, 'one of the Atlantides' (57), was kissed by the beams of the sun, and at the end of the second stanza

> She, in that dream of joy, dissolved away.
>
> (64)

But an action which appears to culminate in erotic annihilation continues in the next stanza as eroticized evaporation and condensation:

> 'Tis said, she first was changed into a vapour,
>   And then into a cloud, such clouds as flit,
> Like splendour-winged moths about a taper,
>   Round the red West when the sun dies in it.
>
> (65–8)

The ambiguously entwined figurative pattern of death and transfiguration extends its range of reference: having been 'dissolved away' in a 'dream of joy' induced by the sun's amorous beams, the Witch's mother is reconstituted as a cloud that attends upon the dissolving or quenching of those very beams as the sun 'dies' in the fire of its own waning light. The temporal progression is completed as the cycle of transformation continues through the rest of the stanza:

> And then into a meteor, such as caper
>   On hill-tops when the moon is in a fit:
> Then, into one of those mysterious stars
>   Which hide themselves between the Earth and Mars.
>
> (69–72)

'Meteor' is the key transitional image here: as a wandering or erratic 'atmospheric phenomenon' it is a plausible thing for a cloud to be changed into, particularly a cloud that has just been compared to a

'splendour-winged moth[ ]'; as a 'luminous celestial body' it is on its
way towards that final metamorphosis 'into one of those mysterious
stars'. That such stars 'hide themselves' returns us to the initial phase of
the metamorphic sequence: the Atlantid has after all 'dissolved away',
figuratively, in a mysterious dreamlike stellification.

The verbal wit of these image sequences based upon the unending
cycle of evaporation and condensation may be seen at its most
extravagant in *The Sensitive Plant*. Among the natural phenomena
perceived through the narrator's exuberantly synaesthetic imagination
in 'Part First' are

> The unseen clouds of the dew which lie
> Like fire in the flowers till the Sun rides high,
> Then wander like spirits among the spheres,
> Each cloud faint with the fragrance it bears . . .
>
> (86–9)

We begin this stanza with the dew suspended between its condensed
and evaporated states: it is already volatizing into 'unseen clouds', yet its
drops still sparkle 'Like fire', as if the evaporating heat were self-
generated. Once 'the Sun rides high', these 'unseen clouds' 'wander
like spirits' – like supernatural beings, but also perhaps like volatile
aromatic spirits. Shelley would appear to be playing upon this latter
possibility in the double meaning of the stanza's last line: 'faint with'
may mean both 'faintly permeated by' and 'on the point of fainting or
swooning because of ' the fragrance of the flower from which it came.
The dew dissolves away or evaporates, but the fragrance which has been
dissolved in it lingers –momentarily.

This image sequence, like many others in the poem, undergoes a
process of inversion or perversion in 'Part Third' when the garden loses
the kind of love and imagination that had previously sustained its
constantly changing perfection. Instead of the fragrant 'unseen clouds'
of dew floating delicately upwards to join their heavenly counterparts,

> . . . hour by hour when the air was still
> The vapours arose which have strength to kill:
> At morn they were seen, at noon they were felt,
> At night they were darkness no star could melt.
>
> And unctuous meteors from spray to spray
> Crept and flitted in broad noonday

Unseen; every branch on which they alit
By a venomous blight was burned and bit.

The Sensitive-plant like one forbid
Wept, and the tears, within each lid
Of its folded leaves which together grew,
Were changed to a blight of frozen glue.

(74–85)

The unmeltability of these corrupt 'vapours', their stagnant opacity,
becomes a sign of their killing strength. In contrast to the 'unseen clouds
of the dew' which sparkle like fire in the morning sun and then float
into the sky, the 'unctuous meteors' here are corrosive marsh-fires (*ignis
fatuus*) that sinisterly 'Crept and flitted in broad noonday /Unseen'. In
the third stanza the previously vital, expansive processes of dissolving
and evaporating are reversed and give way to thickening, condensation
and frozen constriction. The 'Conclusion' skeptically invites us to
understand this reversal and perversion of the garden's original
spiritualized volatility as a function of our own faulty organs of
perception, as an evanescing of our ability to sustain an idealizing
perspective.

In *Prometheus Unbound* the mysterious precipitations of prophetic or
visionary meaning often take shape, as Wasserman has shown in great
detail, through figurative sequences of dissolving, evaporating and
condensing.[15] Such sequences are particularly prominent in the poem's
most intricate transition, the movement from the end of Act I into the
early scenes of Act II. When the Furies in Act I finally 'vanish' (a
tellingly recurrent word in Shelley's stage directions), the Earth
bids ascend:

> those subtle and fair spirits
Whose homes are the dim caves of human thought
And who inhabit, as birds wing the wind,
Its world-surrounding ether . . .

(1.658–61)

As these Spirits approach, they come into being verbally for the reader
through similes of transient condensation and evaporation:

PANTHEA
Look, Sister, where a troop of spirits gather
Like flocks of clouds in spring's delightful weather,

Thronging in the blue air!
> IONE

> And see! more come
Like fountain-vapours when the winds are dumb,
That climb up the ravine in scattered lines.

(1.664–8)

In one of the most intriguing figurative developments in this part of the
poem, Shelley resumes and elaborates this imagery of fluid transformation
as the Spirits begin to speak, and as Panthea and Ione struggle to voice
their experience of the Spirits' voices:

> IONE

And hark! their sweet, sad voices! 'tis despair
Mingled with love, and then dissolved in sound. –
> PANTHEA

Canst thou speak, sister? all my words are drowned.
> IONE

Their beauty gives me voice. See how they float
On their sustaining wings of skiey grain . . .

(1.756–60)

The precarious status of voice in *Prometheus Unbound* is here being
acknowledged both explicitly and implicitly, figuratively, in Shelley's
language. Pure spirit, thought, or emotion enters the realm of sensory
expression by being 'dissolved' in it – by surrendering its pure integrity
even as it gains articulation. Panthea's own voice is momentarily
overwhelmed, though not silenced, by this dissolving of emotion in
sound, and in saying so she picks up the annihilative overtones of
'dissolved' (the rhyming of Panthea's 'all my words are drowned' with
Ione's 'dissolved in sound' catches and arrests the paradox of Panthea's
responsive and expressive vocal inadequacy). Ione, for her part, is able
to remain confident of her capacity to voice her response to the Spirits
by redirecting attention away from their voices, by transferring the
non-destructive implications of 'dissolved' ('held in solution or
suspension') into visual terms: 'See how they float / On their sustaining
wings of skiey grain.' The Spirits' dramatic existence is entirely a
function of voice – their own and those of the two Oceanides who
register their presence – defined figuratively as a continuous cycle of
fluid transformation: dissolvings, vaporizings, condensings.

The same figurative pattern redevelops in the first scene of Act II, as
thoughts of renovation and reunion glow and fade in the minds of the

characters, and as Shelley continues to evoke states of mind hovering at the outer limits of, yet crucially dependent upon, verbalizable consciousness. First there are Asia's opening references to the 'golden clouds' of joy rising up in the mind 'As from the earth' (II.i.10–12), to 'the burning threads / Of woven cloud' that 'unravel in pale air' (II.i.22–3), and to Panthea's 'smiles that fade in tears / Like stars half quenched in mists of silver dew' (II.i.28–9). Then there is that remarkable exchange, one of the most difficult moments in the poem, in which Panthea struggles to tell Asia her 'remembered dream' (II.i.36). She recalls how, 'Before the sacred Titan's fall' (II.i.40), she used to sleep peacefully with Ione in her ocean bowers:

> But not as now since I am made the wind
> Which fails beneath the music that I bear
> Of thy most wordless converse; since dissolved
> Into the sense with which love talks, my rest
> Was troubled and yet sweet . . .

(II.i.50–4)

The commentaries on this passage all testify to its obscurity;[16] it must be said that to some degree Shelley's own grammar and diction fail here beneath the wordless music he imagines Panthea bearing in her role as intermediary between Prometheus and Asia. But whether we take the subject of 'dissolved' to be Panthea herself (from the parallel with 'since I am made the wind') or 'my rest' (on syntactic grounds), it is clear that Shelley associates Panthea's having been 'dissolved / Into the sense with which love talks' with her initial inability to communicate her prophetic dreams vocally. Asia responds to Panthea's reference to 'wordless converse' in a way that is reminiscent of Ione's response in the previous scene, by attempting to circumvent a dependence on voice:

> Lift up thine eyes
> And let me read thy dream. –

(II.i.55–6)

But Panthea continues to speak, and in doing so she completes Asia's unfinished pentameter line with a reference to her own speech, characterizing its pre-visionary condition by reversing the previous image of dissolving into images of condensing and freezing:

> As I have said,
> With our sea-sister at his feet I slept.

The mountain mists, condensing at our voice
Under the moon, had spread their snowy flakes . . .

(II.i.56–9)

These lines, suggesting through their precise meteorological figure a subconscious and mysteriously transforming vocalizing power in the sleeping Oceanides, prepare for Panthea's subsequent account of the one dream she can remember. A radiant Prometheus appeared to her, and love

from his soft and flowing limbs
And passion-parted lips, and keen faint eyes
Steam'd forth like vaporous fire; an atmosphere
Which wrapt me in its all-dissolving power
As the warm ether of the morning sun
Wraps ere it drinks some cloud of wandering dew.
I saw not – heard not – moved not – only felt
His presence flow and mingle through my blood
Till it became his life and his grew mine
And I was thus absorbed – until it past
And like the vapours when the sun sinks down,
Gathering again in drops upon the pines
And tremulous as they, in the deep night
My being was condensed, and as the rays
Of thought were slowly gathered, I could hear
His voice . . .

(II.i.73–88)

This is the kind of writing that makes some readers of *Prometheus Unbound* give up in disgust or despair. But willing attentiveness to the dominant sequence of images will reveal how cogently Shelley articulates this moment of visionary ecstasy through an extraordinary diurnal sequence. Panthea remembers being dissolved and evaporated in Prometheus's radiant love, then 'condensed' again and 'gathered' as the vision of that radiance fades. The sexual dimension of the experience is unmistakable, as it was in *The Witch of Atlas* passage we looked at earlier, and here it is even more powerfully and complexly conceived: dissolving and evaporating suggest mutual interpenetration as well as the momentary annihilation and absorption of individuated consciousness. As 'vaporous fire' and 'warm ether', Prometheus too is dissolved and evaporated in his own incandescence and enters Panthea's element as she does his – vapor or air being the medium in which

Panthea's native waters and Prometheus's fire are able to merge.

In this passage we may again notice that the action of Shelley's meteorological imagery appears to be intricately co-ordinated with the motif of verbal expression and communication. Dissolving and evaporating seem at first to signal a suspension of voice on behalf of what Panthea has called 'wordless converse':

> I saw not – heard not – moved not – only felt
> His presence flow and mingle through my blood . . .

Not until the vision of a radiant Prometheus had 'past' away like the setting sun, leaving Panthea 'condensed' again like 'drops upon the pines / And tremulous as they', could she 'hear /His voice'. Yet Asia's response at this point indicates that to her Panthea's own voice is still partly 'dissolved / Into the sense with which love talks':

> Thou speakest, but thy words
> Are as the air. I feel them not . . .
>
> (ii.i.108–9)

Consistent with her earlier appeal beyond or around voice to an experience that she calls reading, Asia is able to get access to Panthea's dream only by looking in Panthea's eyes 'that I may read his written soul' (ii.i.110). But this act of reading not only generates Asia's own voicing of what she sees, it suddenly gives her access to Panthea's second, hitherto forgotten dream – a dream which speaks with its own voice ('Follow, follow'). It is as if Shelley were allegorizing in this sequence the basic terms of his own dramatic poem, calling attention to the way in which writing and reading generate the fiction of voice and yet depend upon that fiction for their own full realization.

At this point in the scene images of condensing and congealing begin to accumulate, and as they do they come to include both vocal and graphic modes of signification. Metrically the Dream's first utterance completes Asia's description of it:

> 'tis a thing of air
> For through its grey robe gleams the golden dew
> Whose stars the moon has quench'd not.
>   DREAM
>
> Follow, follow!
> (ii.i.129–31)

In Panthea's vision of the 'lightning-blasted almond tree', it is when 'A

wind swept forth wrinkling the Earth with frost' that the leaves are seen
to be 'stamped' with the same message (II.i.134–41). This vision in turn
provokes Asia to envision a scene in which

> . . . the white dew on the new-bladed grass,
> Just piercing the dark earth, hung silently –
> And there was more which I remember not;
> But, on the shadows of the morning clouds
> Athwart the purple mountain slope was written
> *Follow, O follow!* as they vanished by,
> And on each herb from which Heaven's dew had fallen
> The like was stamped as with a withering fire;
> A wind arose among the pines – it shook
> The clinging music from their boughs, and then
> Low, sweet, faint sounds, like the farewell of ghosts,
> Were heard – O *follow, follow, follow me!*
>
> (II.i.148–59)

It is as constantly changing atmospheric phenomena that these visionary
inscriptions and voices in nature arise, fade and transform themselves.[17]
The 'white dew', which at first 'hung silently' on 'the new-bladed grass'
and then left behind its urgent inscription when it fell, finally gets a
voice as it is transmuted synaesthetically into the 'clinging music'
shaken from the boughs of the pines. The imagery here is a
reconfiguration of that moment in Panthea's first dream when her
'being was condensed' like 'drops upon the pines' and she heard
Prometheus's voice again 'Like footsteps of far melody' (II.i.84–89). As
the Dream-voices themselves condense and evaporate, so do their
echoes:

> Echoes we – listen!
>   We cannot stay
> As dew-stars glisten
>   Then fade away –
>
> (II.i.166–9)

The atmospheric transformations in Acts I and II of *Prometheus
Unbound* should ultimately be seen in relation to that much larger
pattern of meteorological figuration which Wasserman terms 'the
breathing earth' – 'The picture . . . of a world repeatedly breathing out
dew, vapor, mist, clouds, earthquakes, and volcanic eruptions', a world
'dynamically exhaling and diffusing from a Power at its unimaginable

center'.[18] What these image-sequences reveal, however, is a more subtly interactive and multi-directional process than that presented in Wasserman's account. The earth inhales as well as exhales, and the atmosphere it breathes undergoes constant transformation, the volatility and transience of which convey as delicately as anything in Shelley's writing what Wasserman might call, borrowing Shelley's own words from the essay 'On Life', 'the different modifications of the one mind'. Even in Act IV, when mind has reunited and reconstituted itself and all existence with it, the same diurnal atmospheric cycle of dissolving, evaporating and condensing persists as both an instance of and a figure for the volatility and temporal flux of experience. The Earth describes its own joyful renovation:

> As the dissolving warmth of Dawn may fold
> A half-unfrozen dewglobe, green and gold
> And chrystalline, till it becomes a winged mist
> And wanders up the vault of the blue Day,
> Outlives the noon, and on the Sun's last ray
> Hangs o'er the Sea – a fleece of fire and amethyst –
>
> (IV.431–6)

III

Shelley's evanescent atmospheric transformations are intimately related, as the passage above from *Prometheus Unbound* shows, to his characteristic handling of effects of color and light on landscape and seascape. The favorite Shelleyan landscape moments are the kindling dawn, the suspended or descending 'purple noon', and the dwindling sunset. In each of these, but especially in the last, light and color dissolve in each other as together they dissolve away in a continuously shifting temporal action. Four lines from a very early poem in the Esdaile Notebook anticipate the direction of later, more detailed passages:

> I joyed to see the streaks of day
> Above the purple peaks decay,
> And watch the latest line of light
> Just mingling with the shades of night.
>
> ('The Retrospect', 19–22)

The double action of dissolving is succinctly indicated in the play of
'decay' against 'mingling'. Even in such early writing as this we can see
Shelley working to catch the drama of fading light, to keep the moment
of dissolution in motion as he arrests and suspends it. These impulses are
evident again in a more richly elaborated sunset in *Queen Mab*:

> If solitude hath ever led thy steps
>   To the wild ocean's echoing shore,
>   And thou hast lingered there,
>   Until the sun's broad orb
>   Seemed resting on the burnished wave,
>   Thou must have marked the lines
>   Of purple gold, that motionless
>   Hung o'er the sinking sphere:
>   Thou must have marked the billowy clouds
>   Edged with intolerable radiancy
>   Towering like rocks of jet
>   Crowned with a diamond wreath.
>   And yet there is a moment,
>   When the sun's highest point
> Peeps like a star o'er ocean's western edge,
> When those far clouds of feathery gold,
>   Shaded with deepest purple, gleam
>   Like islands on a dark blue sea . . .

$$(\text{II}.1-18)$$

Here the sun is 'sinking', yet it 'Seemed resting on the burnished wave';
'the lines / Of purple gold, that motionless / Hung' disguise the sun's
actual movement as its 'broad orb' descends until only its 'highest point
/ Peeps like a star o'er ocean's western edge'. Light in these early sunsets
is characteristically seen in 'lines' suffused with what Turner (in his first
Royal Academy lecture of 1818) called 'Aerial Colours'.[19] Its power,
never more mysteriously beautiful than when it is fading, is essentially
enhancing as it reflects off water and cloud, and as it defines by
throwing into dramatic relief those shapes that intercept it.

Shelley began experimenting with much more radical effects of
dissolving light in *The Revolt of Islam*. In Canto V Laon remembers the
dawning of 'that great day' when the liberated nations gathered to
celebrate their recent victory over the forces of tyranny:

> To see, far glancing in the misty morning,
>   The signs of that innumerable host . . .

> While the eternal hills, and the sea lost
> In wavering light, and, starring the blue sky
>   The city's myriad spires of gold, almost
> With human joy made mute society –

(2062–9)

It is the idea of 'the sea lost / In wavering light' – light which has the
power to dissolve color and shape partly because it is itself dissolved in
the morning mist – that so conspicuously prefigures the great writing
about light in Shelley's later poetry.[20] We might set this morning
passage beside the ominous sunset later in Canto XI, the scene in which
Laon sees Cythna for the last time:

> A cloud was hanging o'er the western mountains;
>   Before its blue and moveless depth were flying
> Grey mists poured forth from the unresting fountains
>   Of darkness in the North: – the day was dying: –
>   Sudden, the sun shone forth, its beams were lying
> Like boiling gold on Ocean, strange to see,
>   And on the shattered vapours, which defying
> The power of light in vain, tossed restlessly
> In the red Heaven, like wrecks in a tempestuous sea.
>
> It was a stream of living beams, whose bank
>   On either side by the cloud's cleft was made;
> And where its chasms that flood of glory drank,
>   Its waves gushed forth like fire, and as if swayed
>   By some mute tempest, rolled on *her*; the shade
> Of her bright image floated on the river
>   Of liquid light, which then did end and fade –

(4234–49)

Shelley pursues his larger purpose in this passage, the symbolic
prophesying of Cythna's apocalyptic immolation in the next canto,
through a sequence of precisely imagined effects of light. Once again it
is when the light of day is dying that it exhibits its most awesome power.
The violent and corrosive power of light over vaporous darkness in this
scene is as Turnerian in its way as is the solvent fusion of light and mist
in the earlier morning description. So is the chasm of light elaborated in
the second of the two stanzas.[21] Here the sea is not so much lost in as
usurped by light, for Shelley writes about the light as if it were a sea – 'a
stream of living beams', a 'flood of glory' whose 'waves gushed forth

like fire', a 'river / Of liquid light'. Cythna herself appears as an extension of this light as it 'did end and fade –':

> Her radiant shape upon its verge did shiver;
> Aloft, her flowing hair like strings of flame did quiver.
>
> (4250–1)

These contrasting moments from Shelley's vast experiment in visionary political epic suggest the growing intensity and complexity of his interest in rendering in words the active power of kindling and dwindling light as the medium of perception, as a force which both constitutes and annihilates the objects of perception.

It was Shelley's stay at Este in the late summer and autumn of 1818 that occasioned his most extended and resourceful attempts to arrest in language the evanescent effects of light on land- and seascape, and to shape them to – and allow them to shape – a poem's entire moral and psychological symbolism. 'Lines Written Among the Euganean Hills' follows the progress of a single day during which the speaker retreats to one of those metaphorical islands in the sea-like plain of Lombardy and looks back eastward on the 'Sun-girt City', Byron's Venice, and on that 'peopled solitude', 'Many-domed Padua'. The day begins with the most finely wrought sunrise in Shelley's poetry, brilliantly built up through the light, swift strokes of frequently enjambed and predominantly trochaic tetrameter couplets:

> 'Mid the mountains Euganean
> I stood listening to the paean
> With which the legioned rooks did hail
> The sun's uprise majestical;
> Gathering round with wings all hoar,
> Through the dewy mist they soar
> Like grey shades, till th'eastern heaven
> Bursts, and then, as clouds of even
> Flecked with fire and azure lie
> In the unfathomable sky,
> So their plumes of purple grain,
> Starred with drops of golden rain,
> Gleam above the sunlight woods,
> As in silent multitudes
> On the morning's fitful gale
> Through the broken mist they sail,

And the vapours cloven and gleaming
Follow down the dark steep streaming,
Till all is bright, and clear, and still,
Round the solitary hill.

(70–89)

The way in which the 'legioned rooks' register, as they are transformed
by, the movement of early morning light may be a deliberate variation
on that moment at the end of the day in Coleridge's 'This Lime-Tree
Bower My Prison',

               when the last rook
Beats its straight path along the dusky air
Homewards, I blest it! deeming its black wing
(Now a dim speck, now vanishing in light)
Had cross'd the mighty Orb's dilated glory
While thou stood'st gazing.

(68–73)

Shelley's rooks start as 'grey shades', their iridescent blackness as yet
untouched by the rays of the sun and lost in the colorless color of the
'dewy mist' through which they soar. As the sun's first direct rays begin
to emerge with the mid-line turn on 'till' and then burst forth after the
dramatically enjambed line-ending, these spectral 'shades' undergo a
transmutation, the suggestiveness of which is both condensed and far-
reaching. No sooner do they catch the early morning light than Shelley
sees them as harbingers of sunset's rich fading brilliance ('as clouds of
even / Flecked with fire and azure'), and even of the stars' transcendent
gleam ('So their plumes of purple grain, / Starred with drops of golden
rain'). The temporal progression of Shelley's figures anticipates that
temporal regression in 'To a Skylark' from the 'pale purple even' back
through 'the broad day-light' and 'the white dawn clear' to 'Night'
when 'The moon rains out her beams' (16–30). If the rooks in
'Euganean Hills' are 'birds of ill-omen' symbolizing 'the black
meaninglessness of life',[22] it is odd that their blackness is shown to
contain a wondrous complexity of vivid color. In them as in the poem as
a whole, brightness and color emerge from the depths of darkness by
virtue of the energy of light. By the end of this single deftly protracted
and sustained sentence, both the birds and the 'broken mists' through
which they 'sail' are 'gleaming'. Then they vanish, and Shelley rounds
off the passage by turning again on 'Till' – this time as an initial rhyme

to reinforce the terminal convergence of 'still' and 'hill'.

Now the speaker sees Venice in the newly risen sun:

> Lo! the sun upsprings behind,
> Broad, red, radiant, half-reclined
> On the level quivering line
> Of the waters chrystalline;
> And before that chasm of light,
> As within a furnace bright,
> Column, tower, and dome, and spire,
> Shine like obelisks of fire,
> Pointing with inconstant motion
> From the altar of dark ocean
> To the sapphire-tinted skies . . .
>
> (100–10)

One of the remarkable things about this poem is the way in which a precise attentiveness to visual experience provides the resources for, and is never betrayed by, abstractly formal or political concerns.[23] The effect of this Turnerian 'chasm of light' is to melt Venice's solid architectural shapes – 'Column, tower, and dome, and spire' – into its own fiery element, to put them into flame-like 'inconstant motion'.[24] What seems like a dissolution of visual structure is, at another level, part of the progress towards a larger formal design: the burning sun and city rise from the 'dark ocean' to the 'sapphire-tinted skies', from one realm of 'unfathomable' blue to another. Visually, and mythologically in the reference to Apollonian sacrifice at the end of the verse-paragraph, Venice may either become part of the sun's vital relation to ocean and sky or be consumed by them. So in the political meditation which follows, the 'Sun-girt City', once 'Ocean's child and then his queen', may soon 'be his prey' (115–18); it may either regain its freedom and 'adorn this sunny land' (157) or perish like 'Clouds which stain truth's rising day / By her sun consumed away –' (161–2).

The central moment in the poem's diurnal structure is of course noon, and it is significant that when it comes it 'descends', reversing the morning's predominantly rising movement:

> Noon descends around me now:
> 'Tis the noon of autumn's glow,
> When a soft and purple mist
> Like a vaporous amethyst,
> Or an air-dissolved star

Mingling light and fragrance, far
From the curved horizon's bound
To the point of heaven's profound,
Fills the overflowing sky . . .

(285–93)

Shelley's noon is an atmospheric event: light and air modify each other and merge into a single effect. The sun's light, which had earlier dissolved and dispersed the morning mists, is now itself dissolved in a 'soft and purple mist' of its own making. The image of 'a vaporous amethyst' suggests the idea of light as a liquified and therefore vaporizable gem which we have already noted in *The Witch of Atlas* ('Each flame . . . is as a precious stone / Dissolved in ever moving light'); 'air-dissolved star' extends these suggestions through a wonderful transformation of that earlier impression of the rooks 'Starred with drops of golden rain' (81). In both similes the luminous and unifying atmosphere is created figuratively through processes of dissolution and disintegration. The speaker characterizes with elegant specificity each discrete entity in his panoramic noontide landscape, and then declares that they all, together with

> my spirit which so long
> Darkened this swift stream of song, –
> Interpenetrated lie
> By the glory of the sky:
> Be it love, light, harmony,
> Odour, or the soul of all
> Which from heaven like dew doth fall,
> Or the mind which feeds this verse
> Peopling the lone universe.

(311–19)

By the end of Shelley's verse-paragraph the 'soft and purple mist' in which noon descends condenses and falls 'like dew',[25] anticipating the poignantly swift transition with which the next verse-paragraph begins:

> Noon descends, and after noon
> Autumn's evening meets me soon . . .

(320–1)

As an image of spiritual completion or fulfillment, Shelley's noon is no more stable or static than any other fading coal; the descending action of its light and atmosphere suggests that its glorious intensity is already passing even as it is realized, already moving towards the dwindling 'crimson light' of 'the sunset's radiant springs' (325–6).

Sunset itself is little more than a point of retrospective reference in the eastward looking 'Euganean Hills'. But in *Julian and Maddalo*, Shelley's other major poem based on his 1818 visit to the Veneto, sunset is the pivotal moment. It inspires an extended and passionate response from the narrator, Julian, as he and Maddalo look west across the lagoon separating the Lido from Venice:

> – Meanwhile the sun paused ere it should alight,
> Over the horizon of the mountains; – Oh,
> How beautiful is sunset, when the glow
> Of Heaven descends upon a land like thee,
> Thou Paradise of exiles, Italy!
> Thy mountains, seas and vineyards and the towers
> Of cities they encircle! – it was ours
> To stand on thee, beholding it; and then
> Just where we had dismounted, the Count's men
> Were waiting for us with the gondola. –
> As those who pause on some delightful way
> Though bent on pleasant pilgrimage, we stood
> Looking upon the evening and the flood
> Which lay between the city and the shore
> Paved with the image of the sky . . . the hoar
> And aery Alps towards the North appeared
> Through mist, an heaven-sustaining bulwark reared
> Between the East and West; and half the sky
> Was roofed with clouds of rich emblazonry
> Dark purple at the zenith, which still grew
> Down the steep West into a wondrous hue
> Brighter than burning gold, even to the rent
> Where the swift sun had passed in his descent
> Among the many folded hills: they were
> Those famous Euganean hills, which bear
> As seen from Lido through the harbour piles
> The likeness of a clump of peaked isles –
> And then – as if the Earth and Sea had been
> Dissolved into one lake of fire, were seen
> Those mountains towering as from waves of flame

Around the vaporous sun, from which there came
The inmost purple spirit of light, and made
Their very peaks transparent.

(53–85)

Through the first twenty-seven lines of this description Julian composes
a scene of arrested picturesque beauty: the sun poised just over the
mountains; the sky, with its rich gradations from 'Dark purple' to
'burning gold', reflected in the lagoon; the Alps seen to the north in
distant atmospheric perspective; the Euganean Hills forming a nearer
western horizon. 'And then –' Shelley has Julian put the arrested
moment in motion, and the scene appears to decompose in the sun's
fading intensity. As it sets, the sun dissolves earth and sea 'into one lake
of fire'; the mountains look as if they arise 'from waves of flame', and
their peaks seem 'transparent'. The sun itself is 'vaporous', as if its own
'inmost purple spirit of light' were being dissolved in the 'Dark purple'
of the evening sky. Julian has described himself as one who loves 'all
waste / And solitary places' (14–15), and his language evokes with
powerful visual exactness the sun's sublime power to lay waste to as
well as to define the forms, contours and textures of landscape and
seascape.

'Ere it fade,'

Said my Companion, 'I will shew you soon
A better station' –

(85–7)

Maddalo's promise here (this the first time Julian has quoted him
directly) may be the subtlest event in the poem. 'Ere it fade' shares a line
with the end of Julian's description and suggests Maddalo's intimate
familiarity with his friend's rapture: the antecedent of 'it' is an
unspoken but shared experience, the subsequent account of which in
Julian's retrospective narrative Maddalo could have predicted.
Maddalo seizes upon Julian's favorite moment of fading and with
masterful irony arrests it from a different angle, 'A better station':

'Look, Julian, on the West, and listen well
If you hear not a deep and heavy bell.'
I looked, and saw between us and the sun
A building on an island; such a one
As age to age might add, for uses vile,
A windowless, deformed and dreary pile;
And on the top an open tower, where hung

A bell, which in the radiance swayed and swung;
We could just hear its hoarse and iron tongue:
The broad sun sunk behind it, and it tolled
In strong and black relief. 'What we behold
Shall be the madhouse and its belfry tower,'
Said Maddalo . . .

                                                        (96–108)

Within the fiction of the poem Maddalo challenges Julian's ecstasy by
reorienting his view of the fading, dissolving scene so that it includes a
form which has not faded or dissolved, which stands 'between us and
the sun' in 'strong and black relief'. But since Maddalo, no less than
Julian, is finally a creation of Shelley's imagination, what this shift in
visual perspective intimates is that Shelley is questioning his own
affinity for moments of fading, dissolving beauty, with all that they
imply aesthetically and philosophically. This change of scene
anticipates symbolically the subsequent confrontation – and interrelation – between Julian's belief in the power of mind to dissolve and
transform all impediments to ideal self-realization, and Maddalo's dark
pessimism about the soul's blindness and limitation. Rhetorically,
Julian's voice as narrator contains Maddalo's voice as well as his own
past voice: we have to imagine the entire poem as the product of a
sensibility shaped by the events Julian narrates. So while it was Maddalo
who led Julian to the 'better station', it is Julian who describes what we
see when we get there. And it is Julian who goes on to describe the
eventual fading of this scene as well:

                            The broad star
Of day meanwhile had sunk behind the hill
And the black bell became invisible
And the red tower looked grey, and all between
The churches, ships and palaces were seen
Huddled in gloom; – into the purple sea
The orange hues of heaven sunk silently.

                                                        (132–8)

IV

It is the movement of wind, not light, over the surface of water that
Shelley imagines in the *Defence* when he wants to evoke those

'evanescent visitations of thought and feeling':

> It is as it were the interpenetration of a diviner nature through our
> own; but its footsteps are like those of a wind over the sea, which
> the coming calm erases, and whose traces remain only as on the
> wrinkled sand which paves it.

Impressions, erasure, traces: these are the main elements of yet another
of Shelley's figures of evanescence, elaborated in various contexts and
degrees of completeness throughout his poetry. In some instances, as in
the passage above, the figure implicitly compares mental experience –
perception, reflection, memory – to the process of writing: 'footsteps',
we recall, was the image Shelley borrowed from Bacon much earlier in
the *Defence* to characterize language in its 'vitally metaphorical'
condition (*PP*, 482).[26] Here, thoughts and feelings are impressed or
inscribed on the mind's conscious surface by the wind of inspiration
only to be erased by 'the coming calm' (the present participle carries a
curious predictive, anticipatory force), leaving behind mere 'traces' of
those agitated configurations at some deeper level of memory. In
moments such as this it is as if the usual Shelleyan discrepancy between
conception and composition had seeped back into conception itself,
rendering what was once prior to and separable from language
vulnerable to the same limitations as composition. Thoughts and
feelings, no less than words, are continually erased and left to survive as
traces of a fullness which is always fading, always on the wane.

There is a strong impulse in Shelley to see the mind as existing in a
world of traces. 'The world is now our dwelling-place,' he wrote in the
original draft of the stanzas 'To William Shelley' (1817):

> Where'er the earth one fading trace
>   Of what was great and free does keep,
> That is our home!
>
>   (2–4)

When the action of erasure is arrested or suspended in Shelley's poetry,
we often find ourselves in the presence of death. Thus, in the *Ode to
Naples*,

> Around me gleamed many a bright sepulchre
> Of whose pure beauty, Time, as if his pleasure
> Were to spare Death, had never made erasure;
>   But every living lineament was clear

> As in the sculptor's thought . . .
>
> (12–16)

Though in this instance the artistic forms expressive of thought have not been erased, their very life – 'every living lineament' – reminds us of the decayed human forms they memorialize or contain. When human artifacts are not in fact erased, the possibility or threat of erasure is what gives them life:

> And where within the surface of the River
>   The shadows of the massy temples lie
> And never are erased – but tremble ever
>   Like things which every passing cloud can doom to die . . .
>
> (*The Witch of Atlas*, 513–16)

'Here lies one whose name was writ in Water' – Shelley must have been fascinated by the words Keats asked to have inscribed on his tombstone.[27] In a 'Fragment on Keats', presumably a cancelled passage from *Adonais*, Shelley actually attempts to transform Keats's epitaph by reversing the terms of the figure he had used in the *Defence* some three months earlier. It is now the wind itself that poses the threat of erasure, a threat ironically forestalled by the fixity of death:

> 'Here lieth One whose name was writ on water.'
>   But, ere the breath that could erase it blew,
> Death, in remorse of that fell slaughter,
>   Death, the immortalizing winter, flew
>   Athwart the stream, – and time's printless torrent grew
> A scroll of crystal, blazoning the name
>   Of Adonais!
>
> (*PW*, 658).

Inscribed in stone (as it eventually was), Keat's epitaph refers to another vanished inscription (his own name which 'was writ') whose antithetical mode of existence epitomizes the transience of literary identity and reputation. Shelley perhaps remembered that in Ovid's *Metamorphoses* the flower that springs from Adonis's blood is called *anemone* because 'the winds from which it takes its name shake off the flower so delicately clinging and doomed too easily to fall' (x.738–9); he tries desperately to turn the myth back against itself by imagining that in Keats's case death paradoxically arrests the nullifying power of both the breath of critical defamation and 'time's printless torrent'.[28] The gesture is daring – we can see just how far Shelley was willing to go in

EVANESCENCE: MELTING, DISSOLVING, ERASING 151

pursuing his own forms of elegiac reversal – and ultimately futile, as he himself certainly realized in excluding these lines from the final version of the elegy.

Within the realm of 'time's printless torrent' erasure is inevitable: the only alternatives for the poet are to accept it and articulate it as a process which points beyond itself to a potential which can only be sensed indirectly and fleetingly, or to imagine a movement beyond time to a condition in which there is no discrepancy between meaning or value and their re-presentation in impressions, prints, images, traces. It is in reference to a timeless realm beyond death inhabitable only by the immortal gods that the Earth in *Prometheus Unbound* describes a

> windless and chrystalline pool
> Where ever lies, on unerasing waves,
> The image of a temple built above.
>
> (III.iii.159–61)

The utopian paradox of 'unerasing waves' – of a clear surface whose reflectivity is not disrupted by its movement – stands in sharp antithesis to the relentlessly erasing waves elsewhere in Shelley's poetry:

> my dream became
> Like a child's legend on the tideless sand,
> Which the first foam erases half, and half
> Leaves legible.
>
> (*Fragments of an Unfinished Drama*, 151–4)

> 'And suddenly my brain became as sand
>
> 'Where the first wave had more than half erased
> The track of deer on desert Labrador,
> Whilst the fierce wolf from which they fled amazed
>
> 'Leaves his stamp visibly upon the shore
> Until the second bursts . . .'
>
> (*The Triumph of Life*, 405–10)

In Shelley's last poem the erasing waves of experience leave Rousseau with traces of tracks and prints, themselves only traces of a vanished immediacy – a nightmare version of those 'evanescent visitations of thought and feeling' which Shelley could characterize in the *Defence* as 'elevating and delightful beyond all expression'.

And yet not beyond *all* expression – for Shelley's most productive
poetic impulse is neither to deny by transcending nor to despair at
moments of fading, dissolving and erasing, but to articulate them as
indispensable images in the drama of human perception and
signification. We find erasure at work in the most paradisal of earthly
settings. It is among the powers possessed by the Lady who sustains the
beauty and harmony of the garden in *The Sensitive Plant*:

> And wherever her aery footstep trod,
> Her trailing hair from the grassy sod
> Erased its light vestige, with shadowy sweep
> Like a sunny storm o'er the dark green deep.
>
> ('Part Second', 25–8)

'Footstep', 'sunny storm', 'dark green deep' – here we have yet another,
earlier version of the 'footsteps . . . like those of a wind over the sea'
from the *Defence*. The Lady simultaneously imprints herself on and
erases herself from the garden as she tends it – her nurturing 'Power'
(II.1) is mysteriously self-effacing, self-concealing. This paradoxicality
is picked up in the witty confusion of darkness and light, in the play of
'shadowy sweep' against the punning 'light vestige'[29] and the oxy-
moronic 'sunny storm'.

Then there is the island 'pleasure-house' to which Shelley invites
Emily at the end of *Epipsychidion*. 'It scarce now seems a wreck of human
art' (493)[30] – an ideal work of human art is what it must originally have
been –

> For all the antique and learned imagery
> Has been erased, and in the place of it
> The ivy and the wild-vine interknit
> The volumes of their many twining stems;
> Parasite flowers illume with dewy gems
> The lampless halls, and when they fade, the sky
> Peeps through their winter-woof of tracery
> With Moon-light patches, or star atoms keen,
> Or fragments of the day's intense serene; –
> Working mosaic on their Parian floors.
>
> (498–507)

The 'antique and learned imagery' at the beginning of this passage is
'erased', only to be rewritten in 'tracery' as a mosaic of light and shadow
on the 'Parian floors'. Hillis Miller says that Shelley 'somewhat

prosaically' describes the 'pleasure-house' in one of the drafts of the preface as 'a Saracenic castle which accident had preserved in some repair'.[31] But as we shall see in a later chapter on rhyme and the arbitrariness of language, there is nothing prosaic about the preservative resources of one form of 'accident' in Shelley's verse: here again he marks the word 'erased' by interknitting it phonetically with coincidental yet pointedly significant near rhymes in 'place' and 'tracery'. The 'lampless halls' of this ruined tower are illumined (not just shaded, as Miller says) by 'Parasite flowers' that depend for their support on a structure whose decay they make visible.[32] When those flowers fade, the 'volumes of their many twining stems' remain to provide a 'winter-woof of tracery' that works 'patches', 'atoms', and 'fragments' of external light into an evanescent 'mosaic'. The passage is a virtuosic elaboration of that image of faded thought and desire in the opening address to Emily:

> In my heart's temple I suspend to thee
> These votive wreaths of withered memory.

(3-4)

In the Ocean-King's 'pleasure-house', Shelley presents us with a sequence of fadings and erasings: an original paradisal imagery is replaced by an interdependent succession of substitutions in which increasingly remote natural phenomena function as artifice. The language invites us to read this description of parasitically organicized and refigured architecture as a visualizing of what Shelley's own verse must be like as it is shaped by and gives shape to the forces of accident, fragmentation, fading and erasure.

V SHELLEY'S SPEED

To many readers nothing has seemed more characteristic of Shelley's writing than its speed. Here is C.S. Lewis, elaborating his 'proposition that Shelley and Milton are, each, the half of Dante': 'You know . . . the air and fire of Shelley, the very antithesis of the Miltonic solidity, the untrammeled, reckless speed through pellucid spaces which makes us imagine while we are reading him that we have somehow left our bodies behind.'[1] Leavis knew this sensation but disliked and mistrusted it; for him, the essential antithesis was between Wordsworth's patient, steady contemplation and 'Shelley's eager, breathless hurry – his verse always seems to lean forward, so that it must run in order not to fall.'[2] More recent critics have continued to see in Shelley 'the swiftness of a spirit too impatient for the compromises without which societal existence and even natural life are just not possible',[3] and have wondered at 'the delighted rapidity with which his creative sensibility fastens on the multifarious and antithetical in experience.'[4]

But where exactly are we to observe this speed that Shelley's readers have so often attributed to him? Looking at the writing itself, we might expect to find it in ideas and images signified by the words on the page, in such formal features of Shelley's language as rhythm, syntax and versification – or, as in many of the instances I want to look at later, in both together. But the tendency has often been to confuse or neglect the stylistic sources of Shelley's speed and to speak instead of mental states in the poet or in the reader. Shelley himself must bear some responsibility for encouraging this tendency with his famous – or notorious – self-projections in *Ode to the West Wind* ('One too like thee: tameless, and swift, and proud', 56) and in *Adonais* ('A pardlike Spirit beautiful and swift', 280). Lewis, for example, appears to be thinking of idea and imagery when he refers to 'the untrammeled, reckless speed through pellucid spaces', but 'untrammeled' and 'reckless' may also suggest some kind of access to the mind of the poet in conception or composition, while the concluding remark that Shelley's speed 'makes us imagine while we are reading him that we have somehow left our bodies behind' shifts the emphasis entirely towards an affective perspective. Leavis does seem to be concerned with the movement of Shelley's verse, but he sees that movement as an immediate consequence of the poet's own 'eager, breathless hurry'. It is clear from what Leavis says elsewhere that he was disturbed by what he took to be Shelley's way of passing his habit of speeding on to the reader: 'the imagery feels right, the associations work appropriately, if (as it takes conscious resistance not to do) one accepts the immediate feeling and doesn't slow down to think.'[5] While Shelley's speed made Lewis imagine that he was leaving his body behind, it made Leavis fear that he was being asked to take leave of his critical intelligence. In neither case are we shown how the experience of speed is generated or transmitted through Shelley's language.

Although there has been some useful localized commentary on effects of speed in Shelley's poetry, little has been done to address the question in a larger, more fundamental way. Ants Oras has written well about how Shelley's images of 'intricately circling speed' suggest the mind's perception of phenomena at once highly organized and dizzyingly complex.[6] But his argument that 'Shelley's vision of complexity . . . is essentially kinetic'[7] stops short of exploring the relation between ideas or images of speed and verse that, as Leavis aptly says, 'seems to lean forward'. Richard Harter Fogle applied the terms 'kinesthetic' (rather than 'kinetic') and 'motor' to two of the eight kinds of 'imagery of sensation' he distinguished in Shelley and Keats. He found a much higher percentage of 'motor' imagery in the former than in the latter,[8] and described Shelley's 'characteristic kinesthetic imagery' as 'peculiarly swift of action, forceful but fleeting in [its] effect, so that sensation is soon past, although momentarily violent'.[9] This blurring together of semantic and affective notions of imagery, along with the failure to clarify the distinction between 'kinesthetic' and 'motor' imagery,[10] makes it difficult to use Fogle's account as a basis for further explorations into this aspect of Shelley's writing.

If we confine ourselves to the disposition of ideas and images, thinking affectively about Shelley's speed may be unnecessary and even confusing: there is no reason to assume that a reference to speed in the language or an abrupt transition from one thought to another will necessarily produce a sensation of speed in the reader. But when it comes to syntax, rhythm and versification, affective assumptions would appear to be unavoidable. Words on the page do not in fact move, no matter what their phonetic and syntactical organization. Movement is possible – one might also say necessary – only in the temporal experience of reading, and in that sense is a function of the reader's eye, mind and voice. Yet it is still an important question of critical emphasis whether one focuses on the formal elements in the text that activate and control movement in the reader, or instead gives priority to an assumed experience or sensation of movement. Consider, for instance, the following comment, in a recent essay by Bernard Beatty, on the opening lines of *Ode to the West Wind*:

> O Wild West Wind, thou breath of Autumn's being,
> Thou, from whose unseen presence the leaves dead
> Are driven, like ghosts from an enchanter fleeing,
>
> Yellow, and black, and pale, and hectic red,
> Pestilence-stricken multitudes: O Thou . . .

> From the beginning of line two until the colon in line five, there is no opportunity for taking breath. Already uncomfortable by line three, we anticipate some sort of closure both because of the sense and the encouraging prospect of a printed space between this and the next tercet. Instead we encounter a dependent line of adjectives which cruelly push the sense in front of them onto the next line. The reader of the poem, provided that he is using more than his eyes, is forced to read the verse at a tremendous speed in order to cope at all and finds himself poised between panic and exhilaration.[11]

Beatty has his eye on details of syntax, punctuation and stanzaic arrangement, but only as cues for a particular kind of vocal performance in which the sensation of speed is a result of needing to breathe. Does this mean that only a vocalizing reader will experience the 'tremendous speed' of these lines? Even if we are reading aloud, would we have to know in advance that 'there is no opportunity for taking breath' in order to read at the pace that Beatty prescribes? And is it in fact true that we are given no chance to breathe at the commas after 'driven' or perhaps 'fleeing' in line 3, or after 'red' at the end of line 4? Beatty's point about breathing and vocal performance is suggestive, since he goes on to relate it to the poem's own emphasis on breath, wind and articulate inspiration. But his account of Shelley's speed is too narrow and presumptive in its affective bias, too sketchily grounded in the formal features of the language, to be wholly convincing.

While the tendency to talk about Shelley's speed in terms of its effect on the reader is both unavoidable and fraught with difficulty, the tendency to see speed as a direct reflection of the poet's processes of thinking and composing is critically mystifying and singularly unproductive, Shelley's poetic self-characterizations notwithstanding. The myth dies hard that Shelley, like the other Romantics, wrote at white-hot speed out of moments of urgent emotional intensity. Shelley himself at times encouraged this belief, as did Byron and even Wordsworth and Coleridge in their own ways. Many of Shelley's manuscripts appear to confirm what he reportedly told Trelawny upon being interrupted during the drafting of 'With a Guitar. To Jane' – that he drafted impulsively but revised with care:

> 'When my brain gets heated with thought, it soon boils and throws off images and words faster than I can skim them off. In the morning, when cooled down, out of the rude sketch, as you justly call it, I shall attempt a drawing.'[12]

Whether apocryphal or not, these words are as much a caution against as an inducement to locating the speed of Shelley's writing in the compositional activity from which it derives. The verbal means through which an impression of speed is generated – a cascade of images, a rush of enjambed endings – may just as well derive from the cool measures of revision as from the rapid, and presumably evaporative, boil that is skimmed for a first draft.

This is how the second section of *Mont Blanc* begins in the Bodleian draft:

> Thus thou ravine of Arve, dark deep ravine –
> Thou many colored, many voiced vale –
> Over whose rocks & pines & caverns sail
> Fast cloud shadows & sunbeams   awful scene
> Where Power, in likeness of the Arve comes down
> From the ice gulphs that gird his secret throne –
> Bursting thro   these dark mountains like the flame
> Of lightning thro the tempest . . .[13]

(12–19)

In the intermediate fair copy discovered among the Scrope Davies papers, Shelley adds some conventional pointing and substitutes a comma for the dash at the end of line 12 and an exclamation mark for the dash at the end of line 13. But he also removes the comma separating 'Power' from its natural 'likeness' in line 16, placing it instead more dramatically after 'awful scene' at the end of the preceding line. And he removes all punctuation from the end of line 17.[14] Then, in the final printed text of 1817, he restores the original dash to line 12, changes the added exclamation mark to a comma in line 13, and places a comma at the end of line 17:

> Thus thou, Ravine of Arve – dark, deep Ravine –
> Thou many-coloured, many-voiced vale,
> Over whose pines, and crags, and caverns sail
> Fast cloud shadows and sunbeams: awful scene,
> Where Power in likeness of the Arve comes down
> From the ice gulphs that gird his secret throne,
> Bursting through these dark mountains like the flame
> Of lightning thro' the tempest . . .
>
> (12–19)

Many of Shelley's revisions in punctuation intensify the impression of the Arve's speed by giving it more dramatic articulation. 'Bursting' conveys a greater sense of force and energy when it follows the pause indicated by the comma of the printed text: the dash in the original draft creates the wrong kind of disjunction between the two main clauses, while the enjambment of the intermediate fair copy leaves the Power of the Arve with nothing to flow against and burst through. However quickly Shelley's first draft may have been written, his revisions encourage an act of reading that accentuates the impression, already there in the draft, of a mind moving rapidly to take in the rapid movements of the 'awful scene'.

Shelley's language is often carefully articulated to convey the idea and the experience of speed, and it is naive to assume that we are just following the tracks of a headlong compositional dash. It is clear in the *Defence* that Shelley is committed to an ideal of speed: if 'the mind in creation is as a fading coal which some invisible influence, like an inconstant wind, awakens to transitory brightness', then it may well be 'an error to assert that the finest passages of poetry are produced by labour and study'. But Shelley goes on in this passage to acknowledge that the quick impulses of inspiration can never be sustained through an entire poem, and perhaps not even through their own articulation:

The toil and the delay recommended by critics can be justly

interpreted to mean no more than a careful observation of the inspired moments, and an artificial connexion of the spaces between their suggestions by the intertexture of conventional expressions; a necessity only imposed by a limitedness of the poetical faculty itself.

(*PP*, 504)

The telling clause here is 'a careful observation of the inspired moments'. It is a consequence of the 'limitedness of the poetical faculty' that the work of composition necessarily lags behind the speed of inspired conception – hence the need for 'careful observation' and 'artificial connexion'. 'Toil and delay' may paradoxically be the only means of recording the fleetingness of the mind's 'inspired moments'. Shelley's speed might best be thought of, then, as the formal verbalized articulation, produced by careful observation and deliberate compositional adjustment, of a mind working rapidly and fluctuantly in a world constituted in part through that mind's own perceptual activity.

I

Speed is important in Shelley's poetry most obviously because it is an idea or experience he frequently writes about. The relation of speed as Shelleyan subject to speed as stylistic feature or effect can be relatively direct, as in the second and third stanzas of 'To a Skylark':

> Higher still and higher
>   From the earth thou springest
> Like a cloud of fire;
>   The blue deep thou wingest,
> And singing still dost soar, and soaring ever singest.
>
> In the golden lightning
>   Of the sunken Sun –
> O'er which clouds are brightning,
>   Thou dost float and run;
> Like an unbodied joy whose race is just begun.

(6–15)

Fogle's comment on the interaction of semantic meaning and rhythmic suggestiveness in these lines is worth looking at in some detail:

These two stanzas are filled with a swiftly rising and swooping movement evoked partly by meaning and in part by sound. The verses have a rocking, alternating movement, from the heavy terminal pauses of the short lines and the long caesural pause in the final Alexandrines. This movement of sound induces in the reader an unusual receptivity to the suggestions of flight in *springest, wingest, soar, float,* and *run.* The rocking motion is accentuated by the parallelism of *singing-soar, soaring-singest*; and by the alternatives *float* and *run,* which balance the swift spasmodic striking-out of feet with a smooth leveling-off of poised wings. The net result is a decided organic sensation of vertiginous flight.[15]

Fogle believes that the rhythm of Shelley's stanzas makes the reader receptive to the suggestions of rapid movement signified by the verbs, but the priority ought to be reversed: it is largely because the key verbs establish the idea of flight that we respond to the co-operations of rhythm as readily as we do. Fogle's account of that rhythm is also curious: the basically trochaic pattern might be said to evoke a rocking movement, but in six of the eight short lines the 'terminal pauses' are made light, not heavy, by the presence of unstressed 'feminine' endings. This rhythm propels us from one line to the next, even in instances where the 1820 punctuation, intent on controlling the ambiguous fluidity of the poem's grammar, does not allow for enjambment:

Higher still and higher
  From the earth thou springest
Like a cloud of fire;
  The blue deep thou wingest,
And singing still dost soar . . .

(7–10)

That semi-colon tells us that we should restrict the reference of the central simile to the preceding lines – but the uninterrupted rhythmic movement, together with the alternating rhyme groupings and the figurative continuities ('Like a cloud of fire' seems even more apt for a shape winging 'The blue deep' than for one springing 'From the earth'), invites us to read the simile anticipatorily as well as retrospectively. There is a similar effect in the movement from the first of these stanzas to the second:

And singing still dost soar, and soaring ever singest.

In the golden lightning
　　Of the sunken Sun –

(10-12)

Grammatical arrangement and especially rhythmic patterning here –
the sequence of unstressed and stressed syllables flows on uninterrupted
from line to line – urge the reader past the separation imposed by
punctuation and stanzaic division. The medial pause within line 10 is at
least as emphatic as the pause at the end of the line; the skylark seems to
keep right on soaring into the prepositional phrase which begins the
new stanza. Like the skylark, the reader floats and runs from stanza to
stanza.

  The ways in which Shelley's thoughts about speed get articulated
within and across the apparent confinements of stanzaic arrangement
demonstrate remarkable stylistic resourcefulness, even in passages
where his sense of urgency becomes coercively melodramatic. Byron
had shown him that the Spenserian stanza, with its traditional
invitations to leisurely rhetorical performance and recapitulative pause,
could be made to yield effects of impulsive quickness.[16] Here is a
transitional sequence from Canto VI of *The Revolt of Islam*; Laon recalls
the sudden appearance of Cythna in a moment when the tyrant's forces
had reclaimed Argolis:

　　I soon survived alone – and now I lay
　Vanquished and faint, the grasp of bloody hands
I felt, and saw on high the glare of falling brands:

　　When on my foes a sudden terror came,
　　　And they fled, scattering – lo! with reinless speed
　　A black Tartarian horse of giant frame
　　　Comes trampling over the dead, the living bleed
　　　Beneath the hoofs of that tremendous steed,
　　On which, like to an Angel, robed in white,
　　　Sate one waving a sword; – the hosts recede
　　And fly, as through their ranks with awful might,
　Sweeps in the shadow of eve that Phantom swift and bright;

　　And its path made a solitude. – I rose
　　　And marked its coming . . .

(2494–507)

Shelley urges the reader into the central stanza by beginning with the conjunctive 'When'. He then characteristically reverses the usual sequence of phenomenal cause and emotional effect: we are asked to respond to the enemy's 'sudden terror' before learning that it was inspired by the 'reinless speed' of Cythna's approach. Again the 'operations of the human mind' are given a striking figurative priority. Yet both the images of psychical and of physical speed receive full support from the handling of rhythm and syntax. The cadence of the lines describing the initial appearance of Cythna's horse hurries us past two unstopped line-endings, offers a brief pause at a comma, then hurtles on past yet another enjambed ending. The transition from horse to rider is managed with great economy as the syntax of the internal couplet is opened out and extended through the phrase 'On which' (the effect is similar to that of the stanza's opening 'When'). The stanza concludes with a propulsive alexandrine initiated by the verb 'Sweeps' and by a repeated dactylic pattern. The rhythmic and syntactical momentum accumulated in this last line carries us past the end of the stanza, which is left grammatically open; we don't come to a full stop until mid-way through the first line of the following stanza.

The most subtle and complicated effects of speed in Shelley's stanzaic writing are to be found not in his manipulations of such long stanzas as the Spenserian and ottava rima, striking though these are, but in his experiments with the shortest of stanzas, the tercets of terza rima. As the examples we have just been looking at suggest, it is virtually impossible to talk about speed without also talking about its opposites – slowness, pausing, stopping. In *Ode to the West Wind*, terza rima tercets function as stanzas within the larger fourteen-line stanzas, and as Paul Fry has recently shown,[17] they serve both to check and to accentuate the poem's articulation of a driving energy in the speaker and in the wild scene before him. Enjambment in the movement from tercet to tercet is one critical factor here: two tercets in the first stanza, three in the second, two in the third, three in the fourth, and two in the fifth end without grammatical pause or stop. But as Fry suggests, it is the particular grammatical structure of these enjambments that shapes our sense of the poem's movement.[18] Both inter-tercet enjambments in the first stanza divide a verb or a verb and its modifier from a direct object:

> O Thou,
> Who chariotest to their dark wintry bed
>
> The winged seeds, where they lie cold and low,

Each like a corpse within its grave, until
Thine azure sister of the Spring shall blow

Her clarion o'er the dreaming earth . . .

(5–10)

The blank separation between tercets may be seen to represent
disruptions in the poem's drive towards continuity and completion. But
the fact that the verse so forcefully springs over these gaps dramatizes
the speed and energy of syntactic connection. In the second stanza each
of the three enjambments between tercets marks a movement from
noun to adjectival prepositional phrase:

Like the bright hair uplifted from the head

Of some fierce Maenad, even from the dim verge
Of the horizon to the zenith's height,
The locks of the approaching storm. Thou Dirge

Of the dying year, to which this closing night
Will be the dome of a vast sepulchre,
Vaulted with all thy congregated might

Of vapours . . .

(20–7)

The reader moves from each of these tercets to the next, and from
fourth tercet to final couplet, on the strong wings of grammatical
expectation and completion. The sense of completion may include an
element of figurative tension, as when Shelley seems to use the
collected energy of 'Vaulted with all thy congregated might' to vault
over the stanzaic separation, only to remind us that this mighty vault is
made of air, 'Of vapours'.

Shelley arranges an even more dramatic effect in stanza III to rouse us
from the reflexive 'summer dreams' evoked in the first three
tercets:

                                        Thou
For whose path the Atlantic's level powers

Cleave themselves into chasms . . .

(36–8)

The speed and power of Shelley's transition here hinges on our encountering the verb 'Cleave' and its fierce alliteration with 'chasms' as soon as we cross the cleavage between tercets. This is the first time in the poem that a tercet has begun with a verb; the fact that the verb is reflexive is part of the extraordinary way in which the Mediterranean's 'summer dreams' – 'Lulled by the coil of his [own] chrystalline streams' – get transformed in the Atlantic's violent response to the West Wind's energy.

The speed of Shelley's terza rima depends on his metrical facility as well as on his dramatic experimentation with enjambment and syntax. In *The Triumph of Life*, as Donald Reiman observes, the 'first word ("Swift"), the first verbal ("hastening"), and the first verb ("sprang") set a rapid pace' which is rhythmically sustained 'by the simple expedient of reducing the number of stresses from five to four per line':[19]

> Swift as a spirit hastening to his task
> Of glory and of good, the Sun sprang forth
> Rejoicing in his splendour, and the mask
>
> Of darkness fell from the awakened Earth.

(1–4)

Reducing the number of stresses in a line may appear to be a 'simple expedient', but as Reiman's own analysis of this and subsequent passages demonstrates, Shelley's varying deployment of that 'expedient' can be subtly intricate. The chariot of Life appears to the speaker 'on the silent storm / Of its own rushing splendour':

> The Shapes which drew it in thick lightnings
> Were lost: I heard alone on the air's soft stream
>
> The music of their ever moving wings.
> All the four faces of that charioteer
> Had their eyes banded . . . little profit brings
>
> Speed in the van and blindness in the rear,
> Nor then avail the beams that quench the Sun
> Or that these banded eyes could pierce the sphere
>
> Of all that is, has been, or will be done. –
> So ill was the car guided, but it past

With solemn speed majestically on . . .

(96–106)

The alternation in this passage of four-stress lines (96, 98, 101, 106) with five-, six- and even seven-stress lines provides a rhythmic analogue to Shelley's counterpointing of speed and blindness. One transition in the middle of the passage merits particular notice:

All the four faces of that charioteer
   Had their eyes banded . . . little profit brings

Speed in the van and blindness in the rear . . .

(99–101)

The heavy, clogged stresses of the first two lines – especially of 'Had their eyes banded' – give way to the propulsive movement of a line which quite literally has speed in the van, in the foremost position, and blindness in the rear. In context the line comments on itself and implicitly challenges the view that Shelley habitually and indiscriminately pursues speed as an end in itself. He is capable of turning critically and even satirically against speed even as his writing evokes it.

While Shelley's stanzaic writing produces especially interesting effects of speed, it is to his writing in blank verse that many readers would doubtless turn for the most extreme, extended instances. The antithesis Lewis proposed between 'Miltonic solidity' and 'the untrammeled, reckless speed' of Shelley is misleading in this regard, since Milton (along with the Miltonic element in Wordsworth) is clearly the dominant influence on all of Shelley's important writing in blank verse except for *The Cenci*, where Shakespeare is more prominent as a model. We tend to assume that Shelley wrote more blank verse than he actually did, in part because rhymed decasyllabic poems such as *Mont Blanc, Julian and Maddalo* and *Epipsychidion* often create the impression of blank verse through their rhythm and syntax. But *Alastor* is his only major work, apart from *The Cenci*, entirely without end-rhyme.

In this as in many other respects, the earliness and the imaginative extremity of *Alastor* make it a seminal text for locating recurrent critical issues about Shelley's writing. Look at the first verse-paragraph of the narrative proper (lines 67-106). The forty lines of verse in this paragraph comprise six grammatical periods. These periods gradually swell in approximate length, from a line and a half, to two and a half lines, to four and a half lines, to more than six lines, to thirteen and a

half lines. Then the process of grammatical distension begins to subside
and incipiently to reverse itself in a concluding sentence of almost
twelve lines of verse. The expansion of grammatical units corresponds
exactly with the movement in the narrative towards fuller and fuller
elaboration of the 'undiscovered lands' (77) explored by the wandering
poet in his 'early youth' (75). Such expansive periods, in Shelley as in
Milton and Wordsworth, ask the reader to take in a great deal of
information in a single grammatical movement. But unless they involve
Milton's kind of suspended syntax and postponement of the verb to
create a sense of momentous grammatical expectation – and Shelley's
periods in this passage do not – there is no reason to think that long
periods are in themselves conducive to effects of speed. The frequency
of enjambment within long periods would appear to be another matter,
but even here one has to be careful about jumping to speedy
conclusions. Twenty-nine of the forty lines in this verse-paragraph, a
remarkably high proportion, are enjambed. Even more remarkably,
twelve of the thirteen and a half lines in the fifth and longest period are
not end-stopped. But seven of those lines have strong internal caesural
pauses; the momentum generated in rounding the ends of lines without
grammatical pause is repeatedly, and often meaningfully, checked:

> or where bitumen lakes
> On black bare pointed islets ever beat
> With sluggish surge, . . .
>
> (85–7)

It is a 'sluggish', not a dashing, 'surge' that laps over the two enjambed
endings and beats against the medial pause of that last line. Elsewhere
too in this passage enjambment conduces to effects other than those of
speed. Consider the concluding image of the verse paragaph, where
enjambment might be thought to function in support of an image of
speed:

> And the wild antelope, that starts whene'er
> The dry leaf rustles in the brake, suspend[20]
> Her timid steps to gaze upon a form
> More graceful than her own.
>
> (103–6)

The most evocative of these three enjambed endings is not the quick
turn in the reference to the sudden movement of the startled antelope.
It is the way in which the antelope's 'timid steps' are momentarily and

delicately suspended on the word 'suspend' at the break between lines 104 and 105.[21] A similar but less dramatic effect of suspended animation is achieved through the positioning of 'form' at the end of the following line. Already in *Alastor* Shelley realizes that enjambed endings may contribute to effects of subtly disjunctive pause as well as of speed and momentum.

Elsewhere in the *Alastor* narrative speed becomes a pervasive characteristic of the ambiguously differentiated actions of pursuing and fleeing, and of that vortical whirling or circling movement emphasized in Oras's study.[22] The movement of Shelley's blank verse reinforces but also complicates our response to the images of driving, spinning compulsion:

> Stair above stair the eddying waters rose,
> Circling immeasurably fast, and laved
> With alternating dash the knarled roots
> Of mighty trees, that stretched their giant arms
> In darkness over it.
>
> (380–4)

Rhythm and syntax work against each other here to confirm the image of the water's speed being checked, circumscribed. Strong grammatical pauses after 'rose' and 'fast' bring to a halt the propulsive syncopated rhythm of 'the eddying waters rose' and 'Circling immeasurably fast' (the third syllable of 'eddying' gets lost altogether in the line's metrical structure; the fourth syllable of 'immeasurably' figures in the line's measure but flits by so fast that it can hardly be heard). Again the momentum encouraged by enjambment gets broken by internal pauses and stops; we round the ends of lines 382 and 383 only to find ourselves brought to a halt. The most pointed contribution of enjambment to this passage involves a mode of iconic suggestiveness unrelated to speed: the trees have to stretch 'their giant arms', as it were, over the break between lines 383 and 384. This kind of sensitivity to the iconic or mimetic suggestiveness of enjambed blank-verse line-endings, as well as to their contributions to effects of onrushing momentum, appears elsewhere in *Alastor*:

> A pine,
> Rock-rooted, stretched athwart the vacancy
> Its swinging boughs, to each inconstant blast
> Yielding one only response, at each pause
> In most familiar cadence, with the howl

> The thunder and the hiss of homeless streams
> Mingling its solemn song, whilst the broad river,
> Foaming and hurrying o'er its rugged path,
> Fell into that immeasurable void
> Scattering its waters to the passing winds.
>
> (561–70)

Like Wordsworth, whose influence is searchingly and ambivalently assessed in the poem, Shelley saw the expressive possibilities of placing 'vacancy' and 'void' at the ends of unstopped lines so that the blank space of the page could visually accentuate their meaning.[23] A different kind of effect is achieved by placing 'pause' at the end of a line where the only pause is created by the line-break,[24] as if the poem's metrical structure alone were registering the uncanny transformation of 'each inconstant blast' into a 'most familiar cadence'. Notice that the enjambments after 'vacancy', 'blast', 'pause' and 'streams' are each followed directly by strong medial pauses after 'boughs', 'response', 'cadence' and 'song'. Throughout the poem it is the interplay between enjambed endings and internal pauses or stops that produces the characteristic movement of the verse:

> Calm, he still pursued
> The stream, that with a larger volume now
> Rolled through the labyrinthine dell; and there
> Fretted a path through its descending curves
> With its wintry speed.
>
> (539–43)

We follow the swelling stream as it rolls powerfully over one line-ending but stop before reaching the end of the next line. Then we descend without pause past two line-endings only to stop in mid-line with the word 'speed'.

What these passages from *Alastor* demonstrate is that the alternation of rapid movement and arrested movement may be more important than speed *per se*. Some of the most remarkable kinetic sequences in Shelley's subsequent poetry turn upon his ability to transform impressions of speed into antithetical moments of suspension or stasis. The lyric 'To Constantia' begins *adagio*: the singer's 'voice, slow rising like a Spirit, lingers / O'ershadowing me with soft and lulling wings' (1–2). But the tempo quickens to a frantic pace almost immediately as the listener–speaker's response outspeeds the music:

My brain is wild, my breath comes quick,
The blood is listening in my frame,
And thronging shadows fast and thick
Fall on my overflowing eyes . . .

(5–8)

Not until the second stanza does the tempo of the music itself accelerate, as if to catch up with the response it has provoked. Yet by the end of the stanza the ultimate effect of this acceleration is to suspend the listener in a kind of reverie which is alternately moving and motionless:

Now is thy voice a tempest, swift and strong,
    On which, as one in trance upborne,
    Secure o'er woods and waves I sweep
    Rejoicing, like a cloud of morn:
    Now 'tis the breath of summer's night
    Which, where the starry waters sleep
Round western isles with incense blossoms bright,
Lingering, suspends my soul in its voluptuous flight.

(15–22)

The relation of the enjambed rhyme-word 'sweep' in line 17 to its companion 'sleep' in line 20 – also enjambed – epitomizes the strange convertibility of speed and suspended movement in this passage. The fact that 'its voluptuous flight' in the last line may refer both to the singer's voice and to the listener–speaker's soul confirms the paradoxical reciprocity upon which the entire sequence depends. This reciprocity extends into the next stanza, where the animated singer seems to breathe for the breathlessly entranced listener:

A deep and breathless awe, like the swift change
Of dreams unseen, but felt in youthful slumbers;
Wild, sweet, yet incommunicably strange,
Thou breathest now, in fast ascending numbers.

(23–6)

Prometheus Unbound contains a series of remarkable images in which rapid motion converts itself into suspension and stillness. In Act I Ione announces the approach of 'two shapes from the East and West':

Twin nurslings of the all-sustaining air,
On swift still wings glide down the atmosphere . . .

(I.754–5)

L.O. Kuhns compared this image to a simile evoking the arrival of
Paolo and Francesca in Canto v of the *Inferno*:[25]

> Quali colombe dal disio chiamate
>   con l'ali alzate e ferme al dolce nido
>   vegnon per l'aere, dal voler portate;
> cotali uscir de la schiera ov'è Dido,
>   a noi venendo per l'aere maligno . . .

(v.82–6)

> [As doves
> By fond desire invited, on wide wings
> And firm, to their sweet nest returning home
> Cleave the air, wafted by their will along;
> Thus issued, from that troop where Dido ranks,
> They, through the ill air speeding . . .]

A comparison of Shelley's 'swift still wings' to Dante's 'l'ali alzate e
ferme' – Cary translates 'wide wings / And firm', although 'alzate'
literally means *raised* – brings out what is original and characteristic in
Shelley's adaptation. It is no contradiction to say that swiftly gliding
wings are 'still' as opposed to beating, but the flicker of antithesis in the
adjectival pairing of 'swift' and 'still' connects this image to a recurrent
antithetical pattern. The most impressive instance, perhaps, comes in
Panthea's Act IV description of the Earth's appearance among 'Ten
thousand orbs involving and involved' (241):

> and they whirl
> Over each other with a thousand motions
> Upon a thousand sightless axles spinning
> And with the force of self-destroying swiftness,
> Intensely, slowly, solemnly roll on –

(IV.246–50)

Shelley's most extravagant vision of speed is both intricately and
concentrically organized and, as we noted previously in examining his
reflexive figures, 'self-destroying'.[26] The image of 'self-destroying
swiftness' is also realized rhythmically and syntactically: the blank verse
moves without pause through three and a half lines until it comes to the
reflexive center of Shelley's vision. Then, as if the swiftness of the verse
had itself become self-destroying, we pause before encountering a line
that rhythmically mimes the intense, slow, solemn motion it names.

One further example from *Prometheus Unbound*, this one more extended and complex in its effect, may serve to confirm our sense of the ways in which Shelley's speed can operate antithetically or dialectically within the total experience of a particular passage. In scene iv of Act II, Asia is commanded by Demogorgon to behold the arrival of the 'immortal Hours' (140) that will bring the liberation of Prometheus:

> The rocks are cloven, and through the purple night
> I see Cars drawn by rainbow-winged steeds
> Which trample the dim winds – in each there stands
> A wild-eyed charioteer, urging their flight.
> Some look behind, as fiends pursued them there
> And yet I see no shapes but the keen stars:
> Others with burning eyes lean forth, and drink
> With eager lips the wind of their own speed
> As if the thing they loved fled on before,
> And now – even now they clasped it; their bright locks
> Stream like a comet's flashing hair: they all
> Sweep onward. –
>
> (II.iv.129–40)

A quintessential instance, one might think, of what Lewis meant by a disembodying 'untrammeled, reckless speed through pellucid spaces', or Leavis by verse that 'seems to lean forward, so that it must run in order not to fall'. But as G. Wilson Knight's comment on the passage indicates, a very different response to this vision of speed is possible:

> speed is plastically presented, and the verse moves slow. . . .
> Motion is frozen into a poetic stillness, time's fleeting moment is
> locked in formal stability, like the figures on Keats's urn.[27]

Wilson Knight's case may be overstated and in some respects inaccurate: the blank verse at the beginning and end of Asia's speech, with its repeated enjambment and emphatically placed verbs of motion ('Stream', 'Sweep'), is anything but slow. Yet it is true that the speech does rely on an arrested iconography of speed:

> in each there stands
> A wild-eyed charioteer, urging their flight . . .
> Others with burning eyes lean forth, and drink
> With eager lips the wind of their own speed . . .

It is possible to imagine both passages as descriptions of painted, carved or sculpted figures, of movement 'frozen into a poetic stillness', as in the 'mad pursuit' and 'wild ecstasy' of Keats's ode. Allowing for their problematic textual status, we might compare the ekphrastic language of some of Shelley's prose descriptions of sculpture he saw in Rome and Florence in 1819. He describes a figure of Pomona: 'A woman in the act of lightly advancing – much care has been taken to render the effect of drapery as thrown back by the wind of her motion' (*CW*, VI, 315). And a Mercury: 'His figure nervous yet light, expresses the animation of swiftness emblemed by the plumes of his sandalled feet. Every muscle and nerve of his frame has tranquil and energetic life' (*CW*, VI, 317). And a series of maenads 'sculptured in moderate relief' on the base of an altar supporting a statue of Minerva: 'Their hair loose and floating seems caught in the tempest of their own tumultuous motion' (*CW*, VI, 323).[28] Shelley was alert to the technical devices through which illusions of speed could be 'plastically presented' (to use Wilson Knight's phrase), and he was undoubtedly drawing on what he knew of such visual effects in *Prometheus Unbound*, as he did later in *Ode to the West Wind*. But it seems to me impossible to respond fully to Asia's speech without sensing that the 'formal stability' Wilson Knight locates is energized and partly destabilized by language that appeals directly to the reader's kinetic imagination. The 'wild-eyed charioteer' may stand there like a sculpted figure, but the unstopped ending of line 133 exerts a fine animating pressure on the stability of 'stands'. And in 'urging their flight', the charioteer links himself with the animation of his wind-trampling steeds. Similarly, Asia's reference to the charioteers' 'burning eyes' encourages us to project ourselves with her into the bodily experience of moving at a tremendous speed. Lewis's remark that Shelley's speed 'makes us imagine while we are reading him that we have somehow left our bodies behind' is singularly inappropriate to the experience this passage offers. The image of a body affected by the wind of its own motion, which appears twice in the 1819 sculpture notes, takes on an extraordinary intensity with the thought that the charioteers 'drink' that wind 'With eager lips', as if refreshed (from the burning wind) and nourished by their own urgency. Shelley's writing evokes the pictorial conventions of formally stabilized, arrested movement but appeals beyond them to sensations, impressions, memories and fantasies that resist being 'frozen into poetic stillness'.

II

While the speed Asia attributes to the 'immortal Hours' in Act II, scene iv of *Prometheus Unbound* is evoked through references to physical posture and sensation, it is simultaneously imagined as a psychical phenomenon, as a condition of the mind and the emotions. The Spirit of the Hour makes this emphatic once it arrives and speaks:

> My coursers are fed with the lightning,
>   They drink of the whirlwind's stream . . .
> I desire – and their speed makes night kindle;
> I fear – they outstrip the Typhoon . . .
>
>   (II.iv.163–70)

Shelley extends this mythology of psychically determined speed in the opening exchange of scene v, where he picks up and elaborates the figures from Asia's speech in scene iv:

> SPIRIT
> On the brink of the night and the morning
>   My coursers are wont to respire,
> But the Earth has just whispered a warning
>   That their flight must be swifter than fire:
> They shall drink the hot speed of desire!
>
> ASIA
> Thou breathest on their nostrils – but my breath
> Would give them swifter speed.[29]
>
>   (II.v.1–7)

Fogle noted the 'light accents and unprecedented use of three-syllable feet' in these lines: 'Sound and meaning move', he says, taking his cue from Shelley's own imagery, 'in breathless unison.'[30] The passage indeed offers a remarkable dramatic enactment of the etymological trope of inspiration as breath or wind; the Spirit's 'coursers are wont to respire', but instead they will be sent speeding on their way, literally *inspired*, in Shelley's mythological fiction, by the Spirit's breath of 'desire'. Speed is figuratively metamorphosed from physical to psychical phenomenon in the flash of a couplet, as Shelley moves from an ontologically conventional comparison appropriate to the Earth's warning – 'their flight must be swifter than fire' – to an image that begins in a physical act and ends in an 'operation[ ] of the human mind' –

'They shall drink the hot speed of desire'. Here again it is not that the figurative movement 'makes us imagine . . . that we have somehow left our bodies behind', but that it makes us re-imagine our ways of distinguishing bodily from mental experience. The appeal to bodily sensation is strongly sustained: 'hot' insists that 'desire' is inseparable from that dimension of mental life (to adapt the terms of Shelley's metaphysics) that we commonly refer to as the body. Yet in a way that calls dramatic attention to a recurrent tendency in Shelley's kinetic figures, the Act II sequence locates the ultimate source of and standard for speed in the operations of mind, of 'Spirit'. 'I desire – and their speed makes night kindle.'

In Chapter II it was suggested that Hamlet's desire for 'wings as swift / As meditation or the thoughts of love' might be seen as one instance of the kind of precedent Shelley claims to have found in Shakespeare for 'imagery . . . drawn from the operations of the human mind'. Hamlet's simile becomes a Shelleyan signature, usually without but occasionally with the kind of irony it takes on in Shakespeare's play. The figure is already there in the parts of *Queen Mab* that Shelley revised and published separately as *The Daemon of the World* (1816):

> The shadows with swift wings
> Speeded like thought upon the light of Heaven.
>
> (II.613–14)

It is still there, in more fully personified form, at the end of Shelley's career:

> Swift as a spirit hastening to his task
> Of glory and of good . . .
>
> (*The Triumph of Life*, 1–2)

Throughout Shelley's poetry the pre-eminent figurative standard for speed is the action of thought or spirit. When the tenor of such figures is a natural, physical event or being, as in the opening of *The Triumph of Life*, the effect may be to approximate, even to identify, that event or being with its implicit spiritual significance. Such figurative situations become increasingly circular, as we have seen, as their fictional contexts become more overtly visionary. Near the end of *The Revolt of Islam*, Laon and Cythna, having spiritually outlived their executions, are borne away to the 'Temple of the Spirit' in a boat made of 'one curved shell of hollow pearl':

> Morn, noon, and even, that boat of pearl outran

The streams which bore it, like the arrowy cloud
Of tempest, or the speedier thought of man,
  Which flieth forth and cannot make abode . . .

(XII.4756–9)

This final journey by Laon and Cythna into a realm beyond the limits of mortal existence anticipates the movement at the end of Act III of *Prometheus Unbound* when Asia and Prometheus retire to a cave 'Where we will sit and talk of time and change / As the world ebbs and flows, ourselves unchanged' (III.iii.23–4). It is relevant to this anticipation that the boat which bears Laon and Cythna to their ultimate spiritual destinies should outstrip all comparisons to physical speed – that the only phenomenon to which their movement can now be compared is 'the speedier thought of man'. Since Laon and Cythna may be said to personify the 'thought of man' in its noblest potential, Shelley verges here on that condition of figurative circularity exemplified most extravagantly in *Prometheus Unbound* when 'the Spirits of the human mind' are said to have 'wings [as] soft and swift as thought' (IV.81, 91).

But not all Shelley's figures of mental speed require an assent to such idealized self-realizing circularity. The language through which Shelley celebrates speed as a sign of mental life and energy often includes just those elements of resistance and difference lacking in some of the more extreme mentalistic similes of *Prometheus Unbound*. Consider the metaphorical life led by the word 'quick' – first, as Ahasuerus uses it in a moment of seemingly abstract intensity in *Hellas*:

Thought

Alone, and its quick elements, Will, Passion,
Reason, Imagination, cannot die . . .

(795–7)

It is the word 'die' that makes us read 'quick' as 'alive' in this passage, and not simply as 'swift'. The ideal Shelleyan convergence of mental life and speed, condensed in the adjective 'quick', needs a context which recognizes death and stasis. This is even more vitally evident in the final stanza of *Ode to the West Wind*:

Be thou, Spirit fierce,

My Spirit! Be thou me, impetuous one!

Drive my dead thoughts over the universe
Like withered leaves to quicken a new birth!

(61–4)

The West Wind's fierce, impetuous speed will bring forth a renewal of seasonal life from the 'dying year' (24) and hasten the coming of 'a new birth' of imaginative and political life by transforming the speaker's 'dead thoughts' into glowing 'words' (67). Here thought needs to acknowledge its own as well as nature's death in order to triumph finally as a doubly quickening power. In *Adonais*, too, the word 'quick' comes alive as part of the figurative interplay between the speed of living thought and the static passivity of death:

> O weep for Adonais! – The quick Dreams,
> The passion-winged Ministers of thought,
> Who were his flocks, whom near the living streams
> Of his young spirit he fed, and whom he taught
> The love which was its music, wander not, –
> Wander no more, from kindling brain to brain,
> But droop there, whence they sprung . . .
>
> (73–9)

Adonais's dreams were once 'living', as the note in the Norton Critical Edition says, but they were also swift, 'passion-winged Ministers of thoughts' that have now ceased to fly 'from brain to brain'. The imagery and diction of this ninth stanza anticipate that critical moment in stanza 22 when the despairing finality with which the stanza begins – '*He* will wake no more, oh, never more!' – is suddenly alleviated by the rousing of Urania from her slumberous passivity:

> Swift as a Thought by the snake Memory stung,
> From her ambrosial rest the fading Splendour sprung.
>
> (197–8)

That familiar initial simile acquires a surprisingly violent urgency in the powerful rhyming of the verbs 'stung' and 'sprung'. The subsequent flight of Urania 'to the mournful place where Adonais lay' (207) – 'Out of her secret Paradise she sped' (208) – enacts mythologically the delayed quickening of imagination in response to death, a quickening that will eventually lead to the full elegiac *peripeteia*.

Elsewhere Shelley subjects the speed of thought not to the absolute stasis of death but to the drag of ordinary temporal existence. Beatrice apprehensively awaits the arrival of the two men who are to assassinate her father:

> How slow
> Behind the course of thought, even sick with speed,

Lags leaden-footed time!

(*The Cenci*, IV.ii.1–3)

In keeping with the corruption of values that pervades the play, the speed of Beatrice's thought sickens her as it races ahead in anticipation of a deed she both desires and abhors. But once the assassins arrive, events quicken ominously to keep pace with thought's dire speed. 'All mortal things must hasten thus / To their dark end', she declares (IV.ii.16–17), and by the end of the scene she is trying to compel 'leaden-footed time' to move at her own desperate pace: 'Come, follow! / And be your steps like mine, light, quick and bold' (IV.ii.42–3).

The speed of thought meets a more subtly modulated resistance in *Julian and Maddalo*:

So, as we rode, we talked; and the swift thought,
Winging itself with laughter, lingered not,
But flew from brain to brain, – such glee was ours –
Charged with light memories of remembered hours,
None slow enough for sadness: till we came
Homeward, which always makes the spirit tame.
This day had been cheerful but cold, and now
The sun was sinking, and the wind also.
Our talk grew somewhat serious . . .

(28–36)

Transition is central to any conception of the ways in which thought moves through language, and Shelley's sensitivity to transition is nowhere more evidently masterful. The unimpeded quickness of intimate conversation in the first three lines begins to give way in the fourth and fifth lines to pressures evoked through apparent exclusion or denial. 'Charged', which may initially be taken to mean 'filled' – or even 'energized' with the 'light' of the 'sunny air' (22) – comes to suggest a burden of heavy rather than of 'light memories' (as in 'the sorrow which consigned / Its charge', *Adonais* 452–3). So potentially does 'remembered hours', which at first seems to form an entirely reassuring couplet with 'such glee was ours'. 'None slow enough for sadness' is on its way to becoming slow enough for sadness with its falling cadence and with the strong pause at the colon after 'sadness'. Then comes the dramatically enjambed turn on 'till we came / Homeward': the postponement of grammatical pause from the end of line 32 to its position after 'Homeward' gives this word arresting power. Finally, the sentence which began with 'swift thought, / Winging itself with laughter' moves to its somber close. The sinking of the sun and the wind supply natural analogues for what is essentially a *ritardando* of thought within and between two minds whose quick, exuberant 'glee' has been tamed by time into melancholy, self-mocking reflection.

III

The image of wings, particularly the epithet 'winged', is Shelley's favorite figure for the speed of mental life. Other instances may be added to those already cited: 'on the wing / Of visions' (*The Revolt of Islam* II.926–7), 'a wingèd band / Of bright persuasions' and 'wingèd Hope' (*Rosalind and Helen*, 746–7, 798), 'Winged Persuasions' (*Adonais*, 110). Not surprisingly, Shelley often has recourse to the same figure when he wants to suggest the capacity of language to match, transmit or extend the speed of thought. A stanza near the end of *The Revolt of Islam* schematically idealizes the relation of 'winged thoughts' to 'winged words' by repeating the epithet. The child of Laon and Cythna speaks to her parents:

> 'Then suddenly I stood, a wingèd Thought,
>   Before the immortal Senate, and the seat
> Of that star-shining spirit, whence is wrought
>   The strength of its dominion, good and great,
>   The better Genius of this world's estate.
> His realm around one mighty Fane is spread,
>   Elysian islands bright and fortunate,
> Calm dwellings of the free and happy dead,
> Whence I am sent to lead!' These wingèd words she said . . .
>   (XII.4720–8)

In later poems 'winged words' appear in a variety of contexts, and often with more powerful indications of metaphorical flight:

> Thy words [a Fury's] are like a cloud of winged snakes . . .
>   (*Prometheus Unbound*, I.632)

>   . . . wingèd words let sail,
> Freighted with Truth even from the throne of God.
>   (*Ode to Naples*, 98–9)

Follow his flight with wingèd words . . .
                         ('Fragment of a Satire on Satire', 25)

   Up from beneath his hand in circling flight
The gathering music rose – and sweet as Love
The penetrating notes did live and move

Within the heart of great Apollo – he
   Listened with all his soul, and laughed for pleasure . . .
These words were wingèd with his swift delight;
   'You heifer-stealing schemer . . .'
                         (*Homer's Hymn to Mercury*, 560–4, 579–80)

This last example whimsically points to the literary and philosophical geneology of the figure we are considering. In Chapter II we saw that one of the features of the Homeric *Hymn to Hermes* that especially engaged Shelley's interest as a translator is the extravagant figurative emphasis it gives to the speed of the infant god's mind. In the sequence quoted above, that speed is transferred first to Mercury's music, then to the words of Mercury's rival Apollo, who has been momentarily charmed out of his vindictive mood by the 'circling flight' of song. This is how the Greek text records Apollo's response to the quickness of Mercury's ingenuity:

τὸν δ' ἔρος ἐν στήθεσσιν ἀμήχανος αἴνυτο θυμόν,
καί μιν φωνήσας ἔπεα πτερόεντα προσηύδα.

                         (434–5)

[But Apollo was seized with a longing not to be allayed, and he opened his mouth and spoke winged words to Hermes.]

'Winged words', ἔπεα πτερόεντα, is a Homeric commonplace; Desmond King-Hele claims that it was 'almost a term of banter between Shelley, Hogg, and Peacock'.[31] Line 435 of the Greek *Hymn to Hermes* is in fact an exact quotation of the most famous Homeric instance of 'winged words'. In Book I of the *Iliad*, a startled Achilles responds to the sudden appearance of Pallas Athene:

θάμβησεν δ' Ἀχιλεύς, μετὰ δ' ἐτράπετ', αὐτίκα δ' ἔγνω
Παλλάδ' Ἀθηναίην· δεινὼ δέ οἱ ὄσσε φάανθεν·
καὶ μιν φωνήσας ἔπεα πτερόεντα προσηύδα.[32]

                         (I.199–201)

[Achilleus in amazement turned about, and straightway knew Pallas Athene and the terrible eyes shining. He uttered winged words and addressed her.]

Shelley must certainly have read Apollo's response to Mercury in the *Hymn* as a parodic variation on this grand epic moment, and it is important to what he does with the Homeric figure for verbal speed that he was familiar with it in playful as well as in grave contexts. It is more specifically important that in Shelley's translation, Apollo's 'swift delight' is what makes his words 'winged'. Shelley here undoes and reworks the Homeric phrase so as to give the speed of thought an originating priority over the speed of language.

Horne Tooke had made the comparative speed of language and thought a fundamental issue in *The Diversions of Purley*. The issue is prominently announced in the full title of Tooke's dialogic treatise, which begins with the Homeric phrase itself: *ΕΠΕΑ ΠΤΕΡΟΕΝΤΑ, or the Diversions of Purley*. Facing the title-page is an engraved frontispiece (which I have borrowed for my own) showing the figure of a seated Mercury in the act of strapping on, or perhaps taking off, his wings. Tooke explains both his Homeric title and his frontispiece near the end of the first chapter.

> B.
>
> I think I begin to comprehend you. You mean to say that the errors of Grammarians have arisen from supposing all words to be *immediately* either the signs of things or the signs of ideas; whereas in fact many words are merely *abbreviations* employed for dispatch, and are the signs of other words. And that these are the artificial wings of Mercury, by means of which the Argus eyes of philosophy have been cheated.
>
> H.
>
> It is my meaning.
>
> B.
>
> Well. We can only judge of your opinion after we have heard how you maintain it. Proceed, and strip him of his wings. They seem easy enough to be taken off: for it strikes me now, after what you have said, that they are indeed put on in a peculiar manner, and do not, like those of other winged deities, make a part of his body. You have only to loose the strings from his feet, and take off his cap. Come – Let us see what sort of figure he will make without them.

H.

The first aim of Language was to *communicate* our thoughts: the second, to do it with *dispatch*. (I mean intirely to disregard whatever additions or alterations have been made for the sake of beauty, or ornament, ease, gracefulness, or pleasure.) The difficulties and disputes concerning Language have arisen almost intirely from neglecting the consideration of the latter purpose of speech: which, though subordinate to the former, is almost as necessary in the commerce of mankind, and has a much greater share in accounting for the different sorts of words. Words have been called *winged*: and they well deserve that name, when their abbreviations are compared with the progress which speech could make without these inventions; but compared with the rapidity of thought, they have not the smallest claim to that title. Philosophers have calculated the difference of velocity between sound and light: But who will attempt to calculate the difference between speech and thought! What wonder then that the invention of all ages should have been upon the stretch to add such wings to their conversation as might enable it, if possible, to keep pace in some measure with their minds. –[33]

In emphasizing the central role of 'abbreviation' in the development of language, Tooke is laying the groundwork for what will become his radical belief, as Hans Aarsleff summarizes it, 'that the operations of mind are really operations of language', that 'all the operations of thought reside in language alone'.[34] But as Aarsleff points out, Tooke begins from a position which had been familiar in linguistic theory since Locke – the position that language develops not simply to communicate thought but to do so 'with dispatch', in order to make the speed of language approximate more fully the speed of thought.[35] This is a position which presupposes, even as Tooke articulates it, an inevitable discrepancy between thought and language. Words deserve to be called '*winged*', he says, in so far as the abbreviations they signify greatly facilitate the speed of discourse; 'but compared with the rapidity of thought, they have not the smallest claim to that title.'

Reading Tooke sometime after December 1812 when he ordered *The Diversions of Purley* from his bookseller, Shelley would have found Tooke's opening stance entirely consistent with his own convictions about the relation of verbal to mental operations. He must also have found that stance more than a little inconsistent with Tooke's later efforts to reduce all mental operations to operations of language – efforts which Shelley, as we noted in Chapter I, explicitly rejects in his *Speculations on Metaphysics*. When Tooke says that 'the invention of all ages' has been 'upon the stretch to add such wings to their conversation as might enable it, if possible, to keep pace in some measure with their minds', he comes very close to that unstable suspension of celebratory confidence in and skepticism about language which is so characteristic of Shelley's reflections on language in the *Defence* and elsewhere.

For Shelley as for the Horne Tooke of the opening chapter of *ΕΠΕΑ ΠΤΕΡΟΕΝΤΑ*, words are inherently 'winged' in comparison to the rudimentary verbal structures whose abbreviated articulation they make possible, and as such they are artificially invented ('arbitrarily produced') by the mind and essential to the quickness of its operations. But despite their being integral to thinking itself, as Locke had recognized, words can never fly as fast as the mind that discovers and uses them. This is one reason why the verbalizing imagination is always 'upon the stretch', as Tooke puts it – and why the mental state of expressive desire is a precondition of linguistic development. That condition is also, Shelley would have hastened to add, a precondition of poetic discourse, the 'winged words' of which are generated not simply by the motive 'to *communicate* . . . with *dispatch*', but also by those aesthetic motives and conditions which Tooke, in defiance of his own Homeric title, was to 'disregard'.

It would not have escaped Shelley's attention that in Tooke's dialogue words are called 'the artificial wings of Mercury', 'that they are indeed put on in a peculiar manner, and do not, like those of other winged deities, make a part of his body'. Shelley consistently images winged words as an aspect of that clothing or veiling of thought in language which is a necessary condition of expression:

> Beside the dimness of the glimmering sea,
>   Weaving swift language from impassioned themes,
> With that dear friend I lingered . . .
>
> (The Revolt of Islam, vi.2335–7)

>   Light the vest of flowing metre
> She wears . . .
>
> (The Witch of Atlas, 37–8)

>   My soul spurned the chains of it dismay,
>   And in the rapid plumes of song

> Clothed itself, sublime and strong;
> As a young eagle soars the morning clouds among,
> Hovering in verse o'er its accustomed prey . . .
>
> (*Ode to Liberty*, 5–9)

Even the 'rapid plumes of song' are a kind of clothing for the soul. And while in the *Ode to Liberty* they enable the soul to 'spurn [ ] the chains of its dismay' by soaring and hovering in verse, in *Epipsychidion* the 'winged words' of Shelley's verse are themselves chains that prevent the soul from soaring to the zenith of its desire:

> The winged words on which my soul would pierce
> Into the height of love's rare Universe,
> Are chains of lead around its flight of fire. –
>
> (588–90)

The speed of the mind will always outstrip the winged words it needs to articulate – even to itself – its flights of desire. This is not an attitude that squares with a view of Shelley as a writer who anticipates modern beliefs that thought is only a mode of language. Yet it is an attitude inseparable from both the achievement and the expressed limitations of speed in his poetry.

VI RHYME AND THE ARBITRARINESS OF LANGUAGE

One of the ways in which the language of *The Triumph of Life* 'disfigures' itself, says Paul de Man, is through rhyme:

> If . . . compelling rhyme schemes such as 'billow,' 'willow,' 'pillow' or transformations such as 'thread' to 'tread' or 'seed' to 'deed' occur at crucial moments in the text, then the question arises whether these particularly meaningful movements or events are not being generated by random and superficial properties of the signifier rather than by the constraints of meaning.[1]

De Man goes on to say that this 'arbitrary element in the alignment between meaning and linguistic articulation' is not in itself responsible for the instability of meaning in Shelley's text, but is instead part of a larger, more pervasive process by which the poem enacts what he calls 'the figurality of all signification'.[2] One may believe that the poem's 'movements or events' resist being dissolved in de Man's 'all'-inclusive formulation and yet find the more restricted question about rhyme worth pausing over and exploring in greater detail. De Man rightly suggests that *The Triumph of Life* raises the question of rhyme in an urgent way. But more needs to be said about how the poem does this – and about how the arbitrariness of rhyme bears upon Shelley's declared conception of language as an artistic medium, and upon other poems that challenge the tendency to ignore rhyme or to take it for granted.

By proclaiming that 'language is arbitrarily produced by the Imagination and has relation to thoughts alone,' Shelley embraces more openly and emphatically than any other Romantic poet the Lockean principle that words are arbitrarily related to the thoughts they signify.

Rhyme would appear to be a mysterious consequence of linguistic arbitrariness as Shelley conceives it.[3] For in rhyme the arbitrariness of language turns back on itself to produce – or to make it possible for the poet-as-arbiter to produce – phonetic or graphemic as well as semantic links among arbitrary linguistic signs. In the *Defence* Shelley speaks of an interdependent phonetic and semantic order:

> Sounds as well as thoughts have relation both between each other and towards that which they represent, and a perception of the order of those relations has always been found connected with a perception of the order of the relations of thoughts.
>
> (*PP*, 484)

Rhyme is the most conspicuous manifestation of the double order of sounds and thoughts Shelley imagines here. And that rhyme can be surprising, suggestive and compelling is due in part to the happy coincidences an arbitrarily established system makes available. To take one of de Man's examples, 'billow' and 'pillow' are arbitrarily related to the thoughts they respectively signify. Both may be felt to carry some strong onomatopoeic force, but that too is subject to arbitrary conventions specific to the English language (the corresponding Spanish words *oleada* and *almohada*, for instance, might be thought even more mimetically suggestive than 'billow' and 'pillow', although they sound nothing like their English counterparts). But that 'billow' and 'pillow' should rhyme – that these two arbitrarily established signs should echo one another phonetically in a way that formalizes their shared reference to softly rounded, swelling shapes in Shelley's passage about an ethereal, dream-like movement over the surface of water – comes as a mysterious gift from the arbitrary resources of language.

To say, as de Man does, that such verbal events are 'generated by random and superficial properties of the signifier rather than by the constraints of meaning' is to obscure the process by which valuable constraints of meaning may be generated by, or discovered within, random verbal resources. Charles Tomlinson puts it this way in the poem that gave Donald Wesling the title for his recent study of rhyme:

> The chances of rhyme are like the chances of meeting –
>   In the finding fortuitous, but once found, binding:
> They say, they signify and they succeed, where to succeed
>   Means not success, but a way forward . . .[4]
>
> (1–4)

If a poet must fashion 'A subtler language within language', as Cythna does on the unstable sands of her island prison in The Revolt of Islam (VII.3112), then the poet who takes his chances with rhyme is taking advantage of a fortunate fortuitousness within the larger arbitrariness of language itself. Even the most imaginative production of rhyme is a matter of finding rather than of creating ex nihilo. Rhyming poets must arbitrate among the arbitrary relations of thoughts and sounds a language offers, knowing that what they find can become (in Dr Johnson's terms) capriciously or despotically instead of productively binding, a constraint on rather than a constraint of meaning.

I want to begin to see what Shelley makes of the chances of rhyme by looking at two poems – one from the very end, the other from the beginning of his career – in which rhyme operates under contrasting formal circumstances, and in which the various implications of his conviction that 'language is arbitrarily produced by the imagination' are tested in confrontations with modes of power that are themselves ultimately arbitrary. The chariot in The Triumph of Life moves relentlessly on in 'a cold glare, intenser than the noon / But icy cold' (77–8), 'on the silent storm /Of its own rushing splendour' (86–7); the great mountain in Mont Blanc gleams coldly and silently in the distance, with its precipices which

> Frost and Sun in scorn of mortal power
> Have piled: dome, pyramid, and pinnacle,
> A city of death, distinct with many a tower
> And wall impregnable of beaming ice.
> Yet not a city, but a flood of ruin
> Is there, that from the boundaries of the sky
> Rolls its perpetual stream . . .
>
> (103–9)

In both these poems, but in radically different ways, the arbitrary links available through rhyme are crucial to Shelley's articulation of the mind's encounter with a power which acts 'in scorn of mortal power'. If the terza rima of The Triumph of Life threatens to impose a despotic or tyrannical arbitrariness of its own with its sequential chain of terminal commitments and obligations (Shelley could not have shared Dante's belief that the number three was the very opposite of arbitrary), then the 'wildly irregular'[5] and unresolved rhyming of Mont Blanc poses the opposite threat of impetuous whimsy and mere randomness. In each case, I want to argue, these are calculated stylistic risks, aspects of

Shelley's attempt to appropriate and shape the arbitrariness of language into a medium both reflective of and resistant to a power that defies the mind's desire for meaning.

I

First – and not just arbitrarily – *The Triumph of Life*: we began with Paul de Man's question about the status of rhyme in that poem, and end-rhyme functions there according to a more immediately recognizable and conventional pattern than it does in *Mont Blanc*. Reiman has already given scrupulous attention to Shelley's rhymes in *The Triumph of Life*; I want to re-examine and extend his comments with an emphasis on rhyme's relation to the question of the arbitrary.

The Triumph opens with a rhyme sequence that moves with anticipatory suggestiveness:

> Swift as a spirit hastening to his task
>   Of glory and of good, the Sun sprang forth
> Rejoicing in his splendour, and the mask
>
>   Of darkness fell from the awakened Earth.
> The smokeless altars of the mountain snows
>   Flamed above crimson clouds, and at the birth
>
>   Of light, the Ocean's orison arose . . .
>
> (1–7)

The perfect coincidence of 'task' and 'mask' reinforces the promise of the opening simile and accentuates, through a contextually established contrast, the sun's luminous un*mask*ing of the darkened earth. But the imperfect coincidence of 'forth' / 'Earth' / 'birth' suggests a dissonant counterplot that foreshadows the sun's disturbingly ambiguous status later in the narrator's 'waking dream' (42). This opening sequence establishes a norm for the play of rhyme in the rest of the poem that is alternately tight and loose, exact and approximate. It also confirms John Hollander's point about how important rhyme can be 'in modulating the effects of terminal cuts' at the end of enjambed lines.[6] Five of the poem's first six lines are enjambed, a proportion only slightly greater than that maintained in the rest of the fragment. In this kind of terza rima, rhyme defines a regular structural pattern which is continually threatened with effacement as lines and tercets are denied grammatical closure. The fact that 'mask' answers to 'task' and 'birth' to 'Earth' offsets the unanswered expectations of closure at the end of the first two tercets. The only line which is grammatically closed disrupts, by virtue of that closure, the integrity of the second tercet; it also ends with the first rhyme word in the poem ('Earth') that fails to answer clearly to its predecessor ('forth'). Rhyming such as this suggests a compositional intelligence fully in touch with the arbitrariness of its expressive medium yet capable of shaping that arbitrariness into, as well as according to, precisely provisional 'constraints of meaning'.

The 'compelling rhyme schemes' instanced by de Man all come from the inset discourse of the distorted figure who 'was once Rousseau' (204). This figure comments on the 'mighty phantoms of an elder day' chained to Life's 'triumphal chair' (252–3): Plato, Socrates, Alexander the Great and Aristotle, who

> 'outlived both woes and wars,
> Throned in new thoughts of men, and still had kept
> The jealous keys of truth's eternal doors
>
> 'If Bacon's spirit [   ] had not leapt
> Like lightning out of darkness; he compelled
> The Proteus shape of Nature's as it slept
>
> 'To wake and to unbar the caves that held
> The treasure of the secrets of its reign –
> See the great bards of old who inly quelled
>
> 'The passions which they sung, as by their strain
> May well be known: their living melody
> Tempers its own contagion to the vein
>
> 'Of those who are infected with it – I
> Have suffered what I wrote, or viler pain! –
>
> 'And so my words were seeds of misery –
> Even as the deeds of others.'

(266–81)

For Reiman, Shelley's handling of rhyme towards the end of this passage is uncharacteristically weak: 'The reduplication of the rhyme in lines 273–82 ("reign/strain/vein/pain" and "melody/I/misery/company") marks the only obvious place where Shelley was unable to compel the unwilling dross to the likeness of the beauty he imagined.'[7] Perhaps – but if the dross of language is so unwilling, why would Shelley have made his task of shaping it unnecessarily difficult by extending rhyme sequences beyond the normal requirements of terza rima twice in succession? Although the incomplete revision of these stanzas means that our judgements about style must be as provisional as the text itself, there is some evidence, at least in the first of these reduplicative rhyme sequences, that Shelley was working towards a moment of extreme intensity in Rousseau's account. The progression from Nature's 'reign' through 'strain' and 'vein' to 'pain' marks Rousseau's uncertain relationship to the great figures he comments on. 'Strain' and 'vein' may both be read as puns whose secondary meanings connect as well as contrast Rousseau's 'pain' with that experienced by 'the great bards of old'. Unlike Rousseau they 'quelled / The passions which they sung', but not without a 'strain' akin to his own suffering; the 'vein' to which their passions were tempered, like his own, pulses physically as well as figuratively under the pressure of 'contagion' and 'infected'. The distinction between words and acts denied by Rousseau's powerful internal rhyme of 'seeds' and 'deeds'[8] has already been partly undermined in the distended end-rhyme sequence in the preceding tercets.

One is encouraged to see an incipient coherence in the rhyming relationships of this obviously unfinished passage by the carefully managed rhyme in the three preceding tercets. Six of the nine rhyme-words in those tercets are verbs, and they organize themselves into four verbs of restraint or withholding ('kept'/'slept'/'held'/'quelled') and two verbs of urgent action ('leapt'/'compelled'). Bacon's liberating effect on the domination of Aristotelian thought is enacted in the play of 'leapt' against 'kept' and 'slept', and of 'compelled' against 'held', rhymes so semantically alert that they may be said to meet (admittedly in an un-Popeian spirit) Wimsatt's criterion: 'The words of a rhyme, with their curious harmony of sound and distinction of sense, are an amalgam of the sensory and the logical, or an arrest and precipitation of the logical in sensory form.'[9] Some of these rhyme-words again exert subtle force on their enjambed line-endings:

'If Bacon's spirit [   ] had not leapt
   Like lightning out of darkness . . .'

The rhyme-word 'leapt' sparks across the line-break to fuse with its adverbial complement in a bond accentuated by alliteration and rhythmic stress. 'Slept', on the other hand, modulates the effect of its line- and tercet-ending by setting up a conceptually pointed *contre-rejet* in 'To wake and to unbar'.

The other rhyme sequences which, in de Man's view, betray the subjugation of meaning to 'random and superficial properties of the signifier' occur in Rousseau's controversial encounter with the 'shape all light':

'And as I looked the bright omnipresence
   Of morning through the orient cavern flowed,
And the Sun's image radiantly intense

  'Burned on the waters of the well that glowed
Like gold, and threaded all the forest maze
   With winding paths of emerald fire – there stood

'Amid the sun, as he amid the blaze
   Of his own glory, on the vibrating
Floor of the fountain, paved with flashing rays,

  'A shape all light, which with one hand did fling
Dew on the earth, as if she were the Dawn
   Whose invisible rain forever seemed to sing

'A silver music on the mossy lawn,
   And still before her on the dusky grass
Iris her many coloured scarf had drawn. –

  'In her bright hand she bore a chrystal glass
Mantling with bright Nepenthe: – the fierce splendour
   Fell from her as she moved under the mass

'Of the deep cavern, and with palms so tender
   Their tread broke not the mirror of its billow,
Glided along the river, and did bend her

  'Head under the dark boughs, till like a willow
Her fair hair swept the bosom of the stream
   That whispered with delight to be their pillow. –'

                         (343–66)

This passage provides a revealing opportunity to watch the compositional will at work as it selects and arranges the arbitrary possibilities of rhyme. Notice the accretion of feminine rhyme, which is far more frequent here than in the poem as a whole. Shelley gradually builds towards the two feminine sequences in lines 359–66 by rhyming on unstressed final syllables at line 343 ('omnipresence') and at line 350 ('vibrating'). The accumulated feminine rhymes, together with the repeated enjambment, help initiate and evoke the gliding, sweeping movement of the 'shape all light'. With the possible exception of 'omnipresence', each of these rhymes is semantically pointed and delicately accommodated to the advances of syntax and figuration. This is true of the masculine rhymes as well, although there is one instance where the demands of terza rima might be thought to assert a momentary despotic control. Would the dew flung upon the earth by the 'shape all light' ever have been transformed into 'silver music' without the pressure exerted on Shelley's figurative imagination by the rhyme-word 'sing'? The answer is yes – this extravagant synaesthetic idea is neither a mere product of the exigencies of rhyme nor a capricious freak, but one aspect of 'that double accompaniment of prismatic color [Iris's scarf] and natural music which repeatedly marks the presence of ideal figures in Shelley's poetry'.[10] Dew and the rain to which it is here compared have in fact sung previously in Shelley's poetry, in a line from Act IV of *Prometheus Unbound* where singing is conspicuously not generated by the demands of rhyme. Ione sees the moon riding in a chariot whose wheels of 'solid clouds, azure and gold' (214),

> as they roll
> Over the grass and flowers and waves, wake sounds
> Sweet as a singing rain of silver dew . . .

(233–5)

The manuscript of *The Triumph of Life* shows that Shelley did try a rhyme-word other than 'sing' in line 354 – but it was 'ring',[11] confirmation that the desire to transmute light and moisture into musical sound was what dominated his arrangement of arbitrary linguistic possibilities into the dazzling progression from 'vibrating' to 'fling' to 'sing'.

'In the finding fortuitous, but once found, binding.' Much of the rhyming in *The Triumph of Life* displays Shelley's ability to find the fortunate within the fortuitous, to build inventively upon what he finds, and thus to bind line to line and tercet to tercet through his own arbitrations of the arbitrary. Some of the poem's rhymes turn out to be binding outside the passage where Shelley, and then the reader, first find them. On nine occasions rhyme groups are repeated and establish bonds between as well as within individual passages. Twice Shelley repeats the same three rhyme words in the same sequence, and as Reiman says about both instances, 'the apparent coincidence, when examined closely, proves to be . . . especially fortunate.'[12] Reiman shows in fine detail how 'beneath' / 'death' / 'breath' in lines 56–61 and 385–90 and 'form' /'storm' / 'deform' in lines 83–8 and 463–8 reinforce complexly infolded parallels between the narrator's initial vision of Life's chariot and Rousseau's recollected experience, and thus contribute to the reader's sense that these two phases of the poem are partial re-enactments of each other. The formal and conceptual relationships among the individual members of these two repeated sequences are precisely judged. Phonetically and syllabically, 'beneath' distinguishes itself from and therefore throws into relief that most ironic of rhyming coincidences, 'death' / 'breath'. (Shelley uses this set of rhymes three times in *Adonais* – stanzas II, XII and XX – but never in this sequence.) 'Form' / 'storm' /'deform', on the other hand, contains an unusual amount of internal phonetic duplication: it begins and ends with what the French call *rime riche*, the repetition of an entire phonetic syllable including the initial consonant. One problem with such rhymes, at least in English poetry, is that they often lack the coincidental or arbitrary dimension of most rhyme and depend instead on very obvious lexical transformations; they fall flat unless there is some strong conceptual point to justify the predictable phonetic duplication. The progression of 'form' through 'storm' to 'deform' introduces the element of the arbitrary by separating 'form' and 'deform' with a word which only coincidentally echoes them. And both instances of Shelley's sequence make a strong conceptual point, for it is the storm of Life's triumph that is responsible for deforming the natural and imaginative forms of perception – actually in the case of the distorted (183) and crippled (544) Rousseau, potentially in the case of the narrator.

Forgetting, obliteration and erasure are powerful forces in *The Triumph of Life*.[13] But the articulation of these forces depends upon the counterforces of remembering, literation and repetition. We can see how important rhyme is to Shelley's marshalling of these counterforces by looking at two passages from Rousseau's inset narrative which are about forgetting, obliteration, erasure. The first passage is transitional from Rousseau's sleep of forgetfulness to the appearance of the 'shape all light':

ague ?

    'I arose and for a space
The scene of woods and waters seemed to keep.

'Though it was now broad day, a gentle trace
  Of light diviner than the common Sun
Sheds on the common Earth, but all the place

  'Was filled with many sounds woven into one
Oblivious melody, confusing sense
  Amid the gliding waves and shadows dun;

'And as I looked the bright omnipresence
  Of morning through the orient cavern flowed,
And the Sun's image radiantly intense

  'Burned on the waters of the well that glowed
Like gold, and threaded all the forest maze
  With winding paths of emerald fire . . .'

                        (335–48)

When some sixty lines later Rousseau remembers drinking from the shape's cup of Nepenthe, rhymed sounds from the earlier passage return to mark the drink's 'oblivious' effect. He

  'Touched with faint lips the cup she raised,
And suddenly my brain became as sand

  'Where the first wave had more than half erased
The track of deer on desert Labrador,
  Whilst the fierce wolf from which they fled amazed

'Leaves his stamp visibly upon the shore
  Until the second bursts . . .'

                        (404–10)

The image of 'tracks' or traces being 'half erased' suggests what happens here to 'space' / 'trace' / 'place' as they are half recalled in 'raised' / 'erased' / 'amazed'. 'Amazed' erases nothing of the forest 'maze' but recalls it entirely – and appropriately, since like Ariadne's thread the sun's reflected image had mnemonically 'threaded all the forest maze / With winding paths of emerald fire'. Such repeated and transformed rhymes are part of Shelley's way of tracing the movements of thought out of one maze and into another, through successive waves of forgetting and remembering.

Many recent accounts of *The Triumph of Life* have emphasized how deeply skeptical it is of human achievement, of imaginative vision, of its own artistic status. De Man extends this skepticism to language itself, to the very principle of verbal signification. But in doing so, he recognizes that Shelley's fragment affirms an irreducible power in the arbitrariness of language, without which language would not be able to question its own mode of meaning: 'The positing power of language is both entirely arbitrary in having a strength that cannot be reduced to necessity, and entirely inexorable in that there is no alternative to it.'[14] One of the ways this 'positing power of language' expresses itself in *The Triumph of Life* is through the positioning of rhyme – through a structuring process in which the arbitrating compositional imagination imposes its will on arbitrary but self-structuring possibilities of language.

II

'Before the chariot had begun to climb
    The opposing steep of that mysterious dell,
Behold a wonder worthy of the rhyme

'Of him who from the lowest depths of Hell
Through every Paradise and through all glory
    Love led serene . . .'

                                                    (469–74)

It is no accident that Shelley should rhyme on the word 'rhyme' in an allusion to Dante, nor was the decision to compose *The Triumph of Life* in terza rima an arbitrary one. But his decision some six years earlier that Mont Blanc was a wonder worthy of rhyme presents a much more challenging formal situation. Shelley's own note says that *Mont Blanc* 'rests its claim to approbation on an attempt to imitate the untameable wildness and inaccessible solemnity from which [his] feelings sprang'.[15] 'Untameable wildness' and 'inaccessible solemnity', without and within, both suggest that blank verse might have been the appropriate form for this subject. Wordsworth (in *The Prelude*), Coleridge (in the 'Hymn Before Sunrise, in the Vale of Chamouni') – and John Hollander too (in a wonderful parody of Shelley's poem called 'Mount

Blank')[16] – all write about Mont Blanc in blank verse. But Shelley's poem, while creating the impression of blank verse with its massive periods and very frequent enjambment, uses rhyme in its 'attempt to imitate' an experience of the untameable and the inaccessible. Why?

The facts about rhyme in *Mont Blanc* are in themselves striking, particularly when measured against what must have been one of Shelley's formal models, Milton's *Lycidas*.[17] Of the 144 lines in *Mont Blanc*, only three end in words which have no rhyme elsewhere in the poem.[18] Three of the 193 lines in *Lycidas* are also unrhymed. There are only fifteen couplets in Shelley's poem, contrasted with thirty-four in Milton's (ten of these contain lines of different length), and six of the fifteen are relatively faint or imperfect. Curiously, however, two of these six imperfect couplets are repeated: 'for ever' / 'river' in lines 9–10 are reversed as 'River' / 'for ever' in lines 123–4; 'down' / 'throne' in lines 16–17 are repeated phonetically though not semantically in 'down' / 'over-thrown' in lines 111–12. Even more curiously, there are eleven instances in *Mont Blanc* of words rhyming with themselves (usually over long stretches of verse), and in three of these eleven instances the same word appears in rhyming position not twice but three times.

One of the remarkable features of this extensive rhyming is the degree to which it is disguised or muted by enjambment. In the text Shelley published in 1817, seventy-three of the poem's 144 lines (one more than half) have no punctuation at the end. In *Lycidas*, by contrast, thirty-three of Milton's 193 lines are without terminal punctuation. In the *Defence* Shelley says of the language of Bacon's prose that 'it is a strain which distends, and then bursts the circumference of the hearer's mind, and pours itself forth . . . into the universal element with which it has perpetual sympathy' (*PP*, 485). The images Shelley uses about Bacon in this passage all have their parallels in the imagery of *Mont Blanc* (*burst* actually appears twice in the poem, at lines 11 and 18). There is much in the syntax and versification of *Mont Blanc* that invites us to apply these images – the recurrent Shelleyan pun on 'strain'; the activities of distending, bursting and pouring – to Shelley's own style. But noticing the rhymes in *Mont Blanc* makes us think differently about the straining swell and flow of Shelley's lines. To treat the poem as if it were written in blank verse is to close our eyes, ears and minds to one of its greatest sources of poetic power.

There is no precedent for Shelley's crossing of extended blank-verse enjambment with irregular rhyme in a poem which raises such fundamental questions about the mind's powers and limitations. That he should rhyme with pervasive and provocative irregularity while going so far to create the feeling of blank verse is in keeping with a poem in which questions simultaneously propose and interrogate, in which the experience of blankness itself is both acknowledged and challenged. Considered from this inclusive perspective, rhyme in *Mont Blanc* is one important way in which Shelley's verbal imagination structures and shapes, without giving a closed or determinate pattern to, an experience which defies structuring and shaping. In a more specific sense, the cognitive play between or among rhyme words shows Shelley taking advantage of the way in which the very arbitrariness of linguistic signs he speaks of in the *Defence* can produce an expressive coincidence and thus a resource for a mind contending, ultimately, with its own and nature's blankness. There is no prior reason, for example, why 'waves' (2) and 'raves' (11) should rhyme. But they do, and the fact affords Shelley a distant yet powerful phonetic link that spans and condenses the relation in this opening verse paragraph between the mad rush of the 'vast river' and the 'everlasting universe of things' to which it metaphorically corresponds. As a dimension of poetic form wrought from the mysterious arbitrariness of language, Shelley's rhyme becomes both a stay against and a means of marking the chaos and blankness which are *Mont Blanc*'s special concerns.

In thinking about the purposes rhyme serves in *Mont Blanc*, we need to look at the way it functions both in terms of its own inherent possibilities and in relation to the syntax and rhythm of Shelley's periods. We must be careful not to isolate rhyme as the vehicle of the structuring, organizing intellect in easy contrast to the sweeping, impetuous emotional energy of the long, overflowing sentences: both are aspects of Shelley's 'attempt to imitate' an experience in which philosophical skepticism and impassioned intuition are held in suspension. Take the second couplet in the opening verse paragraph:

> Where waterfalls around it leap for ever,
> Where woods and winds contend, and a vast river
> Over its rocks ceaselessly bursts and raves.
>
> (9–11)

'For ever' and 'river' here seem at once to confirm the proposition with which the poem opens – 'The everlasting universe of things / Flows through the mind' (1–2) – and yet to convey a certain probing openness, both because the rhyme is partial, imperfect (the imperfection stands out against the initial repetition of 'Where' / 'Where'), and because the absence of any pause after 'river' leaves that line open to flow into the next. This couplet is again left open in part IV, where its reversal shifts the emphasis from 'river' to 'for ever' ('all seems eternal now' the speaker has said in line 75, after first taking in the summit of Mont Blanc). The couplet is followed by 'raves' in line 11, by 'waves' in line 125:

> and one majestic River,
> The breath and blood of distant lands, for ever
> Rolls its loud waters to the ocean waves,
> Breathes its swift vapours to the circling air.
>
> (123–6)

The last word in this passage, 'air', is part of what is perhaps the most striking group of postponed or suspended rhyme-words in *Mont Blanc*. Part II ends with the word 'there', with no immediate companion or echo: 'till the breast / From which they fled recalls them, thou art there! (47–8). That this line appears to be unrhymed is appropriate in a passage about the momentary, precarious apprehension of 'some faint image' (47) of the awesome, personified Ravine of Arve. But 'there' does eventually get its complement in the insubstantial 'air' at the end of part IV. Once this very distant rhyme has been completed, it is immediately confirmed at the end of the first line of part V: 'Mont Blanc yet gleams on high: – the power is there' (127). This is the only point in the poem where a couplet spans two verse paragraphs (although 'raves' and 'Ravine' between parts I and II, both of which contain anagrams of the name 'Arve', and 'feel' and 'streams' between parts III and IV, may seem to foreshadow such a spanning). Yet to link two separate sections together by rhyme in this way is also to pull the couplet apart: every resolution in *Mont Blanc* has at least an undertow of dissolution. The 'there' / 'air' / 'there' sequence is extended a few lines later in part V, but this time the sense of the passage cuts across even the tentativeness of those previous assertions that some presence is 'there': 'in the lone glare of day, the snows descend / Upon that Mountain; none beholds them there' (131–2). The internal rhyme in these lines ('glare' / 'there') illuminates the discrepancy between the mind's power of perception and its limitations in gaining access to reality's ultimate source. The same daylight which renders things visible in the speaker's immediate realm of experience 'glares' upon the snows of Mont Blanc –

but 'there', remote and apart from any beholder, daylight itself seems to lose all connection with human intellection.

The 'there' (48) / 'there' (127) / 'there' (132) pattern is Shelley's finest exploitation in *Mont Blanc* of identical rhyme, of a word rhyming (and re-rhyming) with itself. Homonymic rhyme (punning rhyme, *rime très riche*), in which entire rhyme-words are phonetically identical but semantically different, is a related but distinct phenomenon. Hollander assents to the prejudice against such rhyme when he argues that because of 'the crucial relation between the effect of word stress and the quality of rhyme in English . . . *rime très riche* is always in a sense, *rime pauvre*.'[19] But the two instances of it in *Mont Blanc* indicate how alert Shelley could be to the ways in which even flamboyantly fortuitous rhyme could help him mark the mind's response to the wild and the inaccessible. 'Throne' (17) / 'overthrown' (112) is not a pure example (it is analogous phonetically, though not semantically, to 'form' / 'deform' in *The Triumph of Life*), but given Shelley's politics it might appear to be a suggestive one. The suggestiveness is not, however, exactly predictable. Although earthly thrones, so often the embodiments for Shelley of 'Large codes of fraud and woe' (81), are implicitly included in what will be 'overthrown' by the 'Power' in part IV as it flows down from its remote abode, that 'Power' has itself been imaged as occupying a 'secret throne'. So 'throne' stands distantly and indirectly in relation to 'overthrown' as subject, not object, a relation in keeping with Shelley's skeptical ambivalence towards the 'Power'. The fact that both 'throne' and 'overthrown' form imperfect couplets with 'down' (16, 111) further complicates the suggestiveness of this rhyme group.

The other homonymic rhyme in *Mont Blanc* affords a purer example of this phenomenon and more telling evidence of Shelley's resourcefulness in handling what would appear to be deliberately restricted verbal possibilities. At the beginning of part II, when he first names the Ravine of Arve as the immediate location of his experience, he addresses the ravine as 'Thou many-coloured, many-voiced vale' (13). Twelve lines later, when the first of these compound adjectives is expanded and particularized, the 'vale' becomes, or is seen to contain, a 'veil':[20]

> Thine earthly rainbows stretched across the sweep
> Of the ethereal waterfall, whose veil
> Robes some unsculptured image . . .
>
> (25–7)

'Poetry', Shelley says in the *Defence*, '. . . arrests the vanishing apparitions which haunt the interlunations of life, and veiling them, or in language or in form, sends them forth among mankind' (*PP*, 505). One is again tempted to follow this line of thought and figuration and apply the images in *Mont Blanc* to the poem itself, to see the 'ethereal waterfall' as a metaphor for the poem's own verbal veiling of what may be accessible only to momentary, vanishing intuition. The 'veil' in these lines, as so often in Shelley, has a double valence – it simultaneously conceals and reveals – and the movement from 'vale' to 'veil' is by no means entirely negative (compare the function of Iris and 'her many coloured scarf' in *The Triumph of Life*, 357). There is a sense in which this aspect of the 'vale' hides the 'unsculptured image' behind it; there is also a sense, partly enforced by the verb 'Robes', that the 'veil' is what makes this unspecified ('some'), uncreated image exist for the mind at all. Shelley's homonymic rhyme signals the precarious balance and interaction between skepticism and visionary imagination so important in this section and throughout the poem.

Rhyme in *Mont Blanc* is not, then, as 'wildly irregular' as it has been thought to be. It is sufficiently irregular to help evoke the 'untameable wildness' Shelley spoke of: some of the most interesting rhymes in the poem are so distant and so muted by distended syntax that the reader may find them as 'remote' and 'inaccessible' as Mont Blanc itself. With the three unrhymed lines Shelley's rhyme remains open, partly unresolved. Yet rhyme is there as one of the resources with which the poet verbally counters as well as encounters an experience of threatening power and sublimity. A glance at Shelley's final question, together with the sentence that precedes it, may help to confirm our sense of why he did not ask about Mont Blanc in blank verse:

> The secret strength of things
> Which governs thought, and to the infinite dome
> Of heaven is as a law, inhabits thee!
> And what were thou, and earth, and stars, and sea,
> If to the human mind's imaginings
> Silence and solitude were vacancy?
>
> (139–44)

At the beginning of the poem, 'things' (1) became Shelley's first rhyme-word by finding its phonetic complement in 'secret springs' (4), a phrase which appears prominently and characteristically in the opening section of Hume's *Enquiry Concerning Human Understanding* as a metaphor for

the unknowable first principle 'by which the human mind is actuated in
its operations'.[21] Here at the end of *Mont Blanc*, 'things' finds a rhyme
with a different, apparently less skeptical resonance in 'imaginings',
although the difference diminishes when one takes in the immediate
context of those words: the 'secret strength of things' in line 139; the if-
clause and interrogative syntax surrounding 'the human mind's
imaginings'. 'Thee' in line 140 forms a couplet with 'sea' and thus
supports the initial 'And' through which the final question is joined
logically to what precedes it. And does 'vacancy' belong in this rhyming
sequence with 'thee' and 'sea'? It both does and does not: the '-cy' suffix
rhymes with 'thee' and 'sea', but imperfectly, because it is rhythmically
unstressed and because it is attached to the root *vacan(s)*. Shelley
simultaneously draws that critical last word into and separates it from
the central rhyme of the entire passage – 'vacancy' seems both to yield
to and to resist the rhyming power of the compositional will – and in the
process he makes us conscious of the ambiguous categorizations on
which rhyme depends in the first place.

The rhymes of *Mont Blanc* are part of Shelley's response to a
landscape and to a philosophical tradition – 'to the Arve's commotion, /
A loud, lone sound no other sound can tame' (31–2), and to Hume's
argument that the 'ultimate springs and principles' of phenomenal
reality 'are totally shut up from human curiosity and enquiry', that the
mind's attempts to make sense of them as necessity are nothing more
than arbitrary impositions:

> every effect is a distinct event from its cause. It could not,
> therefore, be discovered in the cause, and the first invention or
> conception of it, *a priori*, must be entirely arbitrary. And even after
> it is suggested, the conjunction of it with the cause must appear
> equally arbitrary.[22]
>
> (*An Enquiry Concerning Human Understanding*, IV.1)

Shelley's irregular rhymes do not tame the wildness of a 'sound no other
sound can tame', nor can they break the inaccessible silence at the
summit of Mont Blanc. But they impose on his and our experience of
both an order of language that accepts the arbitrary and submits it to the
deliberations of art. They are part of the evidence the poem offers that
the arbitrary connections of thought and language need not leave the
'human mind's imaginings' in vacancy.

VII SHELLEY'S LAST LYRICS

' "I have suffered what I wrote," ' says Rousseau in *The Triumph of Life*,

> 'And so my words were seeds of misery –
> Even as the deeds of others.'
>
> (280–1)

These words may mean that Rousseau's writing gave expression to sufferings he had actually lived through – this is certainly what we would expect the author of *The Confessions* to claim. But they may just as well mean that he, and others, eventually lived through sufferings brought about by, or first expressed theoretically and fictively in, his writing. Words can be 'seeds of misery' both because they are sown by and because they sow suffering. Count Maddalo offers a similarly equivocal pronouncement in commenting on the 'wild language' that he and Julian have heard the madman utter:

> 'Most wretched men
> Are cradled into poetry by wrong,
> They learn in suffering what they teach in song.'
>
> (544–6)

Unless he is drawing a contrasting and not a summarizing maxim from what they have observed in the asylum, it is perverse, even for Maddalo, to say that the madman has been 'cradled' by wrong into his tormented discourse. Be that as it may, Maddalo at first seems to place 'wrong' deeds in a clearly anterior position to poetry. But the indeterminate grammar of that last line obscures any sense of even provisional clarity. We expect the line to say that men teach in 'song' what they have already learned in 'suffering', and such a reading is grammatically plausible. But the syntax also encourages a reverse reading: men learn in 'suffering' what they have already taught in 'song' (and notice that the phrase 'what they teach in song' may be the direct object either of 'learn' or of 'suffering'). Like Rousseau, Maddalo holds open the possibility that the words of poetry may be 'seeds of misery – / Even as the deeds of others.'

I begin with these troubled, uncertain broodings about words and deeds, song and suffering, by way of introducing a critical perspective that has been consciously set aside or underplayed in previous chapters, where the aim has been to give priority to the formal features of Shelley's writing and to concepts and attitudes characteristic of his own way of thinking about poetic language. If the advantages of that approach are at all apparent by now, so too is one disadvantage: it has inevitably isolated the poems from historical and biographical pressures that often, we may assume, had as much to do with their coming into being as did Shelley's compositional will and verbal resourcefulness. This is not a matter of apologetic reverence for 'biographical criticism' – of nostalgia for what a deconstructive reader of Wordsworth has called 'mimetical trivia'[1] – but rather of allowing one's primary concern with the work and play of language in the text to remain open to whatever context the text itself makes pertinent. So I want to conclude this study by looking at a group of poems in which Shelley's stylistic choices and performances are inextricably enmeshed in the choices and performances of living.

I

While there is a great deal of critical interest now in *The Triumph of Life*, probably written in May and June of 1822, much less has been said about the shorter poems Shelley wrote during the six months before his death on 8 July. Some have found it easy to dismiss these lyrics as 'slight pieces',[2] 'ariettes' (as Shelley himself once called them) that show us little more than that he could be urbane and melancholy at the same time. Those who have taken the poems more seriously, on the other hand, have sometimes done so in a slightly misleading way. Here is Harold Bloom in *The Oxford Anthology of English Literature*: 'Shelley's heart, when he died, had begun to touch the limits of desire, as his final love lyrics show. A tough but subtle temperament, he had worn himself out, and was ready to depart.'[3] This sort of elegiac despair seems apter to *Adonais* than to the lyrics of 1822; it is an attitude that makes itself felt in these poems, but only in relation to other quite different, even antagonistic, impulses.

For six months Jane Williams was Shelley's muse, lyric focus and – with her husband Edward – primary audience. Four of the 1822 lyrics refer 'to Jane' in their titles; five others are less explicitly, but no less centrally, about her. The Williamses had come to Pisa in January 1821 at the suggestion of Shelley's cousin, Thomas Medwin; in January 1822 they were living directly below the Shelleys in a building called the Tre Palazzi di Chiesa, on the north side of the Arno.[4] They were married only in common law. Jane Cleveland (her maiden name) had been left by a first husband with whom she was apparently unhappy; since living with Williams, a retired lieutenant in the army of the East India Company, she had given birth to two children, the second one after arriving in Pisa in March 1821.[5] Her relationship with Shelley has of course been the subject of much scholarly sleuthing and speculation. When he first met them, Shelley preferred Edward: he was more literary and intellectual (for a time he was taking down daily dictation of Shelley's translation of Spinoza's *Tractatus Theologico-Politicus*), and being an experienced sailor, he was a good companion for Shelley's boating expeditions on the Arno. Shelley at first found Jane 'extremely pretty & gentle' but 'apparently not *very* clever'. Yet even in this letter to Claire Clairmont (16 January 1821) he confessed, having 'only seen her for an hour', that 'I like her very much'. He continued to have reservations, at least when writing to Claire: 'W. I like & have got reconciled to Jane' (14 May 1821). But by January 1822 the reservations had given way to warmly intimate and idealizing affection. He described her to John Gisborne as 'more amiable and beautiful than ever, and a sort of spirit of embodied peace in our circle of tempests', adding 'So much for first impressions!' (12 January 1822).

Just how intimate Jane Williams and Shelley became during the last half-year of his life has been much disputed. Walter E. Peck claimed to have seen an unpublished letter from Shelley to Byron in which Shelley says that he made love to her one evening after they had gone together to a local *festa* near San Terenzo.[6] The letter has never been found or substantiated. More recently, G.M. Matthews has used a combination of literary and biographical inference to argue that Shelley's serious intimacy with Jane Williams 'developed late and very rapidly at San Terenzo towards a crisis', that they became lovers during the latter part of June, and that this was 'the most profoundly disturbing personal experience of Shelley's whole maturity'.[7] Matthews' argument has been countered in extensive detail by Donald Reiman, who insists that there is no evidence from Shelley's writing or from his life to justify our concluding that the relationship with Jane Williams was ever anything but idealizing and 'Platonic'.[8] Others who have looked at the evidence, most notably Judith Chernaik, think that Shelley was in love with her by spring 1822 but that exactly what that love came to must remain a matter of speculation.[9] There are multiple unintended ironies, then, in Newman Ivey White's saying that 'The only authentic record of the high-water mark of Shelley's attraction to Jane Williams is Shelley's own poems.'[10] Poetic fictions lead beyond themselves to actual events and circumstances, which in turn lead back to the poems as our 'only authentic record'. Words themselves may be deeds, it would seem, as well as the seeds of deeds.

While Jane Williams stands at the center of the 1822 lyrics, other figures from what Shelley calls 'our circle of tempests' haunt these poems in ways which have never been taken adequately into account. One of these is certainly Mary Shelley; another is Claire Clairmont. Shelley's relationship to Mary had been under repeated, almost constant strain since the death of their daughter Clara in September 1818, which Mary partly blamed, and with some justification, on a grueling amount of travel designed to put Shelley and Claire in touch with Byron and Allegra in Venice. One source of the strain was Claire herself, whose ambiguous closeness to Shelley had always made Mary uneasy. That uneasiness was sharply exacerbated in August 1821 by the so-called 'Hoppner scandal': Mary learned in a letter from Shelley that Richard Hoppner, British consul-general at Venice, and his wife had been spreading the story 'that Claire was my mistress' and that in the winter of 1818–19 'Clare was with child by me – that I gave her the most violent medicines to procure abortion – that . . . this not succeeding she was brought to bed & that I immediately tore the child from her & sent it to the foundling hospital.' Mary did not believe that Claire had given birth to Shelley's child. But that Claire had been his lover Shelley himself did not explicitly deny ('that is all very well & so far there is nothing new: all the world has heard so much & people may believe or not believe as they think good'). The Hoppner scandal revived Mary's worries about Shelley and Claire just when Shelley's fascination with Emilia Viviani had run its course (her arranged marriage finally took place 8 September 1821).

Mary's alienation from Shelley, which he complained about but also seems to have resigned himself to, is not only understandable but surprisingly temperate, given the circumstances. It was one thing to accept Shelley's principles of non-exclusive love, as Mary seems to have done; it was another to be almost continuously pregnant or nursing while moving from one place to another in a foreign country (she was pregnant five times during the seven years between 1815 and 1822), and then to find herself depicted symbolically in *Epipsychidion* as the 'cold chaste Moon' whose 'soft yet icy flame . . . warms not but illumines' (281–5). Shelley, for his part, could not have turned poetically to Jane Williams without thinking of what it implied about his commitment to Mary – and less directly to Claire Clairmont, whose correspondence with Shelley was often kept secret from Mary during these months.

Then there was Byron, whose shadow is superimposed on those of Mary Shelley and Claire Clairmont in the lyrics of 1822. Mary wrote to Maria Gisborne on 30 November 1821:

> So here we live, Lord B just opposite to us in Casa Lanfranchi. . . .
> Pisa you see has become a little nest of singing birds – You will be both surprised and delighted at the work just about to be published by him. . . . It made a great impression upon me, and appears almost a revelation from its power and beauty – Shelley rides with him – I, of course, see little of him.[11]

The mixture of subdued sarcasm and admiration in this letter is intensely suggestive of the situation in Pisa during the winter of 1821–2. The focus, 'of course', is on Byron, who had arrived on the scene at the beginning of November and whose presence exerted an enormous pressure on what Shelley wrote at this time – and more tellingly perhaps, on what he did not write.

Shelley was remarkably open to Byron's talent and power, in spite of the fact that they had come increasingly to threaten his own personal and poetic self-confidence. This was the fourth time Shelley had lived in Byron's presence:[12] each time his estimation of Byron's greatness grew, along with the sense of his own comparative inadequacy. If we look backwards and forwards chronologically from 1 November 1821, when Byron arrived in Pisa, over equal stretches of Shelley's career, we find that this date marks a striking drop in productivity. The nine months before Byron arrived, from February through October 1821, are filled with major projects conceived and written to completion: *Epipsychidion*, *A Defence of Poetry*, *Adonais*, *Hellas*, along with more than thirty lyrics. The 'Sonnet to Byron', probably written in November shortly after Byron's arrival,[13] marks the interface between this

extraordinary fecundity and a time of relative barrenness. It begins with
what turned out to be a prophetic conjecture:

> If I esteemed you less, Envy would kill
> Pleasure, and leave to Wonder and Despair
> The ministration of the thoughts that fill
> The mind which, like a worm whose life may share
> A portion of the unapproachable,
> Marks your creations rise as fast and fair
> As perfect worlds at the Creator's will.
>
> (1–7)

In the nine months after Byron's arrival, Shelley produced only ten or
so lyrics, some fragmentary translations from Calderon and Goethe, the
Fragments of an Unfinished Drama (*PW*, 482–8), and the unfinished
Triumph of Life, which he was able to begin writing only after he left
Byron and Pisa and moved up the coast to San Terenzo on the Bay of
Lerici. There was also *Charles I*, his only major ambition during that
winter, but that went very haltingly. 'Lord Byron is established now, [&
gives a weekly dinner *deleted*] & we are constant companions,' he wrote
to Peacock in January 1822; 'I have been long idle, – & as far as writing
goes, despondent – but I am now engaged in Charles the 1st & a devil of
a nut it is to crack' (*Letters*, II, 373). Subsequent letters make it clear that
Shelley's imaginative dryness and despondency arose mainly from his
measuring his own achievement and public success against Byron's.
Having told Leigh Hunt that 'particular dispositions in Lord B's character
render the close & exclusive intimacy with him in which I find myself,
intolerable to me,' he goes on to say: 'Indeed I have written nothing for
this last two months. . . . What motives have I to write. – I *had* motives . . .
but what are *those* motives now?' (2 March 1822; *Letters* II, 393–4).

The complex tension and rivalry between Shelley and Byron, the
sources of which were by no means exclusively literary, have been most
recently and fully detailed by Charles E. Robinson and Richard
Holmes. Holmes's account of their favorite pastime, target practice
with pistols, is symbolically suggestive at almost every level:

> The shooting gradually changed from a casual exercise into a
> shared obsession. Byron rode out on a Hussar saddle slung with
> several pistols in decorated leather holsters; Shelley spent several
> hours a week preparing his own targets and carried them round in
> his pockets. . . . he and Byron seemed to have been by far the best
> shots among the party and there was a certain rivalry between the

two. Tom Medwin noted their different styles of shooting: Byron drew a long aim, with a hand that visibly trembled, yet usually produced a high standard of hits. Shelley, on the contrary, took a sudden, rapid aim, with a rock-steady hand – 'all firmness' [Medwin's phrase] – and also produced regularly good shooting. Of the two, one has the impression from Williams's journal that Byron had the edge.[14]

Another anecdote reconstructed by Holmes evokes the drama of Shelley and Byron's literary talks and is more pointedly relevant to Byron's impact on Shelley's poetic self-confidence:

Byron ... always appeared to submit to Shelley's critical judgement on literary matters (it being understood that he regarded *Don Juan* and *Cain* as very great poems). Medwin was immensely impressed by this fact when one morning Byron handed Shelley the manuscript of a poem 'The Deformed Transformed'. Shelley took it over to the window to read, and having read it carefully, returned to where Byron leaned against the mantelpiece and announced that 'he liked it the least of all his works; that it smelt too strongly of "Faust"; and besides, that there were two lines in it, word for word from Southey.' Medwin quailed inwardly at the cool frankness of this judgement, but '. . . Byron turned deadly pale, seized the MS., and committed it to the flames, seeming to take a savage delight in seeing it consume'. Yet in part, this too was a stage device. Byron had another copy safely in his desk, and a revised version was published two years later by Murray.[15]

Robinson's discussion of *The Deformed Transformed* adds a new dimension to Shelley's criticism of the manuscript and to Byron's 'savage delight' in apparently committing it to the flames. Byron's play contains a double transformation suggested to him, Robinson argues, by Shelley, who told Byron about a scene involving a similar device in Calderon's *El Purgatorio de San Patricio*. Unable to go forward with *Charles I*, Shelley had 'at the same time inadvertently given Byron the idea for a new drama' of his own.[16]

Shelley could not win with Byron, and he seems to have known it. His very openness to Byron's ruthless efficacy was bound to erode what confidence he had in, what ambitions he had for, his own major projects. In the 1822 lyrics we can see Shelley turning away from any direct competition with Byron – away from ambitious works on the scale of *Don Juan* and *Cain*, or *Prometheus Unbound* and *Adonais* – towards a more modest and intimate mode that he knew he was good at. But this does not mean that in these lyrics Shelley was able to write free of the pressure of Byron's success, any more than he could have written them without thinking of Mary's unhappiness, or of Claire's continuing dependence on his support and affection, or of his own dependence on their dependence on him. Just how Shelley's last lyrics contend with and accommodate anxieties they often seem to be trying to avoid is one of the questions I now want to pursue.

II

It may have been to try to get away from Byron and the established round of pistol-shooting and talking about each other's poetry that Shelley went for a day-long walk on 2 February with Jane Williams and Mary Shelley in the Cascine pine forest just outside Pisa. He drafted a 116-line poem about this occasion; he then revised the draft, split it into two poems, and gave them to Jane under the titles 'To Jane. The Invitation' and 'To Jane. The Recollection'. It has often been pointed out about both the draft and the revised poems that Mary is nowhere to be seen. True – and yet she haunts every line of these lyrics, which are the most important poems Shelley worked to completion in 1822. Less immediately, Byron haunts them too. The ways in which they are both there in Shelley's writing in spite of, or perhaps through, their apparent absence is part of what needs further consideration.

If we read 'The Invitation' and 'The Recollection' together, we find that Shelley has situated himself rhetorically on either side of the transient moment of lyrical intensity he attempts to define and sustain. One poem looks forward, the other backward, to a moment when he and Jane are together in the natural scene – but that moment itself is always out of reach, always either a wish or a memory. Shelley accentuated this sense of the inaccessibility of the moment of completion or fulfillment when he divided the original poem in two as he revised it. But the division is already there, strikingly, in the unified first draft. After an introductory quatrain, that draft moves through twenty-eight lines of tetrameter couplets that will eventually provide the foundation for 'The Invitation'. Then at line 33, before Jane has ever had a chance to accept the invitation and join the speaker in 'the

wild woods and the plains' (25), we hear that 'the last day of many days'
'is dead' (33, 35). As the speaker calls upon 'Memory' to 'Rise . . . and
write its praise!' (36), rhythm and rhyme-scheme undergo a subtle
adjustment, and then settle into the ballad quatrain that becomes the
new formal idiom for that part of the draft that will become 'The
Recollection'. Although 'The Invitation' insists that 'To-day is for itself
enough' (40), Shelley seems to have felt from the beginning that the
moment with Jane could be articulated only as a prospective or
retrospective construct of the imagination.

He develops the prospective movement of 'The Invitation' through a
subtly muted variation on the *carpe diem* invitation genre that includes
poems like Herrick's 'Corinna's going a Maying'.[17] Where Herrick
urges Corinna into a 'blooming morn' in May –

Rise; and put on your Foliage, and be seene
To come forth, like the Spring-time, fresh and greene;[18]

(15–16)

Shelley invites Jane to join him on a winter morning that is prematurely
and still only incipiently spring-like:

The brightest hour of unborn spring
Through the winter wandering
Found, it seems, this halcyon morn
To hoar February born . . .

(7–10)

Shelley's speaker, like Herrick's, is already in the natural scene;
rhetorically the invitation issues from a temporal sequence that is
already underway (compositionally, of course, the invitation was
written in retrospective anticipation of a past experience). The erotic
impetus and wit of Herrick's poem are muted and displaced onto the
landscape, where they work to release the scene's unobtrusive
autobiographical symbolism:

Bending from Heaven in azure mirth
It kissed the forehead of the earth
And smiled upon the silent sea,
And bade the frozen streams be free
And waked to music all their fountains . . .

(11–15)

'Fairer far than this fair day' (2), Jane herself has been a prophetess of this 'prophetess of May' (17) who has warmed and freed a stream of song that had previously been frozen – almost entirely frozen, one could say, since Byron's arrival at the beginning of November. Characteristically, Shelley reverses the direction in which the basic figurative situation might be expected to move: it is not that Jane's effect on the speaker is like this morning's effect on the winter landscape, but – at the beginning and again at the end of the first verse paragraph – the other way around:

> Making the wintry world appear
> Like one on whom thou smilest, dear.
>
> (19–20)

Within the poem's rhetorical fiction, Jane is being invited to experience the natural enactment of a momentary imaginative reawakening she has already inspired.

Shelley's refined awareness of literary tradition is nowhere more apparent than in 'The Invitation', and it is not at all surprising that Donald Davie once paid it such handsome tribute in the chapter of *Purity of Diction in English Verse* he called 'Shelley's urbanity'. The poem, he wrote, is

> a nonpareil, and one of Shelley's greatest achievements. It maintains the familiar tone, though in highly figured language, and contrives to be urbane about feelings which are novel and remote. . . . We can accept Jane as 'Radiant Sister of the Day', largely because the lyrical feeling has already accommodated such seemingly unmanageable things as unpaid bills and unaccustomed visitors. It is an achievement of urbanity to move with such ease from financial and social entanglements to elated sympathy with a natural process; just as it is a mark of civilization to be able to hold these things together in one unflurried attitude.[19]

If this were all there were to say about the poem, it would be enough to make it a poem worth caring about (in spite of Davie's sour and undetailed retraction of his tribute more than ten years later).[20] But there is, I think, much more that needs to be said. If the poem is an instance of 'urbanity', then that term has to be able to accommodate forces which are darker and more deeply unsettling than unpaid bills and unwanted visitors (threatening though these were to Shelley in 1822). The larger structural pattern of Shelley's approach in 'The Invitation' and 'The Recollection', and in the draft from which they derive, should remind us of a famous stanza from 'To a Skylark':

> We look before and after,[21]
>   And pine for what is not –
> Our sincerest laughter
>   With some pain is fraught –
> Our sweetest songs are those that tell of saddest thought.
>
> (86–90)

The prevailing tone of urbane romantic familiarity in 'The Invitation' is shot through with references to a realm of sadness, anxiety and guilt which Shelley seems – and perhaps only seems – to be trying to set aside or banish.

Look at the second verse paragraph, all of which Shelley added in revision. With its inset 'notice on my door' (29) and wittily personified abstractions, this is the most eighteenth-century section of the poem and predictably the focus of much of Davie's praise. Yet from the beginning the paragraph evokes a world of frustration and disappointment from which it never manages fully to escape. Come away, the speaker says,

> To the silent wilderness
> Where the soul need not repress
> Its music lest it should not find
> An echo in another's mind . . .
>
> (23–6)

The fact that 'find' here does find an echo in the 'mind' that completes Shelley's fluent couplet may be appropriate to the anticipated meeting of minds with Jane, but it also throws into relief the memory or expectation of moments devoid both of music and of responsive echo. Reading a reference to Mary or Byron in these lines is possible but unnecessary to seeing how strongly the speaker's celebration of the moment he longs for with Jane is conditioned by an awareness of its opposite. One of the things Shelley wants to put on hold here is the echo of his own mind:

> Reflexion, you may come tomorrow,
> Sit by the fireside with Sorrow –
>
> (33–4)

But reflection will not stay at home until 'tomorrow' with 'Sorrow': in the final verse paragraph it is right there in the forest with the speaker as he waits for Jane, projected figuratively in

> . . . the pools where winter-rains
> Image all their roof of leaves,
> Where the pine its garland weaves
> Of sapless green and ivy dun
> Round stems that never kiss the Sun –

(50–4)

This scene, beautifully and delicately articulated (the semantic antithesis in the rhyming of 'dun' with 'Sun' precisely condenses the tone of the passage), is potentially one of those arenas of reflexive self-involvement reaching all the way back through Shelley's career to *Alastor*. The image of 'stems that never kiss the Sun' momentarily reverses the opening image of the 'halcyon morn' as 'It kissed the forehead of the earth' (9, 12), and we may feel that Shelley has inadvertently found himself in a spot where Jane's and the spring-like morning's influence will be of no avail. The poem does not linger beside these embowered reflecting pools, however; it moves on to other vantage points, and to a climactic harmony in which the sun's unifying light and warmth prevail. At the end 'Sun' is bound in a couplet with 'one', not 'dun'. But we will return to those pools in 'The Recollection', and their figurative implications will be worked through to a very different conclusion.

'The Recollection' begins by acknowledging that the moment celebrated anticipatorily in 'The Invitation' was an 'evanescent visitation', a 'vanishing apparition' seemingly 'arrested' in advance in the previous poem through the artifice of a fictive invitation, but now traceable only by writing 'The epitaph of glory fled' (6). That rhyme-word 'trace' in line 5 suggests that Shelley may already be recalling his figure of inspiration as 'a wind over a sea' from the *Defence*; the 'epitaph of glory fled' indicates that Wordsworth has displaced Herrick as the text Shelley is now taking as a point of departure. 'The Recollection' has been less admired than 'The Invitation', mainly, I think, because the urbane familiarity of the first poem is much less effective here in muting and disguising the underlying anxiety. Particular elements of the natural scene undergo dramatic transformations. The somber, embowering pines of 'The Invitation' are now seen as

> the pines that stood
> The giants of the waste,

> Tortured by storms to shapes as rude
> As serpents interlaced . . .
>
> (21–4)

Even the day's paradisal calm, although it temporarily soothes the violent impulses now evident in the landscape, is latently threatening. This is precisely what bothered Leavis about the poem. Alert as he always was to Wordsworth's importance for Shelley, Leavis argued that the calm in section 3 of 'The Recollection'

> is the reverse of Wordsworthian; the peace is indeed momentary. What is bound is not the silence, but the impending violation – the chain will break; for 'inviolable' [37] suggests the opposite of what it says, and the characteristic leaning movement conveys the opposite of security. A Wordsworthian atmosphere is never filled with love, and love here is at the same time a sultry menace.[22]

Often in his writing about Shelley, Leavis gets hold of the right point in the wrong way. In the midst of this crotchety denunciation he says just what needs to be said about 'inviolable quietness'. And while 'sultry menace' seems extreme for a passage with a 'busy woodpecker' in it (35), there is latent in the scene an element of erotic intensity that threatens to make the peace, as Shelley says in line 47, 'momentary'. Leavis goes on to object specifically to Shelley's having substituted 'thrilling silent life' (46) for the allegedly more Wordsworthian 'thinking silent life' of the first draft (70). But 'thrilling', with its suggestions of intense arousal and its etymological implication of 'piercing' or 'penetrating', does something much more interesting to 'silent life' than does 'thinking'.[23] Leavis is right about 'the characteristic leaning movement' of this passage: thirteen of the twenty lines lack end-stopping, and the verse accumulates a kind of energy that infuses with suspense the insistence on 'How calm it was!'

> The breath of peace we drew
> With its soft motion made not less
> The calm that round us grew. –
>
> (38–40)

There is a veiled tension or pressure in this intake of breath and in the calm 'that round us grew', much as there is in the prior reference to 'The inviolable quietness'. One feels that the 'leaning' Leavis perceives comes from an urgent striving to hold in check 'Our mortal nature's strife' (48).

The sense of erotic energy and personal anxiety under precarious and perhaps illusory control is important to what Shelley makes of those reflecting pools from 'The Invitation' in the last two sections of 'The Recollection'. At first they may seem innocent enough as picturesque analogues for the idealizing imagination as it attempts to discover a transcendent realm represented there in the natural scene:

> We paused beside the pools that lie
>   Under the forest bough –
> Each seemed as 'twere, a little sky
>   Gulphed in a world below;
> A firmament of purple light
>   Which in the dark earth lay
> More boundless than the depth of night
>   And purer than the day,
> In which the lovely forests grew
>   As in the upper air,
> More perfect, both in shape and hue,
>   Than any spreading there . . .[24]
>
> (53–64)

But the illogically extravagant comparative rhetoric – 'More boundless' and especially 'More perfect' – destabilizes the activity of idealizing reflection by making it seem driven, 'leaning'. 'More boundless' even threatens to undo that binding of 'Our mortal nature's strife' to 'momentary peace' in the previous section. What the process of idealizing reflection is being driven by is revealed in the poem's final section:

> Sweet views, which in our world above
>   Can never well be seen,
> Were imaged in the water's love
>   Of that fair forest green . . .
>
> (69–72)

As Shelley draws out the implications of recognizing that love pervades the poem's 'inviolable quietness' and motivates its idealizing representation, the waters of the pool are darkly personified, the image they reflect becomes delusively untruthful, and the 'atmosphere without a breath' moves with the breath of envy:

Like one beloved, the scene had lent
  To the dark water's breast,
Its every leaf and lineament
  With more than truth exprest;
Until an envious wind crept by,
  Like an unwelcome thought
Which from the mind's too faithful eye
  Blots one dear image out. –

                                                                    (77–84)

Shelley's revisions of and additions to the first draft are particularly revealing in this passage. Lines 77–80, with their darkening confirmation of what love's part in the experience may mean, are entirely new. 'Wandering wind' in the draft becomes 'envious wind' in the revision. Most commentators have identified this wind and the 'unwelcome thought' to which it is compared (in one of the most simply effective of Shelley's reversed similes) with Mary, who has been excluded from the poem but who makes her absence felt here at the end to a frustrated and perhaps guilty Shelley.[25] The question of guilt is ambiguous: How are we to take 'too faithful'? 'Too faithful' to Mary (with an undertone of bitter resentment)? Or 'too faithful' to the actual circumstances of his life? If we are looking for biographical referents, the wind's envy might be Shelley's instead of (or as well as) Mary's, and refer to Shelley's worrying about Byron. After all, that 'Sonnet to Byron' had begun with the grim surmise that 'If I esteemed you less, Envy would kill / Pleasure.'

But no biographical reading alone is adequate to the way in which Shelley finally undoes the reflection imagery as it has evolved through the two poems by reworking the figure of inspiration as 'a wind over a sea' from the *Defence*. There it is the 'coming calm' that inevitably erases the wind's ephemeral imprint on the water's surface. Here the action is reversed: a moment of inspired calm within 'A magic circle traced', as Shelley says in line 44, does not 'erase' but is itself blotted out – the writing imagery is remarkably insistent – by a wind that mocks the breath of inspiration and brings the poem's writing, its activity of 'trac[ing] / The epitaph of glory fled' (5–6), to an end. If there is a way of squaring or reconciling these seemingly incongruous figures of wind and water, it is by recognizing that the 'envious wind' and the disturbing, unwelcome thoughts figured in it are in fact the poem's deep source of inspiration – that both 'The Invitation' and 'The Recollection' are defenses against, and in that antithetical sense are inspired by, thoughts which are only partly excluded from or bound within the 'magic circle' centered around Jane. To 'trace / The epitaph of glory fled' is to rewrite or re-record a death that has already been marked and inscribed. The epitaph traced in 'The Recollection' may be implicit in the elusive ephemerality of the moment described with fictive anticipation in 'The Invitation'.

III

The lyrics of 1822 transgress the boundary separating words from deeds. It is a deed, an act which springs from but also might be expected to cause suffering, for Shelley to make Jane Williams fill in the missing name at the end of 'The Recollection' when he gave the poems to her (this is how the last two lines appear in the British library fair copy):

> Less oft is peace in –––'s mind
>   Than calm in water seen.

Other lyrics too are deeds in that they were not only written for Jane but were shown or given to her as half-furtive, half-open acts of personal communication. Consider three poems also belonging to the early months of 1822. On 26 January, a week before the walk in the Cascine pine forest that occasioned 'The Invitation' and 'The Recollection', Shelley enclosed a seven-stanza poem entitled 'To ––' and beginning 'The serpent is shut out from Paradise' with the following note to 'My dear Williams':

> Looking over the portfolio in which my friend used to keep verses, & in which those I sent you the other day were found, – I have lit upon these; which as they are too dismal for *me* to keep I send them you [who can afford *deleted*].
>
>   If any of the stanzas should please you, you may read them to Jane, but to no one else, – and yet on second thought I had rather you would not [*some six words scratched out*].
>
> (Letters, ii, 384)

The blatantly transparent disguise ('my friend'), divided emotions, insinuatingly underscored pronoun and still legible deletions in this note are all gestures to be found in Shelley's poems of this period as well. 'The Magnetic Lady to Her Patient' can be dated to about the same time.[26] At the top of the first page of the holograph Shelley wrote 'For Jane & Williams alone to see', and on an outer wrapping for the poem, 'To Jane. Not to be opened unless you are alone, or with Williams'.[27] Like the titles of these poems, such inscriptions are hard to keep separate from the poetic texts to which they are attached. Somewhat later, probably in February or March,[28] Shelley gave Jane a guitar accompanied by a beautifully written copy of the 'frightful scrawl' that Trelawny had found him working on in the woods outside Pisa. He now gave this poem the title 'With a Guitar. To Jane'.

These three poems adopt very different lyrical postures and tones of voice. 'The Serpent is Shut Out from Paradise', although the least successful and inventive of the three, presents some revealing difficulties. Parts of it are openly self-pitying; there is little of what Davie would call urbanity in the almost Petrarchan sequence of images with which the poem opens:

> The serpent is shut out from Paradise –
>> The wounded deer must seek the herb no more
>>> In which its heart's cure lies –
>> The widowed dove must cease to haunt a bower
> Like that from which its mate with feigned sighs
>>> Fled in the April hour. –
>> I, too, must seldom seek again
> Near happy friends a mitigated pain.
>
> (1–8)

In the second stanza self-pity takes on a defiant, bitter edge and confronts the limitations of pity – although not, it seems, of self-pity:

> But not to speak of love, Pity alone
> Can break a spirit already more than bent.
>
> (12–13)

What really makes this poem so disturbed and disturbing is the furtive ambiguity of the emotional claims it makes on its immediate audience. As in the note he sent with the poem, Shelley shifts the focus of his attention from both Williams and Jane to just one of them – but to which one?

> Therefore, if now I see you seldomer,
>> Dear friends, dear *friend*, know that I only fly

    Your looks, because they stir
Griefs that should sleep, and hopes that cannot die.

(17–20)

Given Shelley's note, we would expect Williams to see himself as the
singular 'dear *friend*', but the lines that follow hardly make sense unless
the narrowed reference is to Jane.[29] For how long in the poem is this
narrowed reference meant to apply? Does it still hold for the next
stanza, where another added emphasis that looks like bold directness
only heightens a sense of slippery indirection?

    You spoil me for the task
    Of acting a forced part in life's dull scene.
Of wearing on my brow the idle mask
      Of author, great or mean,
   In the world's carnival. I sought
Peace thus, and but in you I found it not.

(27–32)

The autobiographical reference to the role Shelley was forced to play in
Byron's presence is obvious ('serpent' in line 1 alludes to Byron's
favorite nickname for him).[30] 'Idle mask' and the wavering of 'great or
mean' seem to convey weary detachment from that role, but this itself
may be a mask for defensive anxiety ('I have been long idle,' Shelley
wrote to Peacock on 11 January 1822; *Letters*, II, 374). Byron's
influence on the poem may even be reflected in its ottava rima scheme,
which Shelley complicates and partly disguises by varying the line
lengths. But what effect do Jane and/or Williams have on Shelley's
'acting a forced part'? '*You* spoil me for the task' suggests that they made
it more difficult; 'I sought / Peace thus, and but in you I found it not'
suggests that they made it easier.

    This poem dramatizes its own uncertainty in ways that complicate
rather than clarify what it asks of its readers – of Jane and Edward
Williams, but also of us. The flowers the speaker reads in stanza 5 yield
an indeterminate message, yet he 'dread[s] / To speak' and his friends
'may know too well' one of its possible meanings. Is it this unspoken
meaning or the indeterminacy itself that constitutes 'the truth in the sad
oracle'? In the final stanza the vocal manner suddenly does become
urbanely colloquial; the speaker raises the question of resolution and
confesses that he lacks it:

I asked her yesterday if she believed

That I had resolution. One who *had*
  Would ne'er have thus relieved
His heart with words, but what his judgment bade
Would do, and leave the scorner unrelieved. –

(49–53)

Does 'thus' in line 51 refer to the speaker's having 'asked her yesterday if she believed / That I had resolution'? Or does it refer to his present act of confessing his feelings in the poem itself? Either way, these lines are an act against 'her', against Mary: the third-person pronoun is no longer distanced from its biographical referent by being quoted in a folk saying, as in stanza 5. Perhaps it is this gesture, and not the hesitant allusion to 'Griefs that should sleep, and hopes that cannot die' (20) or to truths 'I dread / To speak' (38–9), that makes him feel that he has 'relieved / His heart with words'. What the poem's words leave the reader with is a sense of unrelieved, even unrelievable, frustration.

  'The Magnetic Lady to Her Patient' stands between the consciously indulgent yet constricted self-absorption of 'The Serpent is Shut Out' and that elegant and ostensibly liberating 'ariette', 'With a Guitar. To Jane'. It is the only one of the 1822 lyrics written for more than one voice. Jane herself is made to speak the first four stanzas (she is named in stanza 5); what she says is rhythmically incantatory and, even in its demurrals, erotic:

  'And from my fingers flow
The powers of life, and like a sign
Seal thee from thine hour of woe,
And brood on thee, but may not blend
  With thine.'[31]

(5–9)

Judith Chernaik may be right to say that the biographical 'explicitness of the poem . . . is part of its charm',[32] but the charm is not without its painful equivocations:

'Sleep, sleep, sleep on, – I love thee not –
  Yet when I think that *he*
Who made and makes my lot
As full of flowers, as thine of weeds,
  Might have been lost like thee, –
And that a hand which was not mine
Might then have charmed his agony

As I another's – my heart bleeds
For thine.

(10–18)

Apparently Shelley could rely on Williams to take these words as the
loyal compliment they seem to be and not to feel blamed for making his
lot full of 'weeds', but the grammar is ambiguous and potentially makes
Williams responsible for Shelley's unhappiness as well as for Jane's
happiness. It is also troubling that while Jane's sympathy is made partly
to depend on her imagining her husband in Shelley's unhappy situation,
she stops short in the poem of imagining herself in Mary's, or of taking
her explicitly into account at all. Jane's performance is contradictory: at
the end of the third stanza she tells her patient to 'forget me, for I can
never be thine' (26–7), but at the end of the fourth she claims 'By mine
thy being is to its deep / Possest' (35–6). Much of this veiled tension is
momentarily released in the chatty dialogue at the beginning of the last
stanza:

'The spell is done – how feel you now?'
  'Better, quite well' replied
  The sleeper –

(37–9)

But as the dialogue continues, the tone of relaxed intimacy takes on a
tenser inflection:

    'What would do
You good when suffering and awake,
    What cure your head and side?'
'What would cure that would kill me, Jane,
And as I must on earth abide
Awhile yet, tempt me not to break
    My chain.'

(39–45)

Medwin's comment on these lines gives them a morbid medical gaiety:
'he made the same reply to an enquiry as to his disease, and its cure, as
he had done to me, – "What would cure me would kill me." – meaning
lithotomy' (the surgical removal of stones from the bladder – without
anaesthesia, of course, in Shelley's day).[33] What Medwin deliberately
ignores – it is inconceivable that even he did not get it – is the sexual
implication of these lines. 'The "chain" he must not break', Chernaik
remarks, 'is the chain of life; also, undoubtedly, it is the chain of his

marriage.'[34] Undoubtedly. Shelley gave the poem to Jane with instructions 'Not to be opened unless you are alone, or with Williams'. That Shelley could imagine, even desire, that Jane would read this poem in Edward's presence is the most disturbingly equivocal thing about it.

In 'With a Guitar. To Jane' the frustrated desire, alienation and guilt of those early months in 1822 for once seem to be brought under playfully sophisticated control. The fragility and vulnerability of that control are, however, the poem's most interesting features. 'With a Guitar. To Jane' introduces itself as a lyrical dramatic monologue – 'Ariel to Miranda' (1). And in addition to casting himself, Jane and Williams in roles borrowed from Shakespeare, Shelley also revives the courtly Renaissance tradition, as Richard Cronin has recently pointed out, of writing a poem to accompany and explain a gift presented to the poet's mistress (Herrick is again a possible influence, along with Donne).[35] Yet pain and sadness are not excluded from this archaizing artifice; they are instead suspended within and by it:

> Take
> This slave of music for the sake
> Of him who is the slave of thee;
> And teach it all the harmony,
> In which thou can'st, and only thou,
> Make the delighted spirit glow,
> 'Till joy denies itself again
> And too intense is turned to pain . . .
>
> (1–8)

Joy is inherently unstable and self-destroying by virtue of its very intensity: the idea is certainly familiar in Shelley's writing, but in extending it here to the joy inspired by Miranda's anticipated music, Shelley indirectly links this compliment-*cum*-warning to the Patient's wry reply to the Magnetic Lady: 'What would cure that would kill me, Jane.' Death is a continuous motif in Ariel's song, even though here, as in *The Tempest*, it is made to seem dreamily fictitious by an elegantly deployed fantasy of reincarnation:

> When you die, the silent Moon
> In her interlunar swoon
> Is not sadder in her cell
> Than deserted Ariel;
> When you live again on Earth

Like an unseen Star of birth
Ariel guides you o'er the sea
Of life from your nativity . . .

(23–30)

For a reader who recalls the figure of the 'cold chaste Moon' in *Epipsychidion*, Ariel's comparing himself to the darkened and 'silent Moon' may seem the only instance in the poem where the biographical symbolism darkens as it does in the other lyrics. In *Epipsychidion* the speaker recalls a time when he was dominated by the influence of this 'Moon':

And there I lay, within a chaste cold bed:
Alas, I then was nor alive nor dead: –
For at her silver voice came Death and Life,
Unmindful each of their accustomed strife . . .

(299–302)

Ariel is not entirely free of this lunar influence; the illusory reconciliations of 'her silver voice' echo through his celebration of Miranda's warm, intense 'harmony'.

As it turns out this Ariel, unlike Shakespeare's 'airy spirit', is 'Imprisoned for some fault of his / In a body like a grave' (38–9).[36] His transitory release from this living death must come from Miranda's smiles and from her music. It is this idea that provides the intricate link between the first part of the poem and the second, with its tender etiological account of the guitar's death as a tree and double rebirth through art:

The artist who this idol wrought
To echo all harmonious thought
Felled a tree, while on the steep
The woods were in their winter sleep . . .
– and so this tree –
O that such our death may be –
Died in sleep, and felt no pain,
To live in happier form again,
From which, beneath Heaven's fairest star,
The artist wrought this loved guitar,
And taught it justly to reply
To all who question skilfully
In language gentle as thine own . . .

(43–61)

In so far as it speaks 'In language gentle', art – the guitar-maker's and then Miranda's – transfigures death into an illusion. But we already know that this language may provoke joy so extreme that it 'denies itself again / And too intense is turned to pain' (7–8). Miranda's guitar, like the poem that accompanies it to explain its genesis and potential, speaks a double language, for

> It talks according to the wit
> Of its companions, and no more
> Is heard than has been felt before
> By those who tempt it to betray
> These secrets of an elder day. –

(82–6)

The graceful wit of Shelley's octosyllabic couplets is almost, but not quite, enough to fend off suspicions that 'tempt it to betray' may mean 'tempt it to prove false to' as well as 'tempt it to reveal'. Such suspicions will be particularly hard to banish for a reader with the conclusion of 'The Magnetic Lady to Her Patient' still in her or his mind: 'tempt me not to break / My chain'. Shelley insists that it is not just a question of what 'has been felt before' by the guitar in its antenatal dream of nature's 'harmonies' (62–78), but of what Ariel and Miranda, he and Jane, have felt of 'Our mortal nature's strife' ('The Recollection', 48). Without them the guitar is a 'silent token', even though its music may express 'more than ever can be spoken' (11–12); it can 'echo all harmonious thought' (44), and presumably all dissonant thought as well. They both know that even 'its highest holiest tone' (89) can never be impervious to the strains of desire and loss.

It may seem contrary to emphasize the pessimistic interpretive possibilities of a text which is so clearly crafted to tease its readers, imaginary and actual, out of thinking about them. But I think it essential to recognize that the most urbanely playful writing in Shelley's last lyrics is never proof against the kind of 'unwelcome thought' that blots that 'one dear image out' at the end of 'The Recollection', or that stains all the images in 'When the Lamp is Shattered' – another lyric (if G.M. Matthews is right) that belongs to these early months of 1822. One sequence of images in this latter poem bears particularly on the undertones of vulnerable mortality and death in 'With a Guitar':

> When the lute is broken
> Sweet tones are remembered not –

When the lips have spoken
Loved accents are soon forgot.

As music and splendour
Survive not the lamp and the lute,
The heart's echoes render
No song when the spirit is mute –
No song – but sad dirges
Like the wind through a ruined cell
Or the mournful surges
That ring the dead seaman's knell.

(5–16)

The last line of this passage somberly echoes the last line of Ariel's 'Full fathom five' song from *The Tempest*: 'Sea nymphs hourly ring his knell' (i.ii.405). Jane's guitar, though fashioned 'To echo all harmonious thought', is as subject to silence and dissonance as are the hearts of those that question it, however 'skilfully' (60). The same could be said of the poem itself: Cronin is right to argue that while 'The poem explains the history and qualities of the guitar . . . the guitar acts as a metaphor explaining the genesis and the distinctive qualities of poetry'.[37] These last lyrics suggest that although poems may acquire their own separate existence as verbal forms and fictions, they are never entirely free of the vicissitudes of those who write and read them. Matthews claims that 'When the Lamp is Shattered' 'was undoubtedly written for the "Unfinished Drama" of early 1822' and insists that 'it is ludicrous to treat a song written for private theatricals as if it were the cry of Shelley's own soul'.[38] But thinking of the poem as a piece of dramatic 'artifice, creative play',[39] need not preclude our also thinking of it as a deed, as an act inevitably if indirectly linked to personal motives and consequences. What *if* the poem were written to be performed in private theatricals, possibly (Matthews suggests) by Jane and Mary together? Acting is acting, as Hamlet discovers, despite the interventions of art. And since Shelley never finished the drama and apparently gave Jane a copy of the poem separately, it is difficult not to imagine how it would have been read by the recipient of 'With a Guitar. To Jane'.

IV

'Unwelcome thought[s]' about living and writing continue to emerge in the lyrics Shelley wrote later in 1822, during the last two months of his life. Since early February Shelley and Williams had been planning to find a summer place on the coast above Pisa where they could sail whenever they wanted and be out from under the shadow of Byron and his entourage. They looked for a house in the fishing village of Lerici, but all they could find was a dilapidated building, originally a boat-house, right on the water about a mile from Lerici, near the tiny village of San Terenzo. They were eager to move, however, so on 27 April the four of them – with their children, two servants and, at Shelley's urging, Claire Clairmont – sailed up the coast and moved in.[40]

Being away from Byron was good for Shelley's writing: he may have begun work on *The Triumph of Life* fairly soon after settling in at Casa Magni.[41] But the spectacle of Byron's success continued to oppress him, even at long distance. In February he and Byron had both ordered boats for their summer sailing to be built at Genoa. Byron's was to be much the larger and would be called the *Bolivar*; Shelley, with the financial assistance of Williams and Trelawny, commissioned a sleek twenty-four-foot yacht. Trelawny suggested that the boat be called the *Don Juan*, and Shelley initially agreed. But he eventually decided to assume full ownership of the boat and intended to change its name to the *Ariel*. Yet when the boat finally arrived in Lerici harbor on 12 May, Shelley was appalled to see stenciled on the forward mainsail, in large black letters, the name *Don Juan*. Even if the boat was to have kept the name originally given to it, such a display would have been totally inappropriate.[42] Shelley knew whom to blame, of course, but as he said in a letter to Trelawny of 16 May, there was very little he could do about it:

> The Don Juan is arrived, & nothing can exceed the admiration *she* has excited, for we must suppose the name to have [been] given her during the equivocation of sex which her godfather suffered in the Harem. . . . [*Heavily scratched over*: I see Don Juan is written on the mainsail. This was due to] my noble friend, carrying the joke rather too far; much I suspect to the scandal of Roberts [the shipcaptain charged with getting the boat built to specifications], & even of yourself. . . . though I must repeat that I think the joke was carried too far; but do not mention this to Roberts, who of

course could do nothing else than acquiesce in Lord Byron's request. Does he mean to write the Bolivar on his own mainsail? – [43]

(*Letters*, II, 421–2)

Shelley's allusion at the beginning of this letter to the fifth canto of *Don Juan*, where Juan is threatened with castration unless he agrees to disguise himself as a woman and become Juanna, is revealingly suggestive of the kind of threat he jokingly attributes to Byron's joke. To catch the full force of Shelley's indignant sarcasm, one needs to know that less than a year before, having heard Byron read the fifth canto of *Don Juan* to him on his visit to Ravenna, he wrote in a letter to Mary:

It sets him not above but far above all the poets of the day: every word has the stamp of immortality. – I despair of rivalling Lord Byron, as well I may: and there is no other with whom it is worth contending.

(8 August 1821; *Letters*, II, 323)

Shelley's admiration – even his words ('the stamp of immortality') – had once again come back to haunt him. Byron had stamped the name of his finest achievement on Shelley's boat: so much for 'Ariel'. The joke infuriated and frustrated him: he tried for hours to remove the letters from the sail with turpentine and all sorts of other substances, but it was no use. An entirely new section of sail had to be carefully sewn in to disguise the disfigurement. And after all the fuss, the name *Don Juan* stuck, and even came to be accepted by Shelley himself.

Just how much Shelley's affection for Jane Williams intensified during these two months is a matter of conjecture. But that matters had grown considerably worse between Shelley and Mary is evident from their letters and from Mary's and Edward Williams's journals. Mary was pregnant again, probably since the end of March or the beginning of April, and this in itself might have made her unhappy about living in a run-down boat-house near a remote fishing village, in late spring weather that was oppressively hot even for Italy. And as if the deaths of three previous children were not enough to give her forebodings, she, and Shelley too, had to contend with the fact that just two days before they left Pisa, Allegra died of typhus in the convent where Byron had taken her to live, away from her mother Claire. On many days in late May and early June Mary stayed in the house unwell, while Shelley worked on *The Triumph of Life* and sailed in the bay with Williams, and sometimes with Jane.

On 16 June Mary Shelley had a serious miscarriage and almost bled to death. It was hours before a doctor could be found, and Shelley probably saved her life by getting hold of some ice and making her sit in a tub of it until the bleeding stopped. Two days later he wrote to John Gisborne about the incident with relief and confidence: 'I succeeded in checking the hemorrhage and the fainting fits, so that when the physician arrived all danger was over, and he had nothing to do but to applaud me for my boldness. She is now doing well, and the sea-baths will restore her' (*Letters*, II, 434). But in fact Mary was slow to recover, and so, in a different way, was Shelley – the miscarriage must have disturbed him in ways that the letter to Gisborne does not reveal. A week after the miscarriage, in the middle of the night, he ran screaming into Mary's room (they had slept apart since coming to San Terenzo) claiming that he had been visited by two terrifying 'visions' – he insisted that they were not dreams. Here is Mary's account of what he had told her, in a letter to Maria Gisborne written more than a month after Shelley's death:

> He dreamt that lying as he did in bed Edward & Jane came into him, they were in the most horrible condition, their bodies lacerated – their bones starting through their skin, the faces pale yet stained with blood, they could hardly walk, but Edward was the weakest & Jane was supporting him – Edward said – 'Get up, Shelley, the sea is flooding the house & it is all coming down.' S. got up, he thought, & went to the his [sic] window that looked on the terrace & the sea & thought he saw the sea rushing in. Suddenly his vision changed & he saw the figure of himself strangling me, that had made him rush into my room. . . . talking it over the next morning he told me that he had had many visions lately – he had seen the figure of himself which met him as he walked on the terrace & said to him – 'How long do you mean to be content'.
>
> (15 August 1822; *Letters of Mary Wollstonecraft Shelley*, I, 245)

Even allowing for the effect Shelley's drowning had on Mary's emotions, for the possibility that his death activated her own fictionalizing powers, she gives us a text or scenario that disturbingly reflects what we know of Shelley's life and writing at Casa Magni. I want to use her narrative as both biographical and figurative context for looking selectively at the short poems Shelley wrote at this time.

Of the four or five lyrics generally thought to have been written during the last two months of Shelley's life, two may be dated with relative certainty because they appear in the midst of *The Triumph of Life* manuscript. The three parts of the lyric beginning 'The keen stars were twinkling' were originally drafted out of final sequence on widely separated pages of this manuscript. We know their final sequence because we also have Shelley's fair copy of the poem, which he left in Jane's room with a cryptic and apologetic note ending, 'I commit them to your secrecy and your mercy, and will try to do better another time' (*Letters*, II, 437).[44] The poem celebrates and rhythmically evokes Jane's singing on an evening when 'The keen stars were twinkling / And the fair moon was rising among them' (1–2). Clearly some new pattern of association has momentarily eclipsed the figure of the cold, sad moon in *Epipsychidion* and 'With a Guitar. To Jane'. Once again Shelley's lyric perspectives straddle and place out of immediate reach the actual moment being celebrated. The first stanza, in the past tense, indicates that this moment is being recollected; the second stanza is in the present and also the future tense because it asks Jane to

> Sing again, with your dear voice revealing
> A tone
> Of some world far from ours,
> Where music and moonlight and feeling
> Are one.
>
> (20–4)

The world of ideal lyric unity is explicitly recognized as being 'far from ours', even though Jane has previously evoked it and may do so again. The first draft of the last two lines reads 'Where moonlight & music & feeling / Are *won*' (my emphasis),[45] suggesting that Shelley may have been initially less concerned with a nocturnal version of the unifying ideal we find at the end of 'To Jane. The Invitation', than with the thought of fully possessing, through a performance or exertion of the interpretive will, experiences which here in our world are always 'arising unforeseen and departing unbidden', as he says in *The Defence*.

The other, longer lyric drafted in *The Triumph of Life* manuscript but left unfinished is also a nocturne; it has come to be called 'Lines Written in the Bay of Lerici'. Its position in the manuscript, together with certain correspondences between its imagery and external circumstances worked out in detail by Matthews, suggest that it was written about a week after Mary's miscarriage. (If Matthews' dating is correct, it may even be based on an experience that happened earlier on the very evening when Shelley had his gruesome nightmares.)[46] The first part of the poem, through line 32, works to sustain the memory of an intensely beautiful encounter, presumably with Jane, against a pervasive awareness that the moment has vanished and left the speaker with divided feelings. Until Matthews' work on the poem appeared in 1961, published texts began where the manuscript draft seems to begin, at line 7:

> She left me at the silent time
> When the moon had ceased to climb
> The azure dome of Heaven's steep,
> And like an albatross asleep,
> Balanced on her wings of light,
> Hovered in the purple night . . .
>
> (7–12)

What Matthews noticed was that a group of lines crammed into the space at the top of the manuscript page and obviously written later – lines which before had always been published as a separate fragment – were in fact a new opening to the poem:[47]

> Bright wanderer, fair coquette of Heaven,
> To whom alone it has been given
> To change and be adored for ever. . . .
> Envy not this dim world, for never
> But once within its shadow grew
> One fair as [thou], but far more true.
>
> (1–6)

No one had previously taken these lines to be part of the poem because they address the moon directly and seem to be written in a different key. But Matthews and Reiman agree on the textual status of the lines, and it is only reasonable to accept them as a revised beginning. Yet it is difficult to avoid thinking that they spoil one of Shelley's finest openings. The abrupt simplicity of 'She left me', followed by the image of the moon balanced and hovering at its zenith just before starting its descent, set the tone and direction of the first part of the poem deftly and movingly. Then why did Shelley add the new opening? Matthews says he wanted to parallel 'the fair but changeable and vanishing moon' with 'the fair, unchanging but vanished Jane'.[48] This may be so, but a further effect of the new opening is to disturb or contaminate in advance the image of the moon momentarily hovering at its height. It is as if Shelley had become uncomfortable retrospectively with the suggestion that the moon's suspended balance could be anything other than the delusive display of a 'fair coquette'. Considering the way in which the poem ends, we may have here from a compositional point of view a revised and contrived beginning distorted by an initially unforeseen ending.

Shelley's speaker clings to the memory of Jane's presence by first 'Thinking over every tone' of what she said or sang, and then by extending those thoughts in a way that leaves totally ambiguous whether Jane touched him as well as her guitar:

> And feeling ever – O too much –
> The soft vibrations of her touch
> As if her gentle hand even now
> Lightly trembled on my brow;
> And thus although she absent were
> Memory gave me all of her
> That even fancy dares to claim.
>
> (21–7)

The difference between 'Memory' and 'fancy' is blurred here in a distinctively Shelleyan, un-Wordsworthian, un-Coleridgean way. The uncertainty continues in the next couplet: 'Her presence had made weak and tame / All passions' (28–9) could mean that when he was with Jane he felt no passion, or that having spent his passion in her presence he no longer felt it. The uncertainty is not resolved, and may even be compounded, by our knowing that Shelley first wrote 'Desire & fear' in line 29, then cancelled it in favor of 'passions'.[49] The critical question to ask is what to make of the ambiguity in this part of the poem. It might simply be said that we are dealing with an unfinished, incompletely revised text about which it is inappropriate to make decisive interpretive judgements. But the reader may still wonder whether the ambiguity is not there to disguise or veil the kind of intimacy Shelley's speaker remembers having experienced, the kind of passion he thinks he felt. One may even want to ask whether or not the poem is fundamentally uncertain or confused in its representations of intimacy and passion. Are the evasive insinuations of what 'even fancy dares to claim' and the blurring of 'Memory' and 'fancy' gestures of discretion or of protective self-deception, or of both?

Tentative answers to these questions begin to suggest themselves as the poem turns, dramatically, at line 33:

> But soon, the guardian angel gone,
> The demon reassumed his throne
> In my faint heart . . . I dare not speak
> My thoughts; but thus disturbed and weak
> I sate . . .
>
> (33–7)

Those who always complain when Shelley's speakers say that they are weak or faint rarely make clear whether they are objecting to these emotions *per se*, or to Shelley's way of writing about them. Judith Chernaik is on the right track when she compares this poem to the 'Stanzas Written in Dejection, December 1818 – Near Naples'.[50] But the way in which self-pity is dramatized in that poem – 'I could lie down like a tired child / And weep away the life of care / Which I have borne and yet must bear' (30–2) – is essentially different from this turn in 'Lines Written in the Bay of Lerici'. Here Shelley is 'disturbed' by emotional and imaginative exhaustion, not just 'weak' with it; 'I dare not speak / My thoughts' confesses an unwillingness, perhaps too an inability, to come fully to terms with the 'demon' in his heart.

In the midst of this critical moment of emotional and expressive failure – and also, the reader may feel, as a way of escaping from it – Shelley returns in mid-sentence to the natural scene, and we get another passage of arresting lyric serenity that throws into relief the agitation he has just confessed. He remembers the boats out in the bay and imagines them sailing 'to some Elysian star'

> for drink to medicine
> Such sweet and bitter pain as mine.
>
> (43–4)

'Sweet and bitter pain' sounds Petrarchan: could Shelley have been using sonnet 164 from Petrarch's *Rime*, a sonnet beautifully translated by Surrey, as a way of trying to formalize or stabilize the poem's emotional turmoil at this point?[51] The poem moves towards its close through yet another sequence of delicately rhymed idyllic images:

> And the wind that winged their flight
> From the land came fresh and light,
> And the scent of sleeping flowers

And the coolness of the hours
Of dew, and the sweet warmth of day
Was scattered o'er the twinkling bay . . .

(45–50)

The graceful swing of these couplets, with their repeating 'And'-clauses, may lull us into thinking that the 'demon' has again been banished, this time without Jane's presence or even an explicit memory of her. But then we turn one last corner on 'And' and find him waiting in ambush:

And the fisher with his lamp
And spear, about the low rocks damp
Crept, and struck the fish who came
To worship the delusive flame.

(51–4)

The way in which the predatory violence of this image emerges so unexpectedly from the delicately observed seascape, and through the same syntactic pattern as that of the preceding lines, is like nothing else in Shelley, or in English Romantic poetry. Line 51 is syntactically extended and enjambed much like line 48 – 'And the coolness of the hours / Of dew' – only now the initial phrase after the line-ending, 'And spear', marks a lethal addition to the scene. Then the cadence of the octosyllabic line is disrupted and distorted in 'about the low rocks damp / Crept': notice how the first strongly stressed syllable has crept forward in each line from 'And the físher' to 'And spéar' to 'Crépt'. One effect of the passage is to give the reader a sense of having been lured into a beautiful but deadly situation. To say that, however, is to see Shelley not as most commentators have seen him here, in the role of the helpless fish lured to destruction by the 'delusive flame' (a refiguring of the coquettish moon from the beginning of the poem, as well as a variation on the opening image from 'When the Lamp is Shattered'), but rather as the 'fisher with his lamp / And spear' – or perhaps as both fisher and fish – luring the reader, Jane and himself towards a grim ending.

The poem itself ends with a kind of moral – sardonic, obscure and unfinished:

Too happy, they whose pleasure sought
Extinguishes all sense and thought
Of the regret that pleasure [   ]

Destroying [*or* Seeking] life alone not peace.

(55–8)

Shelley changed his mind about the first word of the last line, and editors disagree about how it ought to read. Matthews, who reads 'Seeking life alone not peace', says that '*Destroying* is firmly cancelled in MS., with a space before the next word, and probably had no connexion with the rest of the line as it stands.' He paraphrases the entire conclusion: 'They are enviably happy who, in exchanging mere placid existence ("peace") for active sensuous enjoyment ("life"), can remain blind to the price they must pay for it (the spear).'[52] Reiman reads 'Destroying life alone not peace', arguing that although 'It is true that the first seven letters of "Destroying" are firmly cancelled', 'Seeking' is written a good distance below 'Destroying' as if it were to have been the first word of a new line. But 'even if one accepts Matthews' reading "Seeking" for "Destroying," ' Reiman concludes, 'the basic implications of the figure are not drastically altered.'[53] This seems an astonishing claim to make – and yet in the context of Shelley's deeply unsettled stylistic performance in this poem, I think that Reiman is right. On one reading ('Seeking'), those who die in the instinctive, unreflective pursuit of pleasure are interested only in living, not in living peacefully; on the other reading ('Destroying'), these same creatures, when they die, lose only their life and not a peacefulness of which they were never aware. In either case, the bitter contrast with what Shelley has to lose is clear. It is nevertheless a remarkable thing to be able to say about a poem that its ending is not 'drastically altered' by the difference between 'Seeking life' and 'Destroying life'. No wonder Shelley left this poem without being able to find the rhyme he wanted for its last word, 'peace'.

Like several of the 1822 lyrics but in a more radically self-questioning way, 'Lines Written in the Bay of Lerici' couples an agitated uncertainty about desire and personal relationships with an agitated uncertainty about writing, about verbal representation. The coupling is important to Shelley's entire career: his writing is often most compelling when it questions, explicitly and implicitly, its own empirical origins and linguistic resources. It is also important to his last great piece of writing, *The Triumph of Life*. The draft of 'Lines Written in the Bay of Lerici', along with a draft of lines 11–18 of 'The Keen Stars Were Twinkling' and other fragments, cancellations and notes, appears at that very point in the manuscript of the ongoing poem where Rousseau claims:

> 'I
> Have suffered what I wrote, or viler pain! –

> 'And so my words were seeds of misery – '

Here *The Triumph of Life* draft appears to break off in the midst of a
tercet, the lyric drafts and other scraps of writing intervene, and then
Rousseau's speech is completed nine manuscript-pages later:

> 'Even as the deeds of others.'

(278–81)

Even if the order of materials in the manuscript does not reflect the
exact order of their composition, it is strikingly suggestive that 'Lines
Written in the Bay of Lerici' should be framed by Rousseau's arresting
internal rhyme: words as 'seeds', words as 'deeds'.[54] Shelley uses
Rousseau to make himself and his readers think about the mutual
entanglements of writing and living. He might also have used Byron.
But he did not dare.

If Shelley had somehow been able to seal off his last lyrics from sexual,
domestic and personal literary perturbations, they would be less
important demonstrations of his distinctive, unsettled brilliance. Their
stylistic range and deftness, their often masterful inventions of voice
and rhythm and stanzaic or couplet arrangement, are the workmanship
of an artist instinctively wilful yet profoundly unresolved about
writing, and about living.

NOTES

INTRODUCTION

1. See Newman Ivey White, *Shelley*, New York, Alfred A. Knopf, 1940, II, 637, who gives 1827 as the date of Wordsworth's pronouncement and cites Christopher Wordsworth, *Memoirs of William Wordsworth*, London, E. Moxon, 1851, II, 474. See also *The Prose Works of William Wordsworth*, ed. Alexander B. Grosart, London, E. Moxon, 1876, III, 463.
2. *PMLA*, 67, 1952, 601.
3. New York, Seabury Press, 1979; see Geoffrey Hartman's Preface, ix.
4. Cambridge, Mass., Harvard University Press, 1965, 168.
5. *SIR*, 19, 1980, 339.
6. ibid., 330.
7. See Canto IV, lines 417–18 of *The Botanic Garden* – 'Each widening scale and bursting film unfold, / Swell the green cup, and tint the flower with gold' – and Darwin's note about how 'The effect of light on plants occasions the actions of the vegetable muscles of their leaf-stalks, which . . . open their calyxes and chorols' (London, J. Johnson, 1791; rpt New York, Garland, 1978, intro. Donald H. Reiman, I, 194–5). Shelley was reading Darwin's poem as early as 1811 (*Letters*, I, 129).
8. Perkins, *Quest for Permanence*, 168.
9. Hogle, 'Metaphor and Metamorphosis', 339.

I THE MIRROR AND THE VEIL: LANGUAGE IN SHELLEY'S *DEFENCE*

1. The discussion of language and representation in Earl J. Schulze's *Shelley's Theory of Poetry: A Reappraisal*, The Hague, Paris, Mouton, 1966, 104–38, is still one of the most helpfully detailed accounts available.

John W. Wright laments the 'Neglect of . . . [Shelley's] distinctive sense of the nature and role of language' in *Shelley's Myth of Metaphor,* Athens, University of Georgia Press, 1970, 4, but in his concern with 'metaphoric apprehension' as 'the fundamental power of the human mind' (22), he himself tends to neglect specific questions of verbal articulation. To a lesser degree, so does Jerrold E. Hogle in his impressive rewriting of Shelley's poetics in terms derived from Jacques Derrida and other post-structuralist theorists ('Shelley's poetics: the power as metaphor', *KSJ*, 31, 1982, 159–97). René Wellek allows that Shelley 'understands the kind of superiority which may be claimed for the poetic medium over that of the other arts' (*A History of Modern Criticism II: The Romantic Age*, New Haven, Yale University Press, 1955, 129), but his treatment of this and other questions about language in the *Defence* is sketchy. So is Earl Wasserman's in *Shelley: A Critical Reading*, Baltimore, The Johns Hopkins University Press, 1971, 214–19, 267–9.

2. *The Violet in the Crucible: Shelley and Translation*, Oxford, Clarendon Press, 1976.

3. Cf. Hogle, 'Shelley's poetics', 184–7.

4. Richard Cronin, *Shelley's Poetic Thoughts*, New York, St Martin's Press, 1981, 9.

5. Cf. William K. Wimsatt Jr and Cleanth Brooks, *Literary Criticism: A Short History*, New York, Random House, 1967, 421.

6. For general discussions of this aspect of eighteenth-century thinking about language, see M.H. Abrams, *The Mirror and the Lamp*, Oxford, Oxford University Press, 1953, 78–84; Stephen K. Land, *From Signs to Propositions: The Concept of Form in Eighteenth-century Semantic Theory*, London, Longman, 1974, 50–74; Murray Cohen, *Sensible Words: Linguistic Practice in England 1640–1785*, Baltimore, The Johns Hopkins University Press, 1977, 122ff.

7. Shelley and Peacock, *A Defence of Poetry, The Four Ages of Poetry*, ed. John E. Jordan, New York, Bobbs-Merrill, 1955, 28, n. 10.

8. See Land, *From Signs to Propositions*, 57. René Wellek argues that there is no evidence of Vico's influence in England before Coleridge in 'The supposed influence of Vico on England and Scotland in the eighteenth century', *Giambattista Vico, an International Symposium*, ed. Giorgio Tagliacozzo and Hayden V. White, Baltimore, The Johns Hopkins University Press, 1969, 215–23. See also Hans Aarsleff, 'The eighteenth century, including Leibniz', *Current Trends in Linguistics*, vol. XII of *Historiography of Linguistics*, ed. Thomas A. Sebeok, The Hague, Paris, Mouton, 1975, Part I, 429.

9. London, Scolar Press, 1972, 41.

10. *On the Origin of Language*: Rousseau's *Essay* and Johann Gottfried Herder's *Essay on the Origin of Language*, trans. John H. Moran and Alexander Gode, New York, Frederick Ungar, 1966, 12.

11. 1783 edition, ed. Harold F. Harding, Carbondale, Ill., Southern Illinois University Press, 1965, vol. I, lecture VI, 112.

12. *The Prose Works of Wordsworth*, ed. W.J.B. Owen and Jane Worthington Smyser, Oxford, Oxford University Press, 1974, I, 160.

13. *Shelley's Myth of Metaphor*, 2, 24.

14. ibid., 31.

15. *The Works of Francis Bacon*, ed. James Spedding, Robert Leslie Ellis and Douglas Denon Heath, London, Longman *et al.*, 1857–74, IV, 337–9. For the Latin text of the passage to which Shelley here refers, see I, 541–3 of this edition. Bacon's actual words in *De Augmentis* III.i, which is cited in Shelley's own note, are 'una eademque naturae vestigia aut signacula, diversis materiis et subjectis impressa' (I, 543). In *The Advancement of Learning* this becomes 'the same footsteps of nature, treading or printing upon several subjects or matters' (III, 349). For evidence that Shelley read both *The Advancement* and the *De Augmentis*, see 'Shelley's notes in his copies of Bacon's *Works*' in Appendix F of Walter E. Peck's *Shelley: His Life and Works*, Boston, Houghton Mifflin, 1927, II, 344–8.

16. *Works of Bacon*, IV, 440–1. For Latin text see I, 653–4.

17. ibid., IV, 433–4. For Latin text, see I, 645–6. For the parallel passage in *The Advancement of Learning*, see III, 396–7.

18. 'Letter on the Deaf and Dumb', in *Diderot's Early Philosophical Works*, trans. and ed. Margaret Jourdain, New York, Burt Franklin, 1916, 175–88, 214–15. See especially 177 ('signs for periods of time and tenses were invented last of all') and 215 ('symbols which in speech denoted indefinite divisions of *quantity* and *time* were among the last to be introduced'). See also H.J. Hunt, 'Logic and linguistics. Diderot as "Grammairien-Philosophe" ', *MLR*, 33, 1938, 219–26.

19. *Considerations concerning the First Formation of Languages* (1761), in *The Early Writings of Adam Smith*, ed. J. Ralph Lindgren, New York, A.M. Kelly, 1967, 239–40. See Land, *From Signs to Propositions*, 85–7.

20. Ed. C. Gregory Smith, London, Everyman's Library, 1967, 292.

21. *A Philosophical Enquiry into the Origin of our Ideas of the Sublime and Beautiful*, ed. J.T. Boulton, London, Routledge & Kegan Paul, 1958, 163, 165. See Dixon Wecter, 'Burke's theory concerning words, images, and emotion', *PMLA*, 55, 1940, 167–81.

22. New York, Garland, 1970, 57, 70.

23. ibid., 90.

24. *The Notebooks of Samuel Taylor Coleridge*, ed. Kathleen Coburn, Princeton, Princeton University Press, 1973, III, 4397. For Coburn's comments on Harris, see her notes to this entry.

25. See *Course in General Linguistics*, ed. Charles Bally and Albert Sechehaze, in collaboration with Albert Riedlinger, trans. Wade Baskin, New York, McGraw Hill, 1966, 67–70.

26. See Hans Aarsleff, 'Leibniz on Locke on language', *American*

Philosophical Quarterly, 1, 1964, 165–88 (this and all other essays by Aarsleff cited below have been collected in *From Locke to Saussure: Essays on the Study of Language and Intellectual History*, Minneapolis, University of Minnesota Press, 1982), and John. W. Yolton, *Locke and the Compass of Human Understanding*, Cambridge, Cambridge University Press, 1970, 196–223. The idea of words as arbitrary signs was not of course original with Locke: among Shelley's favorite writers, the invention of words *ad placitum* is recognized by Dante (*De Vulgari Eloquentia* I.iii.2–3; *Paradiso* XXVI.130–2) and by Bacon (e.g. *De Augmentis Scientiarum* VI.1).

27. All quotations are from *An Essay Concerning Human Understanding*, ed. Peter H. Nidditch, Oxford, Clarendon Press, 1975.

28. See Hans Aarsleff, 'Locke's reputation in nineteenth-century England', *The Monist*, 55, 1971, 392–422, and 'Wordsworth, language, and Romanticism', *EIC*, 30, 1980, 115–26.

29. On 11 August 1810, two months before his matriculation at University College, Oxford, Shelley ordered 'the cheapest edition of Locke on the Human Understanding' (*Letters*, I, 13). There are admiring, enthusiastic references to Locke in letters to Hogg (I, 47) and to his father (I, 50–1) in 1810, in the correspondence with Elizabeth Hitchener in 1811 (I, 100; I, 110; I, 116; I, 136; I, 148), in letters to Godwin (I, 276; I, 303) and to Hogg (I, 335; I, 380) in 1812–13, and in the notes to *Queen Mab* of 1813. In *Shelley at Oxford*, Hogg recalls that 'The examination of a chapter of Locke's *Essay Concerning Human Understanding* would induce him, at any moment, to quit every other pursuit' (London, Methuen, 1904, 71).

30. Apparently Shelley's bookseller at this time, Lackington, Allen & Co., did not immediately fill the order, so he reordered 'Locke on the Human Understanding 8vo' on 5 December 1815 (*Letters*, I, 437).

31. *Prose Works*, I, 124.

32. ibid., III, 82.

33. *Collected Letters of Samuel Taylor Coleridge*, ed. Earl Leslie Griggs, Oxford, Clarendon Press, 1956, I, 625–6.

34. *A Dictionary of the English Language*, London, 1775; rpt New York, AMS Press, 1967. All subsequent references are to this edition.

35. Compare Shelley's use of *arbitrary* and *arbitrarily* in *Speculations on Metaphysics* (*CW*, VII, 60); *Speculations on Morals* (*CW*, VII, 80); *Essay on Christianity* (*CW*, VI, 252); and *A Philosophical View of Reform* (*CW*, VII, 51). On the other hand, *arbitrary* has a neutral or positive sense elsewhere in *Speculations on Metaphysics* (e.g. *CW*. VII, 63: 'It requires no more than attention to perceive perfect sincerity in the relation of what is perceived, and care to distinguish the arbitrary marks by which are designated from the   themselves'), and in the Preface to *Prometheus Unbound* ('The Greek tragic writers, in selecting as their subject any portion of their national history or mythology, employed in

their treatment of it a certain arbitrary discretion', *PP*, 132).

36. A copy of Thomas Taylor's translation of the *Cratylus, Phaedo, Parmenides, and Timaeus of Plato*, with notes on the *Cratylus* (London, 1793), was found among Shelley's books. See *The Shelley Correspondence in the Bodleian Library*, ed. R.H. Hill, Oxford, Oxford University Press, 1926, 47, and James A. Notopoulos, *The Platonism of Shelley*, Durham, N.C., Duke University Press, 1949, 32, 35–6.

37. Scolar Press facsimile of the first edition, 1774–92, 6 vols, Menston, Scolar Press, 1967, II, 196.

38. ibid., II, 197–8.

39. ibid., II, 214.

40. Near the beginning of the *Defence* the 'voice and motions' of 'the child at play' are 'the reflected image' of 'the pleasurable impressions which awakened' them (*PP*, 480). In a later passage mind and the poetry it produces are both seen as mirrors: 'Neither the eye nor the mind can see itself, unless reflected upon that which it resembles. The drama, so long as it continues to express poetry, is as a prismatic and many-sided mirror' (*PP*, 491).

41. 'Letter on the Deaf and Dumb', 194.

42. See Maurice Pope, *The Story of Archaeological Decipherment*, New York, Scribner's, 1975, 43–53. Shelley mentions Warburton only once in an early letter: there is no evidence that he read *The Divine Legation*. Eighteenth-century writers who emphasize the arbitrary and conventional nature of linguistic signs often disparaged what they took to be a crude and inefficient reliance upon natural forms in Egyptian and Chinese writing. See James Beattie, *The Theory of Language* (1788), Menston, Scolar Press, 1968, 311–12, and Monboddo, *Origin and Progress of Language*, II, 428: 'I have spoken elsewhere of the Chinese characters, and have shown them to be no other than natural representations of things'. See Cohen, *Sensible Words*, 98–9.

43. See Stephen K. Land, 'Universalism and relativism: a philosophical problem of translation in the eighteenth century', *JHI*, 35, 1974, 597–600.

44. Preface to *Lyrical Ballads* (1850) in *Prose Works*, I, 135.

45. ibid., I, 146.

46. *Biographia Literaria*, ed. John Shawcross, London, Oxford University Press, 1907, II, 49.

47. Lloyd Abbey, *Destroyer and Preserver: Shelley's Poetic Skepticism*, Lincoln, Neb., University of Nebraska Press, 1979, 45.

48. See Shelley's letter to 'A Lady' written in the spring of 1821: 'Facts . . . are the mere divisions, the arbitrary points on which we hang, and to which we refer those delicate and evanescent hues of mind, which language delights and instructs us in precise proportion as it expresses' (*Letters*, II, 277–8).

49. *Collected Letters*, I, 626.

50. From MS. Egerton 2801, f. 145, quoted in *Inquiring Spirit: A Coleridge Reader*, ed. Kathleen Coburn, London, Routledge & Kegan Paul, 1951, 101. In a revealing investigation of Coleridge's professed linguistic ideals, Frances Ferguson suggests that the 'disjunction between the divine *logos* and the disparate words of human language . . . becomes an acute problem in Coleridge's work' ('Coleridge on language and delusion', *Genre*, 2, 1978, 198).

51. See Wordsworth's note to 'The Thorn', where his account of 'the interest the mind attaches to words, not only as symbols of the passion, but as *things*, active and efficient, which are of themselves part of the passion', is preceded by the recognition 'that an attempt is rarely made to communicate impassioned feelings without something of an accompanying consciousness of the inadequateness of our own powers, or the deficiencies of language' (*Prose Works*, II, 513).

52. ibid., II 84–5.

53. ibid., II, 84. In their note to this passage (II, 114–15), the editors cite Dryden's *Essays*, Pope's *Essay on Criticism*, Johnson's *Lives of the Poets*. In *Academical Questions*, London, W. Bulmer, 1805, Sir William Drummond calls 'figurative language' 'the elegant mantle, which Delicacy throws over all that is gross, or vulgar, or deformed. It is the splendid robe of Fancy, and the graceful dress of the Muses' (408). 'Nevertheless', he goes on to say, 'it is this same license in speech, this free and various colouring of thought, which chiefly helps to perplex us in the study of logic, in the science of metaphysics, and, indeed, in all our enquiries concerning our mental constitution.'

54. That the figure came all too easily to Wordsworth himself is indicated by the fact that in the previous paragraph he originally used the phrase 'clothed in a different manner' but later changed it to 'uttered after a different manner'; see the editors' notes at II, 83 and II, 114. See also his reference to the 'monotonous language of sorrow and affectionate admiration' as a 'veil' in the first *Essay Upon Epitaphs* (II, 66), and the unpublished fragment of *The Prelude, 1798–9*, ed. Stephen Parrish, Ithaca, N.Y., Cornell University Press, 1977, 163: 'Scattering thus / In passion many a desultory sound / I deemed that I had adequately cloathed / Meanings at which I hardly hinted thoughts / And forms of which I scarcely had produced / A monument and arbitrary sign'.

55. *Prose Works*, II, 85. Frances Ferguson points out the oddness of insisting 'upon language as incarnation in essays devoted to epitaphs' and demonstrates the tenuousness of this ideal for Wordsworth in *Wordsworth: Language as Counter-Spirit*, New Haven, Yale University Press, 1977, 28–34. And Stephen Land argues that in his apparent rejection of 'the old dualistic model of language as the "dress of

thought" ', Wordsworth in fact 'emphasized rather than denied semantic dualism' ('The silent poet: an aspect of Wordsworth's semantic theory', *UTQ*, 62, 1973, 160. Land connects this with Wordsworth's 'profound mistrust of words' (163).

56. See Jerome J. McGann, 'Shelley's veils: a thousand images of loveliness', *Romantic and Victorian: Studies in Memory of William H. Marshall*, ed. W. Paul Elledge and Richard L. Hoffman, Rutherford, N.J., Fairleigh Dickinson University Press, 1971, 199–204. Berkeley repeatedly inverts the dress or clothing figure as it appears in Dryden, Pope and Johnson and uses it to express his mistrust of language in the *Treatise Concerning the Principles of Human Knowledge, The Works of George Berkeley, Bishop of Cloyne*, ed. A.A. Luce and T.E. Jessop, London, Thomas Nelson & Sons, 1948–57: 'so long as I confine my thoughts to my own ideas divested of words, I do not see how I can easily be mistaken' (II, 39); 'we need only draw the curtain of words, to hold the fairest tree of knowledge' (II, 40).

57. Notopoulos, *The Platonism of Shelley*, 96–8, emphasizes the Platonic sources of the veil image in Dante and in Petrarch.

58. Slightly misquoted; Dante's actual words are 'perocchè grande vergogna sarebbe a colui, che rimasse cose sotto vesta di figura o di colore rettorico, e poscia domandato non sapesse dinudare le sue parole da cotal vesta, in guisa ch'avessero verace intendimento' (*La Vita Nuova, Le Opere di Dante Alighieri*, ed. E. Moore and Paget Toynbee, 4th edition, Oxford, Oxford University Press, 1924, 223). The translation of Shelley's version of this passage is my own.

59. Cf. Robert F. Gleckner, 'Romanticism and the self-annihilation of language', *Criticism*, 18, 1976, 177–9.

60. See Daniel Hughes's excellent studies of this pattern in 'Kindling and dwindling: the poetic process in Shelley', *KSJ*, 13, 1964, 13–28, and 'Coherence and collapse in Shelley, with particular reference to *Epipsychidion*', *ELH*, 28, 1961, 260–83.

61. Cf. Shelley's comment in an unfinished Preface to his translation of Plato's *Symposium*: 'He despairs of having communicated to the English language any portion of the surpassing graces of the composition, or having done more than present an imperfect shadow of the language and the sentiment of this astonishing production' (*CW*, VII, 161).

62. Jerrold E. Hogle, 'Metaphor and metamorphosis in Shelley's "The Witch of Atlas" ', *SIR*, 19, 1980, 329–32, discusses this passage from the *Defence* and observes that Shelley's image of 'traces' anticipates Jacques Derrida's use of the term in *Of Grammatology*.

63. See McGann, 'Shelley's veils', 204.

64. ' "Unsaying his high language": the problem of voice in *Prometheus Unbound*', *SIR*, 16, 1977, 58.

65. ibid., 52.
66. ibid., 56–60.
67. *Modern Poetry and the Idea of Language*, New Haven, Yale University Press, 1974, 59–61.
68. ibid., 61–2.
69. ibid., 63–7. There is no evidence that Shelley read Humboldt, whose major work on language, *Über die Verschiedenheit des menschlichen Sprachbaues und ihren Einfluss auf die geistige Entwicklung des Menschengeschlechts*, was not published until 1830–5. See Aarsleff, 'Wordsworth, language, and Romanticism', 215 and 226, n. 3. In a review of recent studies of Shelley and Keats, Paul H. Fry suggests that Bruns's and Brisman's emphasis on Shelley's belief in the constitutive power of language might be taken even further with the help of contemporary French theory: 'In the *Defence*, and everywhere in the poetry too, there is much that could be called a Lacanian psycholinguistics in embryo' ('Made men: a review article on recent Shelley and Keats studies', *TSLL*, 21, 1979, 451).
70. *Modern Poetry and the Idea of Language*, 60.
71. 'The problem of voice in *Prometheus Unbound*', 59.
72. *Oeuvres philosophiques de Condillac*, ed. Georges Le Roy, Paris, Presses Universitaires de France, 1947, I, 403b (the translation is mine). See Hans Aarsleff, *The Study of Language in England, 1780–1860*, Princeton, Princeton University Press, 1967, 16–33.
73. *Essay on the Origin of Language*, 10.
74. 'Encyclopédie', in *Oeuvres complètes de Diderot*, ed. J. Assezat, Paris, Garniers, 1875–7, XIV, 429. See Hunt, 'Diderot as "Grammairien-Philosophe" ', 215, 218.
75. *Oeuvres philosophiques de Cabanis*, ed. Claude Lehec and Jean Cazeneuve, Paris, Presses Universitaires de France, 1956, I, 50 (the translation is mine). See Shelley's *Letters*, I, 342.
76. See Hans Aarsleff, 'The tradition of Condillac: the problem of the origin of language in the eighteenth century and the debate in the Berlin Academy before Herder', *Studies in the History of Linguistics*, ed. Dell Hymes, Bloomington, Indiana University Press, 1974, 93–156.
77. Scolar Press facsimile of the 1798, 1805 edition, 2 vols, Menston, Scolar Press, 1968, I, 39 (part I, ch. 2).
78. See Aarsleff, *Study of Language in England*, 37–8.
79. *Origin and Progress of Language*, II, 6. Cf. Stuart Peterfreund, 'Shelley, Monboddo, Vico, and the language of poetry', *Style*, 15, 385–90.
80. Cf. Earl Wasserman's somewhat different assessment of the implications of these lines in *The Subtler Language*, Baltimore, The Johns Hopkins University Press, 1959, 12: 'Shelley clearly understood that meaning is syntactical and that the structure of language is the structure of thought.

... But he also knew that the imagination seeks its own kind of thought by the extraordinary syntactical organization of a special reality.'
81. Ed. Isaac Kramnick, Harmondsworth, Penguin, 1976, 160.
82. *Shelley's Poetic Thoughts*, 4.

II IMAGING THE OPERATIONS OF THE HUMAN MIND

1. *The Letters of John Keats, 1814–1821*, ed. H.E. Rollins, Cambridge, Mass., Harvard University Press, 1958, II, 323.
2. See, for example, Oscar W. Firkins, *Power and Elusiveness in Shelley*, Minneapolis, University of Minnesota Press, 1937; rpt New York, Octagon Books, 1970, 47–55; Richard Harter Fogle, *The Imagery of Keats and Shelley*, Chapel Hill, University of North Carolina Press, 1949, 224–6; Earl J. Schulze, *Shelley's Theory of Poetry: A Reappraisal*, The Hague, Paris, Mouton, 1966, 129.
3. All quotations of Keats's poetry are from *The Poems of John Keats*, ed. Jack Stillinger, Cambridge, Mass., Harvard University Press, 1979.
4. New York, Harcourt Brace, third edn, 1956, 187.
5. Ed. Alex Preminger, Princeton, Princeton University Press, 1974, 363. The article on imagery is by Norman Friedman.
6. *Pathetic Fallacy in the Nineteenth Century*, Berkeley, University of California Press, 1942; rpt New York, Octagon Books, 1976, 27.
7. M.H. Abrams, *A Glossary of Literary Terms*, New York, Holt, Rinehart & Winston, 1957, 76.
8. F.S. Ellis, *A Lexical Concordance to the Poetical Works of Percy Bysshe Shelley*, London, Bernard Quaritch, 1892, 347–8.
9. *An Essay Concerning Human Understanding*, ed. Peter H. Nidditch, Oxford, Clarendon Press, 1975, 403.
10. *The Origin and Progress of Language*, Scolar Press facsimile of the first edition, 1774–92, 6 vols, Menston, Scolar Press, 1967, I, 143.
11. ibid., III, 39–40.
12. See Hans Aarsleff, *The Study of Language in England 1780–1860*, Princeton, Princeton University Press, 1967, 107–8: 'there is no telling what eighteenth-century philosophy would have been like if the word "mind" had been etymologically transparent.'
13. *The Works of Dugald Stewart*, Cambridge, Hilliard and Brown, 1829, IV, 156.
14. Ed. Nidditch, 235–6.
15. ibid., 240.
16. Presumably the 'peculiar style of intense and comprehensive imagery which distinguishes the modern literature of England' to which Shelley subsequently refers (*PP*, 134) does not include 'imagery ... drawn from

the operations of the human mind'.

17. All quotations are from *The Complete Writings of William Blake*, ed. Geoffrey Keynes, London, Oxford University Press, 1966.

18. *The Verbal Icon*, Lexington, University of Kentucky Press, 1954, 103–16.

19. Ch. XVII; ed. John Shawcross, London, Oxford University Press, 1907, II. 39–40.

20. *The Prose Works of Wordsworth*, ed. W.J.B. Owen and Jane Worthington Smyser, Oxford, Oxford University Press, 1974, III, 30–1.

21. All quotations of *The Prelude* are from *The Prelude, 1799, 1805, 1850*, ed. Jonathan Wordsworth, M.H. Abrams and Stephen Gill, New York, Norton, 1979.

22. All quotations of poems other than *The Prelude* are from *The Poetical Works of William Wordsworth*, ed. Ernest de Selincourt and Helen Darbishire, 5 vols, Oxford, Clarendon Press, 1940–9.

23. Quotations of Dante's Italian are from the text established by Giorgio Petrocchi and presented in *The Divine Comedy*, trans. and comm. Charles S. Singleton, Princeton, Princeton University Press, 6 vols, 1970–3. The English translations are from Henry Francis Cary's version of *The Divine Comedy*, New York, The Colonial Press, 1891. Shelley asked Charles Ollier to send him Cary's translation of the *Purgatorio* and *Paradiso*, which had appeared in 1812, on 7 December 1817 (*Letters*, I, 575). In making the same request to Lackington, Allen & Co. on 23 December 1817, he makes it clear that he already owned Cary's translation of the *Inferno*, published in 1805 (*Letters*, I, 586). On Shelley's use of Cary's translation, see Timothy Webb, *The Violet in the Crucible: Shelley and Translation*, Oxford, Clarendon Press, 1976, 282, 324–5.

24. See 'Shelley's notes in his copies of Dante's *Works*', Appendix IV to Walter E. Peck, *Shelley: His Life and Work*, Boston, Houghton Mifflin, 1927, II, 355–61.

25. 'Dante', *Selected Essays*, New York, Harcourt, Brace & World, 1932, 215.

26. *Italy and the English Romantics*, Cambridge, Cambridge University Press, 1957, 64.

27. *Selected Essays*, 205.

28. 'Dante's two "families": Christian judgment and the pagan past', *Italica*, 47, 1970, 28–35.

29. Keats, on the other hand, marked both similes together and underlined them in his copy of the *Inferno*; see Robert Gittings, *The Mask of Keats*, Cambridge, Mass., Harvard University Press, 1956, Appendix A, 153.

30. *The Complete Works of William Hazlitt*, ed. P.P. Howe, London, J.M. Dent, 1931, V, 17–18.

31. See, for example, the 'Observations on Mr Wordsworth's Poem *The Excursion*' published in *The Round Table* (August and October, 1814), *Complete Works*, IV, 112–13.

32. *Shelley and Synesthesia*, Evanston, Ill., Northwestern University Press, 1964, 85. For Dante's influence on Keats's handling of synaesthetic imagery, see Paul D. Sheats, 'Stylistic discipline in *The Fall of Hyperion*', *KSJ*, 17, 1968, 83: 'sensation becomes a process of conscious inference that is far removed from the instinctive outrush of empathy characteristic of the chameleon poet. Keats's attention here moves from the object beheld to the mind that beholds it, and perception results not in self-forgetfulness but in self-consciousness.'

33. All quotations are from *The Complete Signet Classic Shakespeare*, ed. Sylvan Barnet, New York, Harcourt Brace Jovanovich, 1972.

34. *Revaluation*, Harmondsworth, Penguin, 1964, 186–8.

35. Wordsworth echoes Shakespeare's phrase more exactly at the end of Book V of the 1850 *Prelude*, as he celebrates 'the great Nature that exists in works / Of mighty poets. Visionary power / Attends the motions of the viewless winds / Embodied in the mystery of words' (V. 594–7; line 620 of the 1805 text reads, 'Attends upon the motions of the winds'). Then there is Keats's uncanny transformation of Shakespeare's 'viewless winds' into 'the viewless wings of Poesy' in *Ode to a Nightingale* (line 33).

36. *Shelley's Cenci: Scorpions Ringed With Fire*, Princeton, Princeton University Press, 1970, 38–9, 120–1.

37. *Comedias*, ed. A. Valbuena Briones, Madrid, Clásicos Hispánicos, 1974, I, 327 (lines 2019–22). The English translations are my own.

38. Shelley's note is quoted from *Note Books of Percy Bysshe Shelley*, ed. H. Buxton Forman, St. Louis, Mo., Boston Bibliophile Society, 1911; rpt New York, Phaeton Press, 1968, II, 100–2. Quoting from memory, Shelley abbreviates the line and is mistaken about the inflexion of πλάνοις.

39. See *Note Books*, ed. Forman, II, 123–4, for Shelley's draft of these lines and their connection with the passage from Sophocles. See also Neville Rogers, *Shelley at Work*, 2nd edn, Oxford, Clarendon Press, 1967, 173. The frontispiece to Rogers's book, Shelley's drawing from Bod. MS. Shelley adds. c.9 and its accompanying quotation ('The mind . . . a wilderness of intricate paths . . . a labyrinth'), is part of this same motif.

40. Webb, *The Violet in the Crucible*, 15, notes that Trelawny 'records Shelley's habit of making Greek puns at which he "shrieked with laughter" '. On the preservation of literal meaning in metaphor, see Paul Ricoeur, 'The metaphorical process as cognition, imagination, and feeling', *On Metaphor*, ed. Sheldon Sacks, Chicago, University of Chicago Press, 1979, 151–2: 'the self-abolition of literal sense is the

negative condition for the emergence of the metaphorical sense . . . . the metaphorical sense not only abolishes but preserves the literal sense.'

41. See *Note Books*, ed. Forman, II, 101, n. 1.
42. Both Aeschylus and Sophocles are quoted from the Loeb Library texts of their plays. English translations are from *The Complete Greek Tragedies*, ed. David Grene and Richmond Lattimore, Chicago, University of Chicago Press, 1959: *Prometheus Bound* and *Oedipus the King*, trans. David Grene; *Agamemnon*, trans. Richmond Lattimore.
43. A.A. Long discusses this passage and related figures in *Language and Thought in Sophocles*, London, Athlone Press, 1968, 10, 45, 89ff.
44. *Note Books*, ed. Forman, II, 103.
45. *Shelley at Work*, 15.
46. That Shelley studied the language of the *Agamemnon* in considerable detail is evident from his notes on the play; see *Note Books*, ed Forman, II, 128–40.
47. See F.R. Earp, *The Style of Aeschylus*, Cambridge, Cambridge University Press, 1948, 108–9; he cites lines 995–7 of the *Agamemnon* as an example.
48. Greek text and English translation are quoted from the Loeb library edition of *Hesiod, The Homeric Hymns and Homerica*, trans. Hugh G. Evelyn-White, 1914.
49. *The Violet in the Crucible*, 99–100.
50. Again Ricoeur is to the point about the fundamental metaphorizing activity implied in the recurrent Shelleyan idea of Prometheus's 'Methinks I grow like what I contemplate': 'we may say that this instantaneous grasping of the new congruence [in metaphor] is "felt" as well as "seen." By saying that it is felt, we underscore the fact that we are included in the process as knowing subjects. If the process can be called, as I called it, predicative *assimilation*, it is true that *we* are assimilated, that is, made similar, to what is seen as similar. This self-assimilation is a part of the commitment proper to the "illocutionary" force of the metaphor as speech act. We *feel* like what we *see* like' ('The metaphorical process', 154).
51. Cf. Fogle, *The Imagery of Keats and Shelley*, 225–6.
52. Shelley's most extended elaboration of the etymological imagery of *spirit* is *Ode to the West Wind*; see M.H. Abrams, 'The correspondent breeze', *English Romantic Poets*, ed. M.H. Abrams, 2nd edn, London, Oxford University Press, 1975, 43–4.

III REFLEXIVE IMAGERY

1. Harmondsworth, Penguin, 1961, 160–1. One type of reflexive locution, 'the emphatic possessive' formed with *own*, was noticed as characteristically Shelleyan by G. Rostrevor Hamilton, although he was unaware of Empson's remarks (*English*, 5, 1944–5, 149–51). See also the correspondence by E.H.W. Meyerstein (*English*, 5, 219–22) and Arundale Esdaile (*English*, 6, 40).
2. 'Give me that man / That is not passions' slave, and I will wear him / In my heart's core, ay, in my heart of hearts' (III.ii.71–3).
3. *The Verbal Icon*, Lexington, University of Kentucky Press, 1954, 109.
4. *Approaches to Marvell*, ed. C.A. Patrides, London, Routledge & Kegan Paul, 1978, 108–35. Ricks shows that seventeenth-century reflexive imagery can be at once 'witty and mysterious' (119); it opens up 'vistas of regression and involution' (112), sometimes by describing a thing 'both as itself and as something external to it which it could not possibly be' (109), and thus asking us 'to visualize the unvisualizable' (114–15). Since it 'both reconciles and opposes' (109), reflexive imagery can be 'seriously witty' (132) as it glances at 'the metaphysical problem of the One and the Many' (117) or at the political problem of civil war.
5. *Shelley: A Critical Reading*, Baltimore, The Johns Hopkins University Press, 1971, 9, 19.
6. All quotations are from *The Complete Poetical Works of Samuel Taylor Coleridge*, ed. Ernest Hartley Coleridge, Oxford, Oxford University Press, 1912.
7. 'Kindling and dwindling: the poetic process in Shelley', *KSJ*, 13, 1964, 28.
8. *The Romantic Sublime: Studies in the Structure and Psychology of Transcendence*, Baltimore, The Johns Hopkins University Press, 1976, 144.
9. All quotations and English translations are from the Loeb Classical Library edition of the *Metamorphoses*, trans. Frank Justus Miller, London, William Heinemann, 1966.
10. See John Hollander, *The Figure of Echo: A Mode of Allusion in Milton and After*, Berkeley, University of California Press, 1981, 6–14.
11. All quotations are from *Milton: Complete Poems and Prose*, ed. Merritt Y. Hughes, New York, Odyssey, 1957.
12. Reflexive imagery is recurrent in the *Defence*: see the discussion at the end of this chapter.
13. Cf. Peter L. Thorslev Jr, 'The Romantic mind is its own place', *CL*, 15, 1963, 254.
14. See the discussion of this passage in Stephen J. Spector Jr, 'Wordsworth's mirror imagery and the picturesque tradition', *ELH*, 44, 1977, 95–6.

15. Quoted from the text as it originally appeared in the *London Magazine* (1821), ed. Alethea Hayter, Harmondsworth, Penguin, 1971, 107–8.

16. *Medwin's Conversations of Lord Byron*, ed. Ernest J. Lovell Jr, Princeton, Princeton University Press, 1966, 194.

17. All quotations are from *Lord Byron: The Complete Poetical Works*, ed. Jerome J. McGann, 3 vols now in print, Oxford, Clarendon Press, 1980–.

18. See Sheila Emerson, 'Byron's "one word": the language of self-expression in *Childe Harold* III', *SIR*, 20, 1981, 363–82.

19. 'Observations on Mr. Wordsworth's Poem *The Excursion*', *The Round Table* (August and October, 1814), *The Complete Works of William Hazlitt*, ed. P.P. Howe, London, J.M. Dent, 1931, IV, 112–13.

20. See my 'Obstinate questionings: the *Immortality Ode* and *Alastor*', *WC*, 12, 1981, 36–44.

21. 'Wordsworth: Note 2, Shelley and Wordsworth', *Revaluation*, Harmondsworth, Penguin, 1964, 163.

22. *Seven Types of Ambiguity*, 161.

23. Cf. lines 151–4 of *Alastor*: 'He dreamed a veiled maid / Sate near him, talking in low solemn tones. / Her voice was like the voice of his own soul / Heard in the calm of thought.'

24. *Shelley: A Critical Reading*, 260.

25. See Mary Shelley's account of a dream Shelley had in June 1822, less than a month before his death (letter to Maria Gisborne, 15 August 1822, *The Letters of Mary Wollstonecraft Shelley*, ed. Betty T. Bennett, Baltimore, The Johns Hopkins University Press, 1980, I, 245). Her account of this reflexive nightmare is quoted in full on p. 227 of Chapter VII below, where its relation to Shelley's late poems is discussed.

26. Cf. Shelley's 'Sonnet: Political Greatness' (1821): 'Man who man would be, / Must rule the empire of himself; in it / Must be supreme, establishing his throne / On vanquished will, quelling the anarchy / Of hopes and fears, being himself alone' (10–14).

27. *Seven Types of Ambiguity*, 161.

28. See Wasserman's discussion of the 'irradiation of love's light from a cosmic center', *Shelley: A Critical Reading*, 354–8.

29. See, for example, Desmond King-Hele's remarks about the second stanza of *Ode to the West Wind* in *Shelley: His Thought and Work*, London, Macmillan, 1962, 215–16, and F.H. Ludlam, 'The meteorology of Shelley's Ode', *TLS*, No. 3679, 1 Sept. 1972, 1015–16.

30. See the Spirit of the Hour's account of his first vision of the liberated earth in III.iv:

> . . . hate, disdain or fear,
> Self-love or self-contempt on human brows

No more inscribed, as o'er the gate of hell,
'All hope abandon, ye who enter here';
None frowned, none trembled, none with eager fear
Gazed on another's eye of cold command
Until the subject of a tyrant's will
Became, worse fate, the abject of his own . . .

(133–40)

None with firm sneer trod out in his own heart
The sparks of love and hope, till there remained
Those bitter ashes, a soul self-consumed,
And the wretch crept, a vampire among men,
Infecting all with his own hideous ill.
None talked that common, false, cold, hollow talk
Which makes the heart deny the *yes* it breathes
Yet question that unmeant hypocrisy
With such a self-mistrust as has no name.

(144–52)

31. Cf. *Speculations on Metaphysics* II: 'in the great study of ourselves we ought resolutely to compel the mind to a rigid examination of itself' (*CW*, VII, 62); 'We are ourselves the depositories of the evidence of the subject which we consider' (*CW*, VII, 63).
32. *Shelley: A Critical Reading*, 109–15.
33. *Shelley's 'Cenci': Scorpions Ringed With Fire*, Princeton, Princeton University Press, 1970, 136, 137.
34. Cf. *Ode to Liberty* (1820): 'When like Heaven's Sun girt by the exhalation / Of its own glorious light, thou didst arise / Chasing thy foes from nation unto nation / Like shadows' (159–62).
35. Cf. also *Ode to Liberty*, 259–60: 'I heard the pennons of her car'/'Self-moving, like cloud charioted by flame.'
36. Michael Riffaterre's brief comment on the 'symbolic circularity' of the phrase 'in the midst / Of its own darkness' from Wordsworth's 'Yew-Trees' is pointedly relevant: 'the phrase reverses a characteristic representation of epiphany as a self-sufficiency of light emitted and received' ('Interpretation and descriptive poetry: a reading of Wordsworth's "Yew-Trees"', *NLH*, 4, 1973, 240–1). Riffaterre calls this figure a 'syntagmatic tautology . . . whose form is literally a grammatical "uroboros"'.
37. ' "Its own resemblance" ', 123.
38. ibid., 122.
39. *The Starlit Dome: Studies in the Poetry of Vision*, London, Methuen, 1959, 226.
40. 'The philosophy of Shelley's poetry', *Essays and Introductions*, New York, Collier, 1968, 87.

41. Wasserman, *Shelley: A Critical Reading*, 139.
42. 'Essay on Shelley', *The Complete Works of Robert Browning*, ed. Roma A. King Jr, Jack W. Herring, Park Honan, Arthur N. Kincaid, Allan C. Dooley, Athens, Ohio, Ohio University Press and Waco, Texas, Baylor University, 1981, v, 139, 143.
43. 'Prometheus Unbound', *Essays and Introductions*, 423–4.
44. *Shelley's Major Poetry: The Fabric of a Vision*, Princeton, Princeton University Press, 1948, 12.
45. *A Choice of Shelley's Verse*, London, Faber & Faber, 1971, 13.
46. Consider this range of examples from different parts of the *Defence*: 'imagination... may be considered... as mind acting upon... thoughts so as to colour them with its own light, and composing from them, as from elements, other thoughts, each containing within itself the principle of its own integrity' (*PP*, 480); 'Neither the eye nor the mind can see itself, unless reflected upon that which it resembles' (*PP*, 491); 'It is the faculty which contains within itself the seeds at once of its own and of social renovation' (*PP*, 493); 'The imagination beholding the beauty of this order [underlying the institutions of republican Rome], created it out of itself according to its own idea' (*PP*, 494).
47. See *Byron's Letters and Journals*, ed. Leslie A. Marchand, Cambridge, Mass., Harvard University Press, 1979, ix, 189–90. In her 'Note on Poems of 1816', Mary Shelley says: 'There was something in the character of Saint-Preux, in his abnegation of self... that coincided with Shelley's disposition' (*PW*, 536). Trelawny says that 'Shelley loved everything better than himself. Self-preservation is, they say, the first law of nature, with him it was the last' (*Records of Shelley, Byron, and the Author*, ed. David Wright, Harmondsworth, Penguin, 1973, 106).

IV EVANESCENCE: MELTING, DISSOLVING, ERASING

1. See Jerrold E. Hogle, 'Shelley's poetics: the power as metaphor', *KSJ*, 31, 1982, 159–97, esp. 168–72, and 'Metaphor and metamorphosis in Shelley's "The Witch of Atlas"', *SIR*, 19, 1980, 329–31.
2. Wasserman's comments on the idea of 'vacancy' in *Mont Blanc* are relevant here; see *Shelley: A Critical Reading*, Baltimore, The Johns Hopkins University Press, 1971, 229.
3. *Robert Frost: The Work of Knowing*, New York, Oxford University Press, 1977, xvi. The following quotation from 'The Figure a Poem Makes' is from Frost's *Complete Poems*, New York, Holt, Rinehart & Winston, 1968, viii.
4. *KSJ*, 13, 1964, 13–28.
5. ibid., 27.

6. *Ode: Intimations of Immortality*, 143.
7. See T.S. Eliot, *For Lancelot Andrewes: Essays on Style and Order*, Garden City, N.Y., Doubleday, Doran, & Co., 1929, 135–6.
8. *Seven Types of Ambiguity*, Harmondsworth, Penguin, 1961, 156–9.
9. *The Renaissance*, intro. Lawrence Evans, Chicago, Academy Press, 1978, 236; this is a reprint of the 1922 Macmillan and Company edition of *The Renaissance*, taken from the *New Library Edition of the Works of Walter Pater*, 1910.
10. I quote from the text edited by Timothy Webb from Bod. MS. Shelley adds.e.6, fols 339–42, in *The Violet in the Crucible: Shelley and Translation*, Oxford, Clarendon Press, 1976, 313–14.
11. See Webb, *The Violet in the Crucible*, 318. Bloom, *Shelley's Mythmaking*, Ithaca, Cornell University Press, 1969, 271, reads Rousseau's account in *The Triumph of Life* as a 'kind of parody' of the Matilda episode in the *Purgatorio*.
12. 'Shelley's urbanity', *Purity of Diction in English Verse*, London, Chatto & Windus, 1953, 134–7.
13. ibid., 136.
14. See Hogle's strongly Derridean reading of this poem cited in note 1 of this chapter and discussed in the Introduction.
15. See *Shelley: A Critical Reading*, chapter 12, '*Prometheus Unbound*: the breathing earth', 326–58. While Wasserman studies Shelley's figurative and mythopoeic interest in Renaissance conceptions of atmospheric events such as clouds, dew, winds, lightning, comets and rainbows, his primary focus is on the volcanic symbolism associated with Demogorgon. See also Wasserman's comments on the atmospheric symbolism in *Adonais*, 466–9, 482, 488.
16. See especially Susan Hawk Brisman, ' "Unsaying his high language": the problem of voice in *Prometheus Unbound* ', *SIR*, 16, 1977, 79: 'Panthea's first efforts at speech in Act II, scene i, show a surfeit of energy vexing its own articulation . . . . Panthea's message resists her attempts to voice it.' For earlier efforts to contend with Shelley's language here, see *Shelley's 'Prometheus Unbound': A Variorum Edition*, ed. Lawrence John Zillman, Seattle, University of Washington Press, 1959, 423–5.
17. Brisman comments: 'Here the characteristic of mutability so often baffling voice infects instead the medium of writing, which literally consumes itself in air or fire while the message remains inscribed in the mind' (82).
18. *Shelley: A Critical Reading*, 329.
19. See John Gage, *Color in Turner: Poetry and Truth*, New York, Praeger, 1969, 106–16, and James A. W. Heffernan, 'The English Romantic perception of color', *Images of Romanticism: Verbal and Visual Affinities*, ed. Karl Kroeber and William Walling, New Haven, Yale University Press,

1978, 141–3. Gage argues that Turner's 1846 painting *Queen Mab's Cave* is indebted to Shelley's poem – 'the elements and feeling of his treatment are very close to Shelley' (146).

20. Many of Turner's paintings might be cited as analogues here: see, for example, *The Lake, Petworth, sunset*, c. 1828 (Andrew Wilton, *J.M.W. Turner: His Art and Life*, New York, Rizzoli, 1979, catalogue number P284); *Harbour with a Town and Fortress*, c. 1830 (Wilton, *Turner*, cat. P527); and most of the Venice paintings of the 1830s and 1840s – see especially *Venice, the Piazetta with the Ceremony of the Doge marrying the Sea*, c. 1835 (Wilton, *Turner*, cat. P501) and *The Dogano, San Giorgio, Citella, from the steps of the Europa*, 1842 (Wilton, *Turner*, cat. P396). See also the Venice watercolors of 1819 (discussed in Wilton, *Turner*, on pp. 142–4) and of the 1830s and 1840s (Wilton, *Turner*, pp. 231–5).

21. For examples of Turner's handling of the chasm of light, see *The Decline of the Carthaginian Empire*, 1817 (Wilton, *Turner*, cat. P135), *Regulus*, 1828–37 (Wilton, *Turner*, cat. P294), and *Ancient Italy – Ovid banished from Rome*, 1838 (Wilton, *Turner*, cat. P375). See also Wilton's discussion of these last two paintings: *Turner*, pp. 220–1.

22. The first phrase is Donald Reiman's, 'Structure, symbol, and theme in "Lines Written Among the Euganean Hills" ', *PMLA*, 77, 1962, 406; the second is Wasserman's, *Shelley: A Critical Reading*, 199. Cf. Judith Chernaik, *The Lyrics of Shelley*, Cleveland, Case Western Reserve University Press, 1972, 65: 'The description focuses on the rooks' anticipation of the sunrise rather than the sunrise itself; it is as if the poet . . . is granted a sign from the gods. The spontaneous, natural 'paean' of the rooks, their soaring into the sun, contrasts with the 'drifting' of the mariner, the downward motion of the opening section . . . . The image of the rooks in flight not only parallels the poet's sudden joy but anticipates the theme of freedom that is to occupy his thoughts as he mourns the fate of Italy.'

23. Cf. Karl Kroeber, 'Experience as history: Shelley's Venice, Turner's Carthage', *ELH*, 41, 1974, 321–39.

24. Gillian Carey, *Shelley*, London, Evans Brothers, 1975, 78, observes of this passage: 'In the precise observation and assured evocation of light on water and towers . . . he anticipates Turner who painted his first water-colours of Venice the following year' [1819]. Gage also notes 'how close . . . Shelley's incandescent vision of Venice is to Turner's own' (*Color in Turner*, 146). He says that 'Turner seems to have discovered Shelley late in life, in the anthology of modern English poets published by S.C. Hall in 1838 as his last *Book of Gems*' (145–6). The Shelley selections in vol. III of Hall's anthology are headed by an engraving of R.P. Bonington's *Venice* and begin with lines 115–42 of 'Euganean Hills' under the title 'Venice' (Hall changes 'Sun-girt City' in

line 115 to 'Sea-girt city'). It is worth noting that W. Miller, who engraved the Bonington painting that accompanies Hall's Shelley selections, also engraved Turner's own *Sunrise* which appears at the head of the selections from Southey on page 23.

25. Kroeber remarks that 'the syntactic dissolutions of this passage are deliberate; the grammatical fluidity is a linguistic equivalent to the blurring interpenetrations of color by which Turner dissolved to recreate the geometrical structuring of neo-classic painting' ('Shelley's Venice, Turner's Carthage', 338).

26. See Chapter I, pp. 9–10.

27. Letter from Joseph Severn to William Haslam, 1 June 1823, in *The Keats Circle*, ed. Hyder Edward Rollins, Cambridge, Mass., Harvard University Press, 1965, I, 273.

28. See Mary Shelley's 'Note on Poems of 1821': 'the poisonous breath of critics has vanished into emptiness before the fame he inherits' (*PW*, 663).

29. See the discussion of Shelley's interest in Bacon's image of *vestigia* ('footsteps') from the *De Augmentis* in Chapter I, p. 9 above.

30. Daniel Hughes observes of the entire island: 'It is to be identified as an earthly, not a heavenly, paradise, and in itself is a kind of fading coal' ('Coherence and collapse in Shelley, with particular reference to *Epipsychidion*', *ELH*, 28, 1961, 276).

31. 'The critic as host', *Deconstruction and Criticism*, New York, Seabury Press, 1979, 239. For the draft of Shelley's preface, see *PW*, 425.

32. For a somewhat different reading of the parasitic imagery here, see Miller, 'The critic as host', 241–2.

V SHELLEY'S SPEED

1. *Rehabilitations and Others Essays*, Oxford, Oxford University Press, 1939, 28.

2. *Revaluation*, Harmondsworth, Penguin, 1964, 140.

3. Harold Bloom, *The Anxiety of Influence*, Oxford, Oxford University Press, 1975, 131.

4. Miriam Allott, 'The reworking of a literary genre: Shelley's "The Triumph of Life" ', *Essays on Shelley*, ed. Miriam Allott, Totowa, N.J., Barnes & Noble, 1982, 238.

5. *Revaluation*, 173.

6. 'On some aspects of Shelley's poetic imagery', *Acta et Commentationes Universitatis Tartuensis*, 43, 1939, B, No. 4, 53.

7. ibid., 69.

8. Richard Harter Fogle, *The Imagery of Keats and Shelley*, Chapel Hill,

University of North Carolina Press, 1949, 32–6.

9. ibid., 95.

10. The terms *kinetic*, *kinesthetic* and *motor* are not easy to distinguish, particularly with respect to poetry such as Shelley's where external physical phenomena and internal mental responses or sensations are fused. In its most basic sense *kinetic* means 'Of, pertaining to, or due to, motion'. *Motor* means 'Causing, setting up, or imparting motion', and in physiological terminology 'involving or pertaining to, muscular movement'. Thus *motor* would appear partly to overlap in meaning with *kinesthetic*, which refers to 'The sense whose end organs lie in the muscles, tendons, and joints and are stimulated by bodily movements and tensions; the muscle sense'. (References here are to *Webster's New International Dictionary*, 2nd edn.) From Shelley's epistemological perspective, all phenomena of motion or speed would presuppose perceptual experiences of motion or speed.

11. 'The transformation of discourse: *Epipsychidion*, *Adonais*, and some lyrics', *Essays on Shelley*, ed. Allott, 230.

12. Trelawny, *Records of Shelley, Byron, and the Author*, ed. David Wright, Harmondsworth, Penguin, 1973, 115.

13. Quoted from Judith Chernaik's transcription of the draft in *The Lyrics of Shelley*, Cleveland, Case Western Reserve University Press, 1972, 288–9.

14. A transcription of the fair copy appears in Judith Chernaik and Timothy Burnett, 'The Byron and Shelley notebooks in the Scrope Davies find', *RES*, n.s. 29, 1978, 45–9. Since Chernaik and Burnett added 'final pointing' in their transcription, I have consulted a photocopy of the manuscript supplied by Timothy Burnett and the British Library. Thanks are due to Mr Burnett and, for permission to obtain this photocopy of part of the Scrope Davies material, to C.T. Norman-Butler, Local Director of Barclays Bank p.l.c., 1 Pall Mall East, London.

All quotations of the finished version of *Mont Blanc*, here and in Chapter VI, are from the text printed at the end of *History of a Six Weeks' Tour through a Part of France, Switzerland, Germany, and Holland*, London, T. Hookham Jr, C. and J. Ollier, 1817. This entire volume is reprinted in *The Prose Works of Percy Bysshe Shelley*, ed. Harry Buxton Forman, London, Reeves & Turner, 1880, II, 116–204. In thinking about Shelley's punctuation and its consequences for such aspects of versification as enjambment, Reiman's comment in the 'Textual introduction' to *PP* should be borne in mind: 'In his draft manuscripts Shelley often omitted commas at the ends of poetic lines (and sometimes full stops at the ends of stanzas) simply because the natural pause at the end of the line (or stanza) obviated the need for any punctuation at that early stage of composition, when the manuscript was meant merely as a guide to the poet. In his fair copies destined for the press (or for friends to whom the poems were addressed) Shelley is much more careful in punctuating, but even in these he often depended on the natural pause at the end of the line to serve instead of an optional comma' (xv).

15. *The Imagery of Keats and Shelley*, 94–5.
16. I want to thank Professor Susan Fox of Queens College, City University of New York, for a helpful remark about the speed of Shelley's Spenserian stanzas.
17. *The Poet's Calling in the English Ode*, New Haven, Yale University Press, 1980, 213–14.
18. Cf. Donald Reiman's observations on related grammatical patterns in the terza rima tercets of *The Triumph of Life* in *Shelley's 'The Triumph of Life': A Critical Study*, Urbana, Univeristy of Illinois Press, 1965, 88.
19 ibid., 89.
20. The auxiliary 'would' is understood to introduce 'suspend' here, in grammatical parallel with 'would partake' at the end of line 100.
21. Cf. *Epispychidion*, 72–7:
    She met me, Stranger, upon life's rough way,
    And lured me towards sweet Death; as Night by Day,
    Winter by Spring, or Sorrow by swift Hope,
    Led into light, life, peace. An antelope,
    In the suspended impulse of its lightness,
    Were less ethereally light . . .
22. 'On some aspects of Shelley's poetic imagery', 40–53.
23. See Christopher Ricks, 'Wordsworth: "a pure organic pleasure from the lines" ', *EIC*, 21, 1971, 14–17.
24. Ricks comments shrewdly on 'a lengthened pause / Of silence' from the Boy of Winander episode in the 1850 *Prelude* (v.379–80), adding that 'The Concordance shows how often Wordsworth places the word "pause" so that it pauses at the brink of the line' (17).
25. 'Dante's influence on Shelley', *MLN*, 13, 1898, 161–5; cited in *Shelley's 'Prometheus Unbound': A Variorum Edition*, ed. Lawrence John Zillman, Seattle, University of Washington Press, 1959, 408.
26. See Oras, 'On some aspects of Shelley's poetic imagery', 58. Cf. Keats, *Endymion*, I. 797–800: 'But there are / Richer entanglements, enthralments far / More self-destroying, leading, by degrees, / To the chief intensity.'
27. *The Starlit Dome: Studies in the Poetry of Vision*, London, Methuen, 1959, 205.
28. Cf. *Epispychidion*, 106–8: 'and where some heavy tress / The air of her own speed has disentwined, / The sweetness seems to satiate the faint

wind.' On the questionable textual status of Shelley's notes, see E.B. Murray, 'Shelley's *Notes on Sculptures*: the provenance and authority of the text', *KSJ*, 32, 1983, 150–71.

29. Zillman, *Shelley's 'Prometheus Unbound': A Variorum Edition*, 484, quotes a comment from Vida Scudder's edition of the poem, Boston, D.C. Heath, 1892: 'a sense of breathless speed is imparted by the break in this lyric and the swift change of scene, as well as by the abrupt omission of the last line in the concluding stanza.'

30. *The Imagery of Keats and Shelley*, 98.

31. *Shelley: His Thought and Work*, London, Macmillan, 1962, 206.

32. Quoted from the Loeb Classical Library edition of *The Iliad*, London, William Heinemann, 1924. The English translation is Richmond Lattimore's, Chicago, University of Chicago Press, 1951.

33. Scolar Press facsimile of the 1798 edition of vol. I, Menston, 1968, I, 26–9.

34. *The Study of Language in England, 1780–1860*, Princeton, Princeton University Press, 1967, 51, 53.

35. See especially sections III.v.7 and III.vi.32 of Locke's *Essay*.

VI   RHYME AND THE ARBITRARINESS OF LANGUAGE

1. 'Shelley disfigured', *Deconstruction and Criticism*, New York, Seabury Press, 1979, 60.

2. ibid., 62.

3. See Harold Whitehall, 'From linguistics to poetry', *Sound and Poetry*, ed. Northrop Frye, New York, Columbia University Press, 1957, 139: 'Rhyme is in a sense the most mysterious of all sound patterns.'

4. Quoted from 'The Chances of Rhyme' in *Selected Poems, 1951–1974*, Oxford, Oxford University Press, 1978. Cf. Cynthia Chase's brief comment on 'les hasards de la rime' in Baudelaire's 'Le Soleil', 'Reading Hegel with Baudelaire', *SIR*, 22, 1983, 260–1.

5. The phrase is Earl Wasserman's, *Shelley: A Critical Reading*, Baltimore, The Johns Hopkins University Press, 1971, 234.

6. *Vision and Resonance: Two Senses of Poetic Form*, New York, Oxford University Press, 1975, 108–10.

7. *Shelley's 'The Triumph of Life': A Critical Study*, Urbana, University of Illinois Press, 1965, 96.

8. See de Man, 'Shelley disfigured', 47–9.

9. 'One relation of rhyme to reason', *The Verbal Icon*, Lexington, University of Kentucky Press, 1954, 165. Cf. Hugh Kenner, 'Pope's reasonable rhymes', *ELH*, 41, 1974, 74–88, especially Kenner's opening remarks on 'a suspicion that the poet of rhyme is playing with fire, flirting with triviality and unworthy coincidence', and his suggestion

that the 'problem with such effects [of rhyme] seems to inhere in their look of randomness' (74).

10. Glenn O'Malley, *Shelley and Synesthesia*, Evanston, Northwestern University Press, 1964, 82.
11. Reiman, *Shelley's 'The Triumph of Life'*, 185.
12. ibid., 95.
13. See de Man, 'Shelley disfigured', 50–1 and passim.
14. ibid., 62–3.
15. Shelley's note appears at the end of the Preface to *History of a Six Weeks' Tour through a Part of France, Switzerland, Germany, and Holland*, London, T. Hookham Jr, C. and J. Ollier, 1817.
16. The poem is in *Tales Told of the Fathers*, New York, Atheneum, 1975.
17. See Judith Chernaik, *The Lyrics of Shelley*, Cleveland, Case Western Reserve University Press, 1972, 288 n.4. She points out that the rhymes in the Bodleian MS. of *Mont Blanc* are more regularly interwoven than those of the 1817 printed text and suggests that 'Shelley may have been consciously striving in 1817 for the more irregular rhyme effects of *Lycidas*.' I refer here to the text of *Lycidas* in the *Complete Poems and Major Prose*, ed. Merritt Y. Hughes, New York, Odyssey, 1957. For excellent accounts of Milton's rhyming in *Lycidas*, see Ants Oras, 'Milton's early rhyme schemes and the structure of *Lycidas*', *MP*, 52, 1954–5, 12–22, and Joseph A. Wittreich Jr, 'Milton's "Destin'd urn": the art of *Lycidas*', *PMLA*, 84, 1968, 60–70. Wittreich's analysis is particularly relevant to Shelley's rhyming in *Mont Blanc*, since he argues that Milton's 'encompassing scheme' is not confined to patterns within individual verse paragraphs but 'envelops the poem and its various parts in a massive unity' (61). *Lycidas* is listed among the poems read by Shelley and Mary Shelley in 1815, the year before *Mont Blanc* was written (*Mary Shelley's Journal*, 48).
18. The unrhymed words in *Mont Blanc* are 'forms' (62), 'spread' (65) and 'sun' (133). Neville Rogers, *The Complete Poetical Works of Percy Bysshe Shelley*, Oxford, Clarendon Press, 1975, II, 355, says that Locock also counted 'sky' (108) and 'world' (113) as rhymeless. But if we look at the poem as a whole, 'sky' (108) repeats 'sky' at the end of line 60 and rhymes with 'lie' (19, 54), 'by' (45) and 'high' (52, 70); 'world' (113) repeats 'world' at the end of line 49 and rhymes with 'unfurled' (53). *Lycidas* had traditionally been analyzed paragraph by paragraph, in which case there appear to be ten unrhymed lines. But looking at the total rhyme pattern of the poem as Wittreich does yields only three; see 'Art of *Lycidas*', 63, 69–70.
19. *Vision and Resonance*, 118. See Derek Attridge on the different functions of rhyme in English and French verse in 'Dryden's dilemma, or, Racine

refashioned: the problem of the English dramatic couplet', *YES*, 9, 1979, 62–5.

20. Cf. David Simpson, *Irony and Authority in Romantic Poetry*, Totowa, N.J., Rowan & Littlefield, 1979, 233, n.15.

21. Ed. L.A. Selby–Bigge, rev. P.H. Nidditch, Oxford, Clarendon Press, 1975, 14. See also 30, 33, 42, 66. 'Secret springs' receives additional emphasis by forming the poem's first couplet with 'brings' in line 5. If this phrase is a Humean allusion, it developed late in Shelley's revisions; he wrote 'secret caves' both in the Bodleian draft and in the recently discovered fair copy. See Chernaik, *The Lyrics of Shelley*, 288, and Judith Chernaik and Timothy Burnett, 'The Byron and Shelley notebooks in the Scrope Davies find', *RES*, n.s. 29, 1978, 45–9.

22. Ed. Selby-Bigge, 30.

VII   SHELLEY'S LAST LYRICS

1. Cynthia Chase, 'The accidents of disfiguration: limits to literal and rhetorical reading in Book V of *The Prelude*', *SIR*, 18, 1979, 565.

2. See Richard Holmes, *Shelley: The Pursuit*, New York, E.P. Dutton, 1975, 701.

3. Ed. Frank Kermode and John Hollander, New York, Oxford University Press, 1973, II, 400.

4. For the biographical information in this chapter I have relied on Holmes's *Shelley: The Pursuit* and on Newman Ivey White's *Shelley*, 2 vols, New York, Knopf, 1940. Specific citations of these and other biographical sources will be restricted to points of factual and interpretive emphasis or controversy.

5. White, *Shelley*, II, 283.

6. *Shelley: His Life and Work*, Boston, Houghton Mifflin, 1927, II, 199. See White, *Shelley*, II, 626–8.

7. 'Shelley and Jane Williams', *RES*, n.s. 12, 1961, 46–8.

8. 'Shelley's "The Triumph of Life": the biographical problem', *PMLA*, 78, 1963, 536–50.

9. *The Lyrics of Shelley*, Cleveland, Case Western Reserve University Press, 1972, 162–3.

10. White, *Shelley*, II, 627.

11. *The Letters of Mary Wollestonecraft Shelley*, ed. Betty T. Bennett, Baltimore, The Johns Hopkins University Press, I, 209. Hereafter cited parenthetically in the text.

12. They had been together during the summer of 1816 on the shores of Lake Leman, during the late summer and early autumn of 1818 in and around Venice, and during August of 1821, when Shelley visited Byron in Ravenna.

13. See Charles E. Robinson, *Shelley and Byron: The Snake and Eagle Wreathed in Fight*, Baltimore, The Johns Hopkins University Press, 1976, 201, 204–8, 276 n. 61.
14. *Shelley: The Pursuit*, 686.
15. ibid., 689.
16. *Shelley and Byron*, 213–16.
17. On this point I am indebted to an essay written by Mary Laity for a graduate course at Rutgers University in the spring of 1972.
18. Quoted from *The Complete Poetry of Robert Herrick*, ed. J. Max Patrick, Garden City, N.Y., Doubleday Anchor, 1963.
19. *Purity of Diction in English Verse*, London, Chatto & Windus, 1953, 146.
20. 'Shelley and the Pforzheimer Foundation', *New Statesman*, 27 November 1964, 840–1.
21. This line ironically echoes *Hamlet* IV.iv.36–9: 'Sure he that made us with such large discourse, / Looking before and after, gave us not / That capability and godlike reason / To rust in us unused.' See *PP*, 228 n. 7.
22. *Revaluation*, Harmondsworth, Penguin, 1964, 165.
23. See Davie, *Purity of Diction*, 145: 'As Dr. Leavis notes, the changes ("thrilling" for "thinking", "being" to "fair form", and "lifeless" for "breathless") are all in the direction of eroticism.' Wordsworth himself might well have understood Shelley's changing 'thinking' to 'thrilling'; see 'Lines Written in Early Spring': 'the least motion which they made / It seemed a thrill of pleasure' (15–16). Mary Shelley quotes from this poem in a letter to Claire of 2 April 1821, which also includes a note by Shelley (*Letters*, II, 279; *Letters of Mary Wollstonecraft Shelley*, I, 187).
24. Robert Frost echoes and transforms this passage from 'The Recollection' in 'Spring Pools'; see Richard Poirier, 'Frost, Winnicott, Burke', *Raritan: A Quarterly Review*, 2, 1982, 120, and *Robert Frost: The Work of Knowing*, New York, Oxford University Press, 1977, 14–19.
25. See, for example, Chernaik, *The Lyrics of Shelley*, 174.
26. See White, *Shelley*, II, 345–6, and Holmes, *Shelley: The Pursuit*, 627.
27. See Chernaik, *The Lyrics of Shelley*, 257.
28. Shelley wrote to Horace Smith on 25 January 1822, asking him 'to buy a good pedal harp' in Paris (*Letters*, II, 378). On 24 March 1822, Shelley wrote to Claire: 'Horace Smith has lately declined to advance 6 or 7 napoleons for a musical instrument which I wished to buy for Jane at Paris' (*Letters*, II, 400). Then on 11 April 1822, he concluded a letter to Smith by saying, 'I have contrived to get my musical coals at Newcastle itself' (*Letters*, II, 412).
29. See the note by Reiman and Powers, *PP*, 448.
30. See Robinson, *Shelley and Byron*, 210–11, and John Buxton, *Byron and*

Shelley: The History of a Friendship, New York, Harcourt Brace, 1968, 196.

31. Quotations from 'The Magnetic Lady to Her Patient' and 'When the Lamp is Shattered', neither of which is included in *PP*, are taken from the texts in Chernaik, *The Lyrics of Shelley*, 254–9.

32. *The Lyrics of Shelley*, 164.

33. *The Life of Percy Bysshe Shelley*, rev. text, ed. H. Buxton Forman, London, Oxford University Press, 1913, 270; see Holmes, *Shelley: The Pursuit*, 627.

34. *The Lyrics of Shelley*, 165.

35. *Shelley's Poetic Thoughts*, New York, St Martin's Press, 1981, 243–5.

36. Shakespeare's Ariel, as Prospero explains, had been confined by the 'foul witch Sycorax' 'Into a cloven pine; within which rift / Imprisoned thou didst painfully remain / A dozen years' (I.ii.258, 278–80): 'It was mine art, / When I arrived and heard thee, that made gape / The pine, and let thee out' (I.ii.292–4). Shelley adapts this idea to the genesis of the guitar but retains and transforms, in a characteristic way, the notion of Ariel's imprisonment.

37. *Shelley's Poetic Thoughts*, 245.

38. 'Shelley's lyrics', *The Morality of Art: Essays Presented to G. Wilson Knight*, ed. D.W. Jefferson, London, Routledge & Kegan Paul, 1969, 206–7.

39. ibid., 209.

40. Holmes, *Shelley: The Pursuit*, 709–13.

41. For evidence that Shelley was working on *The Triumph of Life* in May and June of 1822, see Reiman, *Shelley's 'The Triumph of Life'*, Urbana, University of Illinois Press, 1965, Appendix D, 244–50, and, most recently, Betty T. Bennett and Alice Green Fredman, 'A note on the dating of Shelley's "The Triumph of Life" ', *KSJ*, 31, 1982, 13–15.

42. On the naming of Shelley's boat, see White, *Shelley*, II, 366, and Holmes, *Shelley: The Pursuit*, 716–17.

43 Jones's note on the scratched-over portions of this letter is significant: 'The following reading is highly conjectural. It is based mainly upon what Shelley *must* have said, as judged by what Mary actually did say in her letter of 2 June 1822 to Maria Gisborne [*Letters of Mary Wollstonecraft Shelley*, I, 236]. Trelawny himself must have scratched the lines out. When he published the letter . . . he omitted the entire passage relating to the name on the mainsail. . . . One would therefore suspect that he as well as Byron had some responsibility for disfiguring Shelley's boat' (*Letters*, II, 422 n. 2).

44. See Reiman's discussion of the drafts in relation to the fair copy in *Shelley's 'The Triumph of Life'*, 245–6, and in *PP*, 451 n. 4.

45. For the variants between draft and fair copy, see Chernaik, *The Lyrics of Shelley*, 260–1.

46. 'Shelley and Jane Williams', 40–1, 44–6.
47. ibid., 40–1.
48. ibid., 41.
49. ibid., 43; see also this and other cancellations noted by Chernaik, *The Lyrics of Shelley*, 273–6.
50. *The Lyrics of Shelley*, 175–6.
51.

> Or che 'l ciel et la terra e 'l vento tace
> et le fere e gli augelli il sonno affrena,
> notte il carro stellato in giro mena
> et nel suo letto il mar senz' onda giace,
>
> vegghio, penso, ardo, piango; et chi mi sface
> sempre m'è inanzi per mia dolce pena . . .
>
> (1–6)

The quotation is from *Petrarch's Lyric Poems*, trans. and ed. Robert M. Durling, Cambridge, Mass., Harvard University Press, 1976. Cf. Surrey's 'Alas! So All Things Now Do Hold Their Peace'.

52. 'Shelley and Jane Williams', 44.
53. 'The biographical problem', 538.
54. See Reiman, *Shelley's 'The Triumph of Life'*, 175, 247.

INDEX OF SHELLEY'S WORKS DISCUSSED

NAME AND SUBJECT INDEX

Darwin, Erasmus iv
Davie, Donald 130, 210, 211, 217
dead metaphor 7, 8–9, 18, 19
death: and erasure 149–51; and rebirth 175–6; Shelley's view of 110–11
de Man, Paul ii; Shelley's rhyme 184, 185, 187, 188, 190; on *Triumph of Life* 194
De Quincey, Thomas 92
Derrida, Jacques ii
Dickens, Charles 81
Diderot, Denis 11, 19, 38
dissolving, imagery of 122, 125–9, 130, 139, 140; *see also* meteorological imagery
Don Juan (yacht) 225–6
Donne, John 221
dress, language as 24–7, 182–3
Drummond, Sir William 11, 46

Eliot, T. S.: on Dante 56, 57–8, 60; on Shelley i
Empson, William: on grammar 124; on reflexive imagery 79, 80, 81, 82, 85, 97, 102, 103, 106–8, 110
enjambment 143, 162, 166–8, 177, 187, 195
erasing, imagery of 122, 149–53, 192
Este, Shelley visits 142
etymological imagery 47, 48–9, 73, 74
evanescence 119–22, 131, 148–9, 151
evaporation *see* meteorological imagery
expression, media of 4–6, 30

Fogle, Richard Harter 155, 159–60, 173
footsteps, imagery of 6, 9, 31, 149
Forman, Buxton 68
freezing *see* meteorological imagery
Frost, Robert 121
Fry, Paul 162

Gisborne, John 203, 227
Gisborne, Maria 227
Godwin, William 22, 40
Goethe, J. W. von 206
Greek poets, mentalistic imagery 55, 66–72

Harris, James 14–15
Hazlitt, William 58, 60, 94–5
Heaney, Seamus 81
Herder, Johann Gottfried 4, 38
Herrick, Robert 209, 212, 221
hierarchy of expressive media 5, 19–20
hieroglyphs, words as 19
Hogle, Jerrold iii, v, 8
Hollander, John 187, 194, 198
Holmes, Richard 206–7
Homer 27, 71, 179
Homeric *Hymn to Hermes* 71–2, 179–80
Hoppner, Richard 204
Horne Tooke, John 1, 38, 39, 47, 48, 180–2
Hughes, Daniel 87, 122
Humboldt, Wilhelm von 35
Hume, David 199, 200
humour 111
Hunt, Leigh 206

ideas, and objects 11, 46, 78
'image', Shelley's use of 45
imagery: allegorical 52; definition 43, 44–5; etymological structure 48, 73, 74; figurative 44, 45, 46, 49; function of 44, 45–6; influences upon Shelley 50–72; mentalistic 43–5, 47, 52–5, 73–8; meteorological 129–39; reflexive 79–81, 82; reversed 44, 60, 61, 76–7; of sense experience 43–4; synaesthetic 107, 132, 138, 191
'imagery', Shelley's use of 45
incarnation, language as 26, 27, 47, 63
intellectual philosophy, Shelley's commitment to 23, 46

Johnson, Samuel, *Dictionary* iv, 17, 43, 186
Jones, Sir William 1
Jordan, John E. 5

Keats, John 42, 150, 171, 172
King-Hele, Desmond 179
Knight, G. Wilson, 112, 171, 172
Kuhns, L. O. 170